On the Path toward One Another

"In a world marked by tension and suffering, one in which mutual distrust threatens to overwhelm, we can teach each other something important: as rational and spiritual beings we are gifted by the Almighty God with mutual trust. The purpose of this book, *On the Path Toward One Another,* is to show us how to strive toward that goal: mutual trust while walking a spiritual path toward God through one another, a path followed by believers in both religions, both Islam and Christianity. The conversation that this book demonstrates deserves the support of every open-minded person who believes in a common humanity that is guided and protected by God, the Almighty."

—Dr. Mustafa Cerić, Grand Mufti emeritus of Bosnia

"Encounters between Christianity and Islam always remain encounters between a Christian and a Muslim." Thus begins an insightful dialogue between a Benedictine and a Muslim scholar, spanning the most pressing fundamental topics for both religious traditions. A penetrating dialogue between two observant religious figures breathes life into what can too often become stale academic debate. A worthy read for beginners and proficient alike."

—Anna Bonta Moreland, Professor of Humanities and the Anne Quinn Welsh Endowed Chair and Director of the Honors Program at Villanova University

"Two masters meeting: Germany's most widely read spiritual teacher from the Catholic tradition and Germany's finest philosopher of religion from the Islamic tradition. Finally! The hope of Vatican II is coming true: they are listening to each other, enjoying their otherness, learning from their counterpart; and they have started walking together toward a world of brothers and sisters."

—Prof. Felix Körner, SJ, Nikolaus Cusanus Chair in Theology of Religion, Central Institute for Catholic Theology, Humboldt University of Berlin

"Together, Christians and Muslims comprise the world's largest number of people of faith — literally billions of believers. With false perceptions and apprehensions rife, it is critical for those of both faiths to understand each other's beliefs and values. Now at last there is a book that answers the pressing questions of Muslims about Christianity and the essential questions of Christians about Islam. We could not have asked for two more credible guides: Ahmad Milad Karimi, a devout Muslim philosopher; and Anselm Grün, a Benedictine monk, a mystic and the author of some three hundred texts on Christian life. Their book has been born not out of judgmentalism or argument, but out of humility. Yet their book moves beyond reducing each religion to the simple bromide that all paths lead to the same God. Grün and Karimi show us that in our undeniable differences, there lies beauty and truth, also strength. As they point out, we can indeed live out our faiths differently and still be united in a search for God that leads not to 'a' path, but to the much deeper work of heart and soul that allows for 'turning oneself into the path.'"

—Judith Valente, author of *How to Live: What The Rule of St. Benedict Teaches Us about Happiness, Meaning and Community,* and *Atchison Blue: A Search for Silence, A Spiritual Home and a Living Faith*

"Amidst theological attempts to create dialogue through the lowest common denominator, this book stands apart. Grün and Karimi's sober engagement with the difficult issues that arise from embodied faith while maintaining fidelity exemplifies why transformative encounters flourish amidst meaningful differences. Pedagogically, this is a phenomenal text for the classroom to contemplate how one could mirror such engagement with fidelity to scripture, how to ask questions about embodied faith, and an openness to transformation. As a Reformed and Evangelical comparative theologian, although I would articulate some theological positions differently, I commend the sensitivity that Grün and Karimi take to present their responses to the other."

—Dr. Alexander E. Massad, Assistant Professor of World Religions, Wheaton College, Wheaton, IL

On the Path toward One Another

A Christian and a Muslim in Conversation

By
Anselm Grün and Ahmad Milad Karimi

Published in the United States by New City Press
202 Comforter Blvd., Hyde Park, NY 12530
©2023 New City Press (English translation)

Translated by Peter Dahm Robertson
from the original German edition, *Im Herzen der Spiritualität: Wie sich Muslime und Christen begegnen können,*
©2019 Verlag Herder GmbH, Freiburg im Breisgau, Germany
Foreign rights represented by Vier-Türme-Verlag, Münsterschwarach, Germany

Unless otherwise noted, all quotations from the Qur'an are taken from Oxford World Classics *The Qur'an: A New Translation,* by M. A. S. Abdel Haleem (2021), accessed at https://archive.org/details/oxford-worlds-classics-the-quran-a-new-translation-by-m.-a.-s.-abdel-haleem/page/n35/mode/2up

All biblical quotations are from *New Revised Standard Version Bible,* copyright ©1989 National Council of the Churches of Christ in the United States of America. Used by permission.
All rights reserved worldwide.

ISBN 978-1-56548-572-3 (paperback)
ISBN 978-1-56548-573-0 (e-book)

Library of Congress Control Number: 2023943075

Printed in the United States of America

Contents

Prologue: Paths toward One Another—Awe and Gratitude 9

Introduction: Motives and Goals 13

"Stumbling Blocks" on the Road
to One Another—Provocations for Dialogue 23
    "Stumbling Blocks" for Christians 24
        1. Who Represents True Islam? 24
        2. The Muslim View of God 26
        3. The Qur'anic Understanding of Revelation 28
        4. Salvation and Redemption 31
        5. Religion and Society in the Purview of Islam 33
        6. The Question of Violence 35
    "Stumbling blocks" for Muslims 38
        1. Truth of the Dogmas and the Question of "True Christianity" 38
        2. God Becoming Human—a Provocation? 40
        3. The "One God," the Theology of the Trinity,
           and Jesus as God's Son 42
        4. The Danger of Deifying Humankind 44
        5. Original Sin—Salvation by the Cross 45
        6. The Social Role of Christianity 49
        7. Christianity's History of Violence 51

Horizons and Fields of Spirituality 55
    Where Do We Come From? 57
        1. The Muslim View of Createdness 57
        2. The Christian Idea of Creation 61
    Origin and Goal of our Life: God 65
        1. The Muslim Conception of a God 65
        2. How Christians Speak of the Threefold God 71
    Living from the Source: The Holy Scriptures as a Guide 75
        1. The Christian Approach to Holy Scripture 75
        2. The Qur'an as Divine, Aesthetic Event 79
    The Prophet: Testimony of One Called by God 85
        1. How Do Christians Conceive of Prophecy? 85
        2. Muhammad as "Seal of Prophecy" 89

Jesus—Prophet or Savior? 96
1. My Prophet Jesus 96
2. Jesus, Son of God 100

Mary: A Special Woman 107
1. The Muslim View of Mary 107
2. The Christian View of Mary 111

The Spiritual Challenge: Life as a Battle of the Spirit 117
1. The Spiritual Battle as Path toward God 117
2. Spiritual Battle as the Great Jihād 121

On the Significance and Meaning of Prayer 125
1. Christian Prayer as Personal Encounter with God 125
2. Bringing God to Mind—a Muslim Understanding of Prayer 129

Spiritual Sites—Church and Mosque 135
1. The Christian House of God 135
2. The Mosque as House of Prayer 138

Pilgrimage and the Journey of Life 142
1. The Christian View of Faith as a Pilgrimage 142
2. On a Journey to the Near-Far God:
   Pilgrimage in a Muslim Framework 147

A Path to Freedom: Fasting 152
1. On the Meaning of Fasting in Christianity 152
2. Fasting: A Central Pillar of Islam 156

Mercy: Core of Spirituality 161
1. God has Mercy on the Merciful 161
2. Mercy: Attribute of God and Command for Human Beings 164

Love: Longing and Fulfillment 169
1. Love: The Foundation of Christian Faith 169
2. Only the Lover Is Truly Spiritual 173

Tolerance and Truth Claims 178
1. The Meaning of Christianity's Claim to Absoluteness 178
2. A Muslim Perspective on Tolerance and Truth Claims 183

Mission or Testimony? 188
1. The Christian Call to Mission 188
2. A Joint Mission 191

What Ought We to Do? Law and Ethics 195
1. Religion, Ethics, and Law from a Muslim Perspective 195
2. Ethics and the Spiritual Path from a Christian Perspective 200

The Individual and the Community 205
    1. The Individual and the Community
       from a Christian Perspective 205
    2. The Individual and the Community
       as Understood by Islam 208

Men and Women: The Relationship between the Sexes 213
    1. The Relationship between the Sexes
       from a Christian Perspective 213
    2. The Relationship between the Sexes
       in the Muslim Tradition 218

How to Live: The Art of Spiritual Living 224
    1. Experiencing Reality through the Spirit
       as the Art of Spiritual Living in Islam 224
    2. The Art of Spiritual Living in the Christian Tradition 228

Mysticism and Secular Society 233
    1. Hearing God's Word and Finding New Action 233
    2. Shaping the World as a Spiritual Task in Islam 238

Suffering: God's Will? 242
    1. Christian Answers to the Question of Suffering 242
    2. Suffering as a Spiritual Challenge in Islam 248

Life, Dying, and Death 253
    1. Christian Thought on the Connection between
       Living, Dying, and Death 253
    2. A Muslim Interpretation of Living, Dying, and Death 257

What Do We Hope for? Where Are We Going? 262
    1. Muslim Expectations of the Beyond 262
    2. Christians' Hope for the Beyond 267

Conclusion: Stories as Means of Approach 271
    Ahmad Milad Karimi 273
    Anselm Grün 277

Bibliography 281

Prologue

Paths toward One Another
—Awe and Gratitude

Anselm Grün and Ahmad Milad Karimi

In conversation with one another, we sought paths toward each other and found them. Actual encounter is the most important of these paths toward the other. "All actual life is encounter," as the Jewish philosopher of religion Martin Buber says.[1] Encounter does not gloss over differences. The difference is perceived, and points of contention are voiced, as well. Differences can remain, but they do not need to become opposition. The path toward one another is not without stumbling blocks that have accumulated on that path over the course of history. Sincerity involves looking at those stumbling blocks too. And perceiving what divides us must also be a part of any encounter that takes place on an equal footing. Only this perception enables true encounter. We can do justice to what divides us if we listen to one another, if we want to learn from one another and are willing to see those parts of the other that are worthy of awe. Meanwhile, encounters between Christianity and Islam always remain encounters between a Christian and a Muslim. Mutual respect forms the basis of this path we share.

In our encounter, we experienced how in dialogue between religions, spirituality is what actually unites us above and beyond all theological differences. These are spiritual traditions that find one another, Sufism and Christian mysticism, which belong together. When we exchange views about spiritual experiences, it is not a matter of being right, but of jointly experiencing the grandeur of God, his love, and his

---

1. Martin Buber, *I and Thou,* translated by Walter Kaufmann (New York: Charles Scribner's Sons, 1970), 62.

healing nearness. Theological clarity is necessary too, of course. In Christianity and in Islam, we each have a different language for talking about God, about Jesus and Mary. And these languages cannot simply be leveled into uniformity. But in a conversation in which we really listen to one another, we can nonetheless approach each other. And then we feel that God is beyond all our words and metaphors, beyond our language; that God is the inexpressible mystery toward which we are all journeying.

Looking back, one important experience for us was this: whenever the question of God comes to the fore, the foreignness of the other recedes. We both see ourselves as journeying toward the God beyond all dogmatic determinations. But the question of God is not primarily one of reconciling the "one God" of Islam with the "threefold God" of Christianity. Instead, the central question is to what kinds of experiences faith in God leads in Islam and in Christianity respectively, and how this faith shapes concrete life. It is, then, a matter of experiencing salvation and redemption, experiencing being accepted and loved. But it is also about caring for one another, about love for one's neighbor and about responsibility for the world. Experiences of God are meant to be interrogated as to the meaning they can provide. They are meant to be contemplated in light of today's fundamental human experiences, such as the experience of an inner rift, of uprootedness, of being afraid and overwhelmed, of a directionless and meaningless life.

Throughout our dialogue, we kept being filled with awe at how the attempt to explain one's own faith to the other and lay bare one's own foundational experiences brings us closer together. We could sense that all of us—Christians and Muslims alike—are dependent on God's love and that it is God who leads us to a fulfilled life. In the process, our experience was: listening to the other's experience of faith clarified one's own faith and deepened one's own spirituality. Again and again, therefore, this encounter filled us with gratitude for the fact that we were able to speak to one another in a way that was respectful towards each other and open to the richness of the other religion's spiritual tradition.

Prologue

When we listen to one another openly, without trying to immediately represent our position as the "better" or "more logical" one, we can discover treasures that each religious tradition carries within it, while also being awed at the richness of spiritual experience and lived wisdom in the other's and our own religion. Suddenly, we feel kinship where before there seemed to be only strangeness.

In our conversation and in this book, we have thought about essential matters: about the divine, the holy, the true and the beautiful, about faith and unbelief, about prayer and prayer spaces, about the responsibility of the faithful, about shared mission, and about the art of living. Such reflection is made in the face of the other but from out of one's own tradition. Our dialogue was not about being in the right, nor about setting oneself above the other and preaching. Instead, it was important to first see oneself from the perspective of the other, rediscovering oneself, at times also questioning one's own ideas critically and standing in awe of one's own tradition. But it was always also about the other person, about the respective other faith, about the heart of its spirituality: about the beauty of Christianity, the fragility of Jesus, the purity of Mary, and a God who himself is love and mercy. It was about the mystery of the cross, which remains a persistent thorn to both Christians and Muslims: in the question of how we understand it and can make it comprehensible to one another.

By explaining our spiritual path to one another, we also try to find a language in which we can pass on to the people of today—to the faithful and non-believers, to Muslims and Christians—the richness of our spiritual tradition in such a way that that richness shapes the people and society of tomorrow. Encounter from the heart of spirituality points to the future because spirituality contains within it an inexhaustible openness.

But what also became clear is the path that still remains before us. The beginnings of a path have been made; the encounter shows that we have a joint mission for creatively shaping an open society—which can remain open only if it is supported by shared values. In such an open society, the suffering of people and a respect for their dignity would come first; refugees would be seen first of all as people; minorities and the weak would not be left to fend for themselves; aging could occur with dignity; religious freedom would be an important good. Only together can we stand up responsibly for what is good and just, for the preservation of life and creation. Only together will we learn to accept gratefully what is our own and pass it on convincingly.

We have made a start. But the path leads on. The goal is not just that Islam and Christianity get to know one another further and each continues to listen closely to what the other is trying to say. Beyond that, it will be important to develop a shared practice for deepening what we have in common. Both religions have been given peace as a central task by God. We must therefore advocate for peace together, rather than falling back into old patterns of religious warfare. Today, we should more strongly take up our shared responsibility for the one world, so that this world becomes more humane and merciful and opens itself up to God, who seeks the salvation of all humankind.

Introduction

Motives and Goals

The Importance and Timeliness of Dialogue with Islam

Anselm Grün

In our modern world where cultures and religious traditions live so closely side by side, overall peace is not possible without peace between religions. If religions are set against one another, if people fight one another in the name of religion, then conflicts escalate, even if they may be rooted in non-religious origins. Nowadays, such a vigorously stoked ideological battle can truly annihilate the entire world.

For years now, the media have been full of news about radical Islamists. Global terrorist activities are giving the entire religion a bad name and in turn evoke generalized, aggressive counter-reactions. Even if many Muslims in the West say, *Those are not real Muslims*, it must still be said, *They understand themselves to be, they pray five times a day, and they cast their actions in religious terms*. Their political actions are shaped by religion. Moreover, they propagate enmity towards the "infidels." Even if they are misunderstanding Islam and misusing religion, and even if we know that the history of Christianity has seen even violent conflicts between Christians similar to what we are today seeing between Sunnis and Shiites, it is still important first to understand what the motives and forces behind all this are. What are the criteria for differentiating? What is truly the core of this religion? Are there actually any bridges across which we can find connections?

Confrontation cannot be a path to the future, nor can mutual isolation. After all, it is not merely a question of the globalized world. Growing numbers of Muslims live in our society too—they are our neighbors. Just like we Christians, they live their religion, essentially in the same secular society. And yet, most of the time, both religions are merely living alongside one another without any interaction. So where can we find inner paths toward one another, toward mutual understanding—paths not on the level of theologians, associations, or religious institutions, or wherever abstract intellectual, political, or legal/organizational matters are negotiated, but where spiritually and religiously open people can be reached on a level that actually touches their everyday lives?

In this process, it is important to avoid taking pointedly different positions opposite one another. At first, it is simply about understanding. Only when we understand one another can we deal honestly and fairly with each other. And only in this way can we avoid larger conflict, as well. Dialogue, then, is the precondition for peace between religions on all levels.

I know, of course, that "the one (true) Islam" does not exist. In Malaysia in particular, I myself encountered the wide variety within this religion. For example, in eastern Malaysia, the relationship between Muslims and Christians is quite good. But I could sense potential aggression in western Malaysia, where an intolerant, authoritarian Islam inspired by Saudi-Arabian Wahhabism holds sway.

For me personally, the encounter with such realities and dialogue with Muslims is a relatively new subject. It is also due to the trend of ever more Muslims living among us in my native Germany. We now have several dozen refugees in our monastery, most of whom are Muslims. In part, that means completely natural communal experiences. On the eve of All Saints' Day, as we were remembering the dead in the cemetery, the refugees joined in with their song, speaking their prayers and lighting candles. Or another impression: On Maundy Thursday, during the ritual washing of the feet, the abbot washed the feet of the Muslim refugees as well. And thereafter, at their wish, they washed his feet too. In that moment, one could feel lived tolerance and respect for one another's tradition. But of course, I have also had other experiences. One example of aggressively expansionist self-confidence is the story told to me by a Christian woman, whose Islamic neighbor said to her: "In ten years, you won't have any more say here, by then everything will be Islamized." That creates fear.

In terms of my own biography, my socialization was entirely Catholic and within the world of the Catholic Church. But the Second Vatican Council brought a great opening toward the world of other religions and an attention to their truths. Already in our studies, of course, Judaism was important. And when the earliest interreligious dialogues were held in the 1960s and 1970s, our focus was more on Buddhism than on Islam. We practiced Zen meditation and engaged with eastern spirituality.

Naturally, I had also read Sufi mystical texts, which continue to touch me deeply in their focus on the immediate experience of God. What fascinated me about Islam were, first of all, the external matters, such as the faithfulness to prayer and praying five times a day, which is familiar to us monks, as well. That is one thing. Regarding theology, from the point of view of a Christian conception of God, I had always had a somewhat ambivalent impression of the Muslim understanding of God and the often apparently fatalistic subjugation to God's will. To me, dialogue between Christianity and Islam seemed at first like something relevant to the Middle Ages: We knew of course that Thomas Aquinas was influenced not only by the Jewish philosopher Maimonides but also by Muslim thinkers such as Avicenna and Averroes, and that there was a rich history of mutual exchange of ideas. I freely admit that this fruitful dialogue seemed to me primarily a matter of history. Other than that, for example during my student days, I had little in the way of deeper encounters with Islam.

But just as in the 1960s we arrived, through the detour of Zen meditation, at Christian meditation and then at the monks' Jesus Prayer—that is, we rediscovered our own tradition through dialogue with Buddhism—I now hope, of course, that dialogue with Islam will reveal something for our own spiritual path as well. Opening one's own religion toward another tradition, the perception of the other, is always also an opportunity for adapting, clarifying, and enriching one's own position.

This is important to me: We should not intermix the religions but should understand what the respective other's path is. After all, the same essential questions—starting with Greek philosophy—concern and occupy us: Where do we come from? Where are we going? What supports us, and from what do we live? Back then, I wanted to know how Buddhists would answer these questions. That forced me to find the answer that I would give, what my tradition had to say on the matter. My interest in Islam today is similar: What are the fundamental questions of this religion? And what are its answers? I consider such learning and openness to be enriching. So where do we start? In my dialogue with Daoism, I realized something essential: "Dao" is the everyday. And spirituality too is an everyday matter: Doing what is in front of us, no nonsense. If a religion makes a claim of truth—Christianity as well as Islam—that is in its nature. But that is not all that determines the relationship between the two religions.

We Christians say: Jesus is the actual revelation. But we do not say that we have the entire truth. And we know that we too have our particular lens of Western culture through which we view the world.

We start, first of all, by perceiving one another. Dialogue with other religions can make our lens clearer, our view broader. One result of dialogue with Islam after all can be that we look at Jesus differently. And then perhaps differently at Mohammed. In interreligious encounters, too, we should bear in mind that faith is never static or a rigidly fixed set of dogmatic determinations. All our paths always go toward God. Being on a journey is the very essence of faith. This movement is made clear already in the Bible. The story of salvation begins with Abraham, in the passage which reads: "Go from your country and your kindred and your father's house" (Gn 12:1). The Church Fathers read this as the description of a threefold departure: from dependencies, from old habits, and from bonds that will not let me go. Faith means a departure from the visible. The mystics, too, have seen this path as one of ascent to God, for example St. John of the Cross in his *Ascent of Mount Carmel*. Being on such a path always also means changing. In the Gospel of Luke, Jesus is the divine wanderer who is with us on our path, walking alongside us and occasionally giving his divine gift: the message of love. Finally, the Second Vatican Council used the image of a path to describe the Church as the wandering people of God. And this wandering always also means journeying together with others. The journey of a religion is always toward the one God. There is only one God, although we have different images of him. Coexistence between religions, including fruitful coexistence between Christianity and Islam, then, is just such a path toward this last, shared goal.

What Makes the Encounter between Muslims and Christians Sensible—and What is the Goal of our Shared Path?

Ahmad Milad Karimi

If spirituality means living from a shared spirit and an existence in that spirit, then how can two different spiritual paths (the Christian and the Islamic), two different life paths of the spirit, really encounter one another in such a way that the result is not merely informative and clarifying, serving to reduce existing tensions, but actually has the effect of mutual enrichment?

From an Islamic perspective, it is easy to justify why such a dialogue is not just sensible but practically an inner necessity. Islam can hardly understand itself without a lasting connection to Christianity and Judaism. In the Qur'an, Jews and Christians are explicitly emphasized as those who have Scripture. For our own self-discovery, then, we Muslims need relation—not just an abstract relation, but a lived relation—including to Christianity.

We need people who bear within them the living testimony of Christendom, in order to better understand our own sources, such as the Qur'an, through encounters with these people. For the Qur'an is filled with Christian wisdom and Christian statements that must be understood. Fundamentally, the Islamic path—if it is to be walked—cannot be followed without Christianity, nor of course without Judaism. For me personally, there is an added level as well: Though I was born in Afghanistan, I also partly grew up in my native Germany; the encounter with Christianity has meant a great deal to my life. I studied in Freiburg, and my academic teacher was a Catholic theologian. From him, especially in engagement with Christianity, I have also learned a great deal about Islam. To begin with, I had to engage with Christian theological discourse as well. And precisely because the religion in which I myself grew up was the one and the only true one for me, it was a painful discovery for me that Christianity, too, advocates a very sophisticated and convincing logic and a great theology.

Through this important lived encounter I learned that honoring others can be an Islamic virtue. Of course, it is not a matter of mixing the different traditions. It would be a misunderstood and inappropriate dialogue if its goal were to convince or "take over" the other. To me, the beautiful thing, including about my engagement with my own religion, is that I discovered that both religions are borne up by the same questions: What do we hope for? Where does the path of life lead? What is the meaning and the goal of our existence? What should we do? What determines our actions? What do we actually mean when we speak of devoting ourselves to God? The answers may be very different. Christians, from their perspective, can say: The center of my faith community, the supporting basis of my life, is Jesus of Nazareth. And I as a Muslim can say: The center of my community is the Qur'an or the Prophet Muhammad. What is most significant is that our questions are the same. And our stance seems important to me as well: That we do not possess the truth, even if we are convinced that our own path is true. We are entitled to make that claim. But if we pretend as though we do possess the truth, our path is blocked already.

The path of spirituality is also a path of living in spirit, to the extent that we conceive of our own path as a path in the first place—as a path to truth, as a longing. The following example shows that Islam, too, knows the spiritual experience of the path, for there are two phenomena that have shaped this religion's understanding of itself from the very beginning: Before Muhammad is anointed Prophet, he makes his way upward, goes up to a mountain cave. Symbolically speaking, in other words, he walks a path from many-ness to oneness. This path into reclusiveness is also a reason why he is visited by the Angel Gabriel and why the Qur'an is revealed to him. The other defining—practically identity-determining—feature in Islamic spiritual history is Muhammad's path from Mecca to Medina, that is, his experience of flight. The Islamic calendar begins with this path, away from tribal culture, away from the bonds that have shaped his path, toward faith and another, new bond. The Arabic word for flight is *hijra*. *Hijra* means severing a bond, un-binding. Through this *hijra*, Muhammad receives what is described by the word *'aqīda*, literally "binding": faith. *'Aqīda*, the bond between human being and God, is realized only if we un-bind ourselves, detach from all the other things which surround us. This reveals a parallel tenet in Islamic spiritual history that can be found in the Hebrew Bible and Christian theology as well: faith as setting out in order to travel on the path of God.

But in addition to the image of the path, another thing is important to me in this dialogue: that I, as a young philosopher, get to hold with a spiritual master of the Christian tradition experienced in its wisdom. That is the attitude of the student, which I have come to know in my own tradition. This attitude of the student is significant particularly in the mystic tradition. There is no Sufi, no mystic tradition that is not familiar with or fails to cultivate this teacher–student relationship. I consider that important for myself, and at the same time it seems to me very Islamic. To some extent, the relationship between the teacher and the student also represents to me the relationship between Christianity and Islam.

I conceive of my path as Muslim as insight into my own position as a student: being a student means wanting to learn, being capable of learning, and open to experiencing or gaining something valuable from someone else, as well. Incidentally, that is also a description of what in its innermost version makes up a spiritual path: being the path oneself, not merely setting out on a path, but turning oneself into that path. If, as a religious person, I want to keep remaining a learner, this presupposes that my religion must be shaped by humility and not by a feeling of superiority which is actually pride. Religion must carry within it an inner openness. It cannot be dictated from above and must not be doctrinally petrified, but must occur in lived practice. It is my belief that this is among the fundamental features of Islam. And this paves the way for a dialogue in which we can truly approach one another.

To prevent misunderstanding: This teacher–student relationship does not mean enslavement or false obsequiousness. But it does speak to a need and a longing to experience enrichment by listening to one another. And another thing is important to understand beforehand: when someone says that what I have just said is an idealistic view of Islam, but the reality in Islamic states such as Saudi Arabia is very different, my position is the following. First off, it is important to see and to name an ideal—and I am not alone in doing so. Furthermore, is Saudi Arabia an Islamic country? One should bear in mind the conditions there: all our holy sites have been taken over by sects that actually pervert our religion, women hardly have rights, human rights are ignored, those of different faiths have no rights, Islam is turned into a business (in the sense of commercial tourism), the Kaaba looks like a minor Manhattan ruled by bad taste. All this has nothing to do with the values or the spirit of Islam, and those should be taken as the measure of the historical character of a religion. Islam, of course, is also always a historical phenomenon, and so it appears in different forms in the context of different societies. Europe is a perfect example that shows how especially we Muslims in Germany, in Europe, in Bosnia live our lives as European Muslims.

I myself am a staunch defender of the German constitution, and I love the sharia; I am also a strictly praxis-oriented Muslim and live an authentic Islam. Such a claim is not idealistic in the sense that it is some purely romantic idea; it is the very real precondition for a dialogue that lays open its foundations. In the process, I refer to the mystical tradition of Islam, that is, to an inner understanding. And the Islamic path does not see mysticism as a marginal phenomenon. Quite to the contrary, its entire orthodoxy is permeated by mysticism, extending all the way back to theologians from the twelfth century. The mystical theologian Abū Ḥāmid al-Ghazālī, finally, says very clearly why these two traditions belong together.

If it were only a matter of fulfilling the ritual prayers without also having internalized these prayers, then nowadays one could—speaking provocatively—simply program a robot to do it. The robot would be much better at keeping the prayer times and, ideally, could even speak the prayer out loud. What truly matters, obviously, is one's own spiritual path. Something we in Islam owe to our mystic tradition is the shaping of a particular stance within the religion: a stance toward faith, a stance toward creation, a stance toward God, a stance toward our neighbor which is continually being shaped. And even if the goal is perfection, that does not mean that we would at some point be perfect. Rather, the idea is that we will always long for God. The mystic ʿAṭṭār, who examined different levels of mysticism, says that seeking is not something with which we are ever at an end in order to reach the next step; rather we remain seekers at each step, which means that the spiritual path can never be walked in a straight line; rather, it runs in a spiral which could be said to always support us.

"Stumbling Blocks" on the Road to One Another —Provocations for Dialogue

If a dialogue is to be successful, it makes sense to bear in mind similarities but also to gain clarity on differences. And it is important to look at potential stumbling blocks on the path toward the other. Certainly there are factual differences but also subjective experiences that shape our perceptions. There are historical, societal, and cultural factors and contingencies that influence mentalities, attitudes, and actions. And there are certain points of view that may prove to be prejudiced. That too can loom large in a process of dialogue, can determine conversations, and can make it more difficult to find agreement—or it can be resolved through listening. For the sake of mutual approach and progress, it makes sense to start by noting these "stumbling blocks" and to look at, exchange ideas about, and finally clarify any disconcerting points.

That is the purpose of the following "provocations": the expression "stumbling blocks" refers to subjects perceived as controversial and which are not unimportant details but address something fundamental. Nevertheless, some of these subjects are discussed only briefly here. That occurs where the concomitant questions are more thoroughly covered in the later chapters.

"Stumbling Blocks" for Christians

Answers by Ahmad Milad Karimi

I. Who Represents True Islam?

Islam has become a feared entity, while also remaining an unknown quantity for many. What is Islam really—with reference to its history, but also with reference to the societies shaped by Islam today? Rigidly conservative Muslims and aggressive fundamentalists, just as much as representatives of a more mystical interpretation of Islam, claim to refer back to the authentic Qur'an and true Islam. So who represents true Islam?

It is already problematic to speak of Islam as a uniform entity. Islamic tradition itself is shaped, both culturally and historically, by a wide variety of readings and interpretative horizons. For over a thousand years, contradictory positions have managed to coexist side-by-side and compete with one another argumentatively. The fixation with a "true Islam," no matter who might originate or hold it, is above all one thing: inimical to tradition. It is reported that the Prophet Muhammad himself prophesied the plurality of Islamic ways of life and that he saw this plurality as a mercy, that is, felt it to be positive.[1] Islam's unity has always also meant a unity in diversity. Within Sunni Islam alone there are several legal schools that accept, tolerate, and respect one another, although their different methodologies lead each of them to different and mutually contradicting results.

What is more, there are also several genuine theological schools that in some cases reach completely different conclusions and results but nevertheless lay claim to authority. And this is not merely a historical fact; it has a religious basis as

---

1. See J. Suyūṭī: *Jāmi' aṣ-ṣaghīr fī aḥādīth al-bashīr an-nadhīr*, Cairo 1373/1954, 28.

well: according to Islamic belief, the truth is God himself, and God alone can lay claim to truth. Our understanding of truth must never be mistaken for truth itself. Because at best all it is and all it remains is an apparent truth, something that seems to us to be true knowledge. Accordingly, Islamic history soon reached the conclusion that while we cannot possess truth, we can do everything in our power to get as close to it as possible.[2] This approaching to and striving for truth was to be fought for—including in scientific ways. That meant that there was a religious interest in speaking about one's own religious convictions in ways that would be comprehensible to all, testable, and thus valid in all cases. This created a rivalry over the plausibility of the different religious ideas. But plausibility also meant that the convictions should not only be reasonably communicable but also practically implementable—based on a statement by the Prophet Muhammad that religion is there to ease life, not to make it more difficult.[3]

In Islam, in other words, philosophers strive for truth by seeking to probe truth itself; theologians strive for truth by seeking to recognize truth; ethicists seek truth in order to shape their actions according to it; and mystics in Islam strive for truth by seeking to lovingly experience what is true. Given this background, one cannot ask which discipline represents

---

2. In his main work the philosopher Al-Kindī writes programmatically: "We ought not to be ashamed of appreciating the truth and of acquiring it wherever it comes from, even if it comes from races distant and nations different from us. For the seeker of truth, nothing takes precedence over the truth." Ya'qub ibn Ishaq al-Kindi, *Al-Kindi's Metaphysics: A Translation of Ya'qub ibn Ishaq al-Kindi's Treatise "On First Philosophy,"* trans. Alfred L. Ivry (Albany: State University of New York Press, 1974), 58.
3. A companion of the Prophet reports: "An Arab of the desert stood up and urinated in the mosque. When the people seized him the Prophet, God's blessing and peace be upon him, said to them: 'Let him be and pour a bucket of water—or a little more—on his urine, for your task is to make it easier for people, not harder!'" Ṣaḥīḥ al-Bukhārī, chapter 4, Ḥadīth no. 220.

"true" Islam because none of them lay any claim to truth in and of itself. But all are concerned with truth, though each in their own way and with their own humility. True Islam, which does not "exist," is the yearning for what is true in Islam.

But despite all the openness inherent in Islam, not every conviction can be considered equally Islamic. Because even Islam sees a clear boundary beyond which fundamental insights, principles, goals of the religion are being disrespected. When fundamentalist groups today claim to have the only true Islam (a claim by which they are already disqualifying themselves on principle), then what they proclaim and (seek to) institute as Islamic is simply—to use a "modern" metaphor—not competitive in the marketplace. Destruction, disrespect, killings and abuse, rape, exploitation, devaluation of creation, persecution of those with different beliefs (inside their own faith and in other faiths) and the like have always counted and still count as clear violations of the fundamental pillars of Islamic religiosity.

2. The Muslim View of God

From the outside, it seems that in Islam God has an inflexible, punishing nature. Does this not contradict all the discussion of his love for humankind? And is faith in a God who does what he will and cannot be grasped by our human categories not automatically faith in a despotic God? If there is such overemphasis on his absolute oneness and transcendence, how could he be a God in whom we can place our trust and our hopes and to whom we can devote our lives?

There is undoubtedly a deplorable habit of overemphasizing the wrathful nature of divine reality, so that—both inwardly and outwardly—a distorted idea of God can prevail. But there is also the other deplorable habit of speaking about God as if he were the kind and friendly grandfather from next door.

Islam's idea of God—if we can even speak of an idea in this context—follows an entirely different path. In Islam, it is fundamentally impossible to speak of God as one would speak of a human being. God cannot be compared with or put in relation to anything else. Initially, this makes it more difficult to speak of God. But it also makes it easier to reach the insight that whoever reduces God to a particular idea, a particular characteristic, is missing the reality of God. God does, however, have characteristics that we can glimpse in the way he acts in regard to the world. In the Qur'an, a wide variety of characteristics of God is mentioned in different contexts and on different levels of meaning. But these never give the impression that one might be able to recognize the mystery of God by, as it were, uncovering him and "knowing what there is to know" about him.

The impression of an inflexible, punishing God is qualified not just by the fact that greater qualitative and quantitative weight is given to descriptions of God's clemency, his forgiveness, and his mercy. The qur'anic testament also never mentions God's punishment except in the context of his justice. The more strongly and intensely imagery of God's punishment is enmeshed in the Qur'an—that is, the more closely it is linked to core qur'anic themes—the more prominent is God's will to preserve humankind from precisely this punishment. The punishment of God is not meant to provoke fear, but rather to admonish, to warn, and to reveal what it means to go wrong. Nor is the nature of the punishment ever self-referential in the sense that God punishes humankind in order that they finally recognize that he is God. It is always about the people themselves: "Whoever purifies himself does so for his own benefit" (Qur'an 35:18).

Emphasis on God's absolute oneness and transcendence, furthermore, does not mean that because God did not adopt a human face he knows nothing of my pain and my human experience of suffering. God is not part of the world but is nevertheless present in his own creation. Nothing moves without him: "No leaf falls without His knowledge " (Qur'an 6:59). His knowledge permeates everything, including my humanity; he is closer to me than I am myself.[4] When I suffer, God does not suffer with me; he is within me while I relate to my suffering: "I am near," he declares of himself in the Qur'an.[5] He is with me by supporting me, giving me hope and strength, encouraging me toward life and the good, so that even in difficult hours of my life I can practice patience and grow—with God. This "over-nearness" of my creator is overwhelming, precisely because he remains God and does not become a part of my human and "worldly affairs."

Nevertheless, the statement that God does what he will can create the impression that he is an arbitrary God not bound to my human yardsticks and conditions. This is an understandable impression. But to say that God has absolute freedom of will is intended to express first of all the unpossessable nature and second the unconditional nature of the immanent God. All that he wills and does, he wills and does in his divinity, so that it leaves me not desperate but trustful.

Nowadays we speak of God in an off-hand manner that robs the word of its true value, for example when we speak of someone as a "soccer god," as a "goddess of beauty," or as a "divine singer." Islam, in contrast, seeks to develop an appropriate attitude in the face of the sublime God; an attitude not expressing fear of an unyielding super-power, but showing gratitude and expressing deeply felt reverence.

3. The Qur'anic Understanding of Revelation

Since Muslims understand the Qur'an to be God's last word, it often seems to make sense to read and interpret it not in its historical context but as an immediate instruction on how to act today. Is such an attitude not just as cogent as its consequences are problematic? Or is the Qur'an ambiguous? But if so, how

---

4. See Qur'an 11:61, among others.
5. Qur'an 2:186.

can it offer guidance? What is right and what is wrong? There are unmistakable passages in the Qur'an calling, for example, for the destruction of non-believers or that are unmistakably directed against Jews. Does that not instruct readers to act out aggression? How can the Qur'an as divine revelation be both the foundation and reference point of love and simultaneously the same for rejection, even hate? Is it not possible to cleanse the Qur'an of its hateful passages in some more modern way?

To us Muslims, the Qur'an is considered the pure word of God. But because this word of God does not want to be mere word, it is not only pure information but also good news to all people. It wants to be understood as such a joyful message. Accordingly, the essence of the Qur'an is that of a message delivered in the language of the people to whom it was first addressed. A linguistically mediated message—and what is more, one that is phrased in rhyming prose, with rhythm and sonority—by its very nature can never be subject to only one interpretation. It is this very multiplicity of meanings, expressed in many parables, imagery, metaphor (that is, in a language of symbols) that has been highly valued in the tradition of Islamic spirituality. But if the Qur'an is reduced to one message, one idea—even if this idea is meant to be the idea of love!—then the nature of the Qur'an as revelation of God has been manipulated. Because merely speaking of love says nothing, and can even become oppressive if the love is misunderstood. For Muslims' understanding of themselves, it is therefore incredibly important that the Qur'an be preserved as it is: as the Qur'an with all its challenges and mysteries, all its wisdom and impositions. But what we must continue to work on again and again is our interpretation of the Qur'an. Not every qur'anic verse is normative in nature. To say that the Qur'an is a book of law is simply wrong. The Qur'an, rather, is much more: laconic, suggestive, at times fragmentary, but again and again also dialogic, philosophical, sophisticated, and spiritually fulfilling.

In order not to run the risk that the Qur'an be reinterpreted as a message of hate—which in fact is occurring at the present time—we are enjoined to develop criteria and interpretative principles. That has been common practice in our Islamic tradition, and that is how one should deal with the Qur'an today, as well. It would therefore be a complete theological absurdity to interpret the Qur'an however one would like according only to one's taste, or to simply delete those sections that are difficult to follow with our understanding today, in effect pasting together a "Qur'an within the Qur'an." It is righteous, on the other hand, to develop interpretive methods for the Qur'an as a whole from within the text, such as *surah* by *surah* or according to subjects, if these methods firstly do justice to the context of the revelation, secondly do not ignore the rich tradition of exegesis but rather consider it in its respective historical context, and thirdly reveal categories that account for the respective normative core of the verses. Furthermore, the fundamental nature of the Qur'an's multiplicity of meanings must be preserved. One and the same passage of the Qur'an can be read completely differently from different perspectives. As an example, the qur'anic verse known as the Verse of Light—which states that God is the light of the heavens and the Earth, "light over light"—has been interpreted very differently by different Muslim philosophers, theologians, and mystics. Here, one cannot speak of a single interpretation, much less one that would be definitive for all time. Such an essentialist understanding distorts the openness of the Qur'an, which does not seek to be ideological, set in stone, or one-dimensional, but rather open, inspiring, purposely multifaceted, guiding without being rigid.

A God who himself chose a poetic, almost playful form of revelation would not have revealed to humankind a single understanding, but rather unending worlds of understanding: "And if all there is in trees on the earth were pens, and the sea, after it had been exhausted, received seven more seas in addition, the words of my Lord would still not come to an end" (Qur'an 31:27).

4. Salvation and Redemption

Even if Muslims say that Islam is not a religion of salvation, does the Qur'an not also say that human beings need guidance and must be liberated from entanglements, meaninglessness, and circumstances that are irredemptive?

Islam's view of humanity is shaped by the idea that every human being that is born carries salvation within them.[6] Neither does sin cleave to us nor are we by our mere nature as human beings weighed down by original sin in whatever form. This fundamental sinlessness is the reason why Islam is a stranger to the theology of the cross, which circles around questions of betrayal, sacrificial death, guilt, sin, and redemption and sees the crucifixion as a necessary act for the salvation of humankind. It is due to this sinlessness that the Qur'an says that the children of Adam are honored.[7] The honor of human existence is free from original sin and, according to Muslim conviction, does not require cleansing of sin by a divine act on the cross.

At the same time, human life is entangled in sin again and again. Lack of orientation and entanglement in irredemptive circumstances can overshadow our life. And not all sin can be amended in this world. When we sin, our act may be irreversible; it may leave behind wounds and scars that cannot be healed. Not infrequently it is we who cannot forgive ourselves and, in extreme cases, can no longer live with our own guilt. But we can also become victim of a sin or experience suffering that to us seems like a coincidence that has no immanent or eschatological meaning. Islam does not ignore these questions—quite the contrary. The Qur'an is understood as guidance and orientation

---

6. On this question, see Ahmad Milad Karimi, "Zur Frage der Erlösung des Menschen im religiösen Denken des Islam" [On the question of salvation of human beings in Islamic religious thought], in Klaus von Stosch and Aaron Langenfeld (eds.), *Streitfall Erlösung* [The dispute over salvation] (Paderborn: Brill, 2015), 17–38.
7. See Qur'an 17:70.

in life. Not only the practice of forgiveness but also dealing adequately with guilt and the vicissitudes of life are meant to be learned. But judging guilt is always an individual as well as a collective matter. A person can be more angelic that the angels together or more bestial than any animal, the mystical theologian Abū Ḥāmid al-Ghazālī tells us.[8]

As the Prophet Muhammad tells us, we are meant to live our lives in forgiving and hoping for forgiveness. For everything is brought before God.[9] And the Eternal will lead us to our truth. As human beings, we need redemption and salvation—this much is beyond debate. But the force that redeems and saves is God alone, as the incomparable source of all hope and all trust. We can have no specific knowledge as to how God produces retributive justice, how he cleanses us and takes away our guilt without mocking the victims of our sins. That is why trust in God is simultaneously the highest expression of religious humility.

We cannot presume automatic salvation, which would minimize our specific actions, our historical deeds in our lives for which we have responsibility. In this context, faith in the justice of God is a clear guide. Even God's forgiveness, which is mentioned remarkably often in the Qur'an, does not represent blind acquiescence to what we have done and failed to do in life. Rather, it is a considered forgiveness that does justice to the story of our life, as well. God's justice is not undercut by his forgiveness. Human beings are meant for salvation. God himself ensures it by creating in human beings an orientation toward God (Arabic: *fiṭra*) and reveals himself to human beings in order that they may orient themselves toward the good.[10]

For the beauty of forgiveness lies precisely in the fact that we cannot possess it, cannot calculate or derive it ahead

---

8. See Abū Ḥāmid al-Ghazālī, *The Alchemy of Happiness*, translated by Claud Field (London: John Murray, 1910), 20. Accessed at: https://archive.org/details/alchemyofhappine00algh/mode/2up.
9. See Qur'an 2:210.
10. See Qur'an 30:30.

of time. Rather, we hope for our salvation with and through God, in his visage.

5. Religion and Society in the Purview of Islam

In some Western countries, the growth of Muslim communities is stoking the fear that integration will fail and societal peace is in danger. After all, Islam—both historically and in many places to this day—made the all-encompassing claim to rule over all areas of life and to control or at least regulate social and political life as well. This has necessarily led to conflicts in a pluralist, secular society.

Fear of a religion that seeks to regulate all areas of life is justified. When Islam is interpreted in this way, it is no longer being conceived of as a religion but as a totalitarian system. This totalitarian claim, extending across the political, legal, and social realms and incapable of distinguishing between religion and culture, is what marks Islamism: Islam is being "islamized."[11] This image perfectly describes fundamentalist practice. Indeed, the specific way this is occurring terrifies Muslims as well. But critics who have a conception of Islam that at its core is the same as the fundamentalists' view of themselves face a dilemma: In the first place, such critics themselves do not distinguish between culture and religion. Secondly, they are speaking of Islam in essentialist terms, without recognizing intra-Islamic plurality. These critics are desperately trying to cast totalitarian Islamism as Islam itself. And fundamentalists identify the very same Islamism as Islam. In between these two

---

11. On the concept of an "islamization of Islam," see Aziz Al-Azmeh, *Islams and Modernities*, 3rd ed. (London: Verso, 2009) and Thomas Bauer, "Islamisierung des Islams" [Islamization of Islam], *Aus Politik & Kultur* no. 11, 178–180. Available online at: https://www.kulturrat.de/wp-content/uploads/2016/04/pdf_Islam_AusPolitikUndKultur_Nr11.pdf

positions stands "the" religion of Islam in all its ambiguity, in all its diversity, in the complexity of how it is lived by different people in different worlds.

It is this diversity that a majority of Muslims still affirm and support. Of course, the reality of global Islam is that it is often imprisoned in cultural spaces that are shaped by cultural poverty, by too few educational opportunities, by a lack of security in life, by economic hopelessness, by eroded infrastructure, and by an absence of peace. Neither is Islam the solution for all these problems, nor, on the other hand, is it their cause. The world is simply too complex for that, so that dialogue between religions is an urgent need in this context, as well.

Muslim life takes part in pluralist society, which is pluralist and tolerant of ambiguity not because these values are mandated from above or imposed from outside, but because they stem from the sum of shared experience. Among the convictions that create meaning in secular European society, for example, the religions of Judaism and Christianity play a constitutive part, as Islam self-evidently does as well. When we speak of European culture, we are also speaking about a Europe in which Islam plays a significant role. Culture is rooted in knowledge, and the history of Islamic thought has contributed significantly to the history of European science—in the areas of medicine, natural science, mathematics, and especially philosophy. Muslims have lived in Europe since the eighth century: in Spain, Sicily, Hungary, Turkey, Poland, and Lithuania. Even historically speaking, Europe has never been fully Christian. The politics of integrating Muslim migrants or refugees is threatened not because a Muslim community is growing or because it is a part of pluralist societies, but because and to the extent that migrants and refugees are reduced to the attribute "Islamic." These people are also Muslims, but they are more than Muslim. Their behaviors, their enculturation, their education, their sensitivity to diverse ways of life, their degree of affinity for democracy and their affirmation of the rule of law trace back to a multiplicity of factors. Failure to recognize this by instead reducing everything unilaterally to Islam will not produce results.

Obviously, Islam contains norms (prohibitions, commandments, etc.) specific to the religion. But these are not to be seen as rivals to the authority of the state. Instead, they concern, for example, the spiritual and ethical dimension of human beings. Accordingly, the idea of a theocracy in an Islamic context is highly dubious, as well as unsupportable by argument. In all cases where Islam is articulated as a justification for endangering the public peace, the state must intercede vigorously. Doing so will be in the interests of Muslims, as well.

6. The Question of Violence

Current news that highlights the terror of Islamist groups or that calls attention to Islam's bellicose history from its earliest beginnings leads many to link Islam and violence—not just historically, but in some essential way. Can Islam even be meaningfully distinguished from violent or at least potentially violent Islamism?

Muslims can be terrorists, but terrorism is not Islamic; Muslims can commit violence, but violence in and of itself is not Islamic; Muslims can be unjust, but injustice is not Islamic; Muslims can shape an ideological movement out of Islam, but the ideology is not Islamic; Muslims can inflict pain and suffering on other people and instill fear and horror in the world, but the subjugation of others is not Islamic. In short, Muslims can fail in their religion, but failing in religion is not part of the religion itself.

Nowadays, Islam's ugliest interpretation and practice cannot be missed. This makes it all the more essential to distinguish, because once we stop distinguishing between Islam as a religion inherently conceived in pluralism on the one hand and the ideology of Islamism on the other, we are adopting the worldview of those whose worldview we reject. We are pinning Islam down to a particular interpretation. This in itself is an act of violence, and above all can have no basis in theology. The essentialist reduction of the religion of Islam to a single—completely distorted—reading contradicts the reality of an Islam that has traditionally always been shaped by a diversity of opinions, interpretations, and readings all of which strove for plausibility in an argumentative competition, while coexisting and attempting to achieve mutual respect.

And yet we cannot wave away the acts of violence some Muslims do in the name of Islam by simply declaring them un-Islamic. Every Islamism has something to do with Islam—as an uncompetitive and thus primitive reading of Islam, but of an Islam that cannot be reduced to Islamism. For all the openness and polyphonic nature of Islam, this is a religion with clear, unmistakable ground rules. There are principles that must be followed if one makes the claim to speak of Islam.

One of these fundamental principles is that violence as an end in itself is always unacceptable. Accordingly, the use of violence might serve the goal of justice or of defending life and peace. The difficulty, then, is that both justice and defense are not simply and self-evidently given but must be interpreted first. This interpretation is a complex and historically contextual matter. For one thing, historical accounts of violence with religious connotations (whether in a battle, in a war of expansion, or in an individual's violent act) cannot be explained outside the historical context.

History is at work in all things that occur, including and especially in religious contexts; so we must always also interrogate the circumstances and constellations that prefigure every violent action. These preconditions and immediate causes, however, cannot be unilaterally traced back to religion, but rather are always complex entanglements. For example, when Germany militarily defends itself in the Hindu Kush, at first glance, the very idea sounds absurd unless the historical context of this "defense" is considered. Additionally, in Islam, the fundamental principle regarding violence has been unmistakably decided: violence must never be religiously motivated. It may be justified only if justice, peace, or life are threatened and it is exercised to preserve or defend these.

Islam becomes Islamism when the religion is abused to legitimize violence; when the spirit of preservation is perverted into the lust for destruction; when the humility demanded in judging others slips into superiority towards or disrespect of them; when diversity of life is suppressed and withers away; when talk of justice and peace serves violence—and not the other way around, as the Islamic maxim dictates.

"Stumbling Blocks" for Muslims

Answers by Anselm Grün

I. Truth of the Dogmas and the Question of "True Christianity"

Some groups in Western societies, motivated by xenophobia or misinterpretations of Christianity, have been mobilizing against Muslims or more generally against Islam. So who represents true Christianity? Who possesses the truth about Jesus as described in Church dogma?

In the first place: dogmas are true in the sense of the Greek term for truth *aletheia*, which, as the German philosopher Martin Heidegger has translated the term, means "un-concealedness." This conception of truth does not refer to true propositions. Rather, this kind of truth means: the veil that lies over all of reality is lifted and beneath it we recognize something of the deepest reality. We look on the foundation of being. Something becomes clear to us without our being able to cloak it in what we might call mathematically clear language. Nor is truth something I have or can possess. Truth can occur to, can arise in a person. Dogmas, then, are not prescriptions, not expressions of bossiness, but rather an attempt to provide a framework within which truth can shine out. Dogmas are interpretations that in turn require interpretation themselves. To me, dogmatics is the art of keeping open the mystery. Dogmatic statements, which at first glance can often appear incomprehensible, seek to open our thinking toward the absolute mystery (to use Karl Rahner's term for God): the indescribable and ungraspable mystery of the invisible God.

No one can lay claim to possessing true Christianity. And whenever one person believes he or she alone is in the right and has grasped the truth, skepticism is appropriate. To correctly understand Jesus' message as transmitted in the Gospels, we must confront ourselves with it, must let ourselves be challenged by it. Jesus' words, of course, are not dogmas in the sense of precisely defined truths. They are words with which we must grapple in order for them to make sense in our lives. There are—both historically and still today—different answers to this challenge. There are many traditions. There are positions that call themselves conservative or progressive, as well as different spiritual directions. Each has a purpose. For example, there is the mystical approach, or a more political emphasis, there are feminist stances or those from liberation theology. Franciscan, Benedictine, and Ignatian spirituality—they all emphasize some particular aspect in particular historical or societal situations. But none of them can claim to possess the single true interpretation of Christianity. We all are forever searching, on our journey. On that road, it is good to live from tradition on the journey through history. But if I seek to prescribe what is historically developed, I am no longer on a journey to God but rather am remaining in a security that faith cannot give me in this manner. I am looking for security not in faith, but in external things.

To me, the essence of Christianity is shown in Jesus' question to his disciples. In answer to the question "Who is Jesus of Nazareth?," Peter answers: "You are the Messiah, the son of the living God." The Messiah seeks to lead others into freedom. Living means that we are all children, sons and daughters of God. Jesus is closest to us wherever aliveness blooms—not where there is narrowness. Those who seek to be in the right and who judge others, who claim to be alone in their possession of truth and who use this claim to legitimize violence, are misusing Christianity and have failed to understand the words and deeds of Jesus. In the monastic tradition, there are four criteria for assessing whether something is the will of God or is the will of one's own super-ego: The will of God always leads to greater aliveness, to greater freedom, to greater peace, and to greater love. The spirit of Jesus is wherever these four criteria are given. Where anxiety and narrowness are in the foreground, what is speaking is not the will of God but rather one's own superego.

2. God Becoming Human—a Provocation?

Christianity says that God became a human being. Does this conception of God not damage the absoluteness and sublimity of God? What makes it necessary for the Lord of all the worlds to have become a human being, specifically, a man, and of all men precisely Jesus of Nazareth?

There is of course no necessity whatsoever for God to become a human being. God's incarnation in Jesus Christ is a historical event, but it remains a mystery how we should understand that in Jesus Christ, God himself is speaking to us. We Christians believe that throughout history, God has repeatedly spoken to the Jewish people through the prophets. To us Christians, too, Jesus is a prophet. But he is more than the prophets of the old covenant. We believe that in Jesus Christ, God communicated himself to humankind in a new and insuperable way. Karl Rahner, in this context, speaks of the absolute self-communication of God in Jesus Christ. It is precisely in God's descent to us human beings that the mystery of our faith is revealed. But God descended to us in Jesus Christ so that we ourselves might have the courage to descend into the depths of our soul, into what C. G. Jung calls the shadow realm of our soul. Whenever we talk about how God became human, it is always connected with how we ourselves can become human. It remains a mystery, however, how we are to understand the junction of God and human being in Jesus Christ. The Church Fathers of the earliest centuries grappled with and also argued over this mystery. They defined dogmatically how we should understand the relationship between God and human being in Jesus Christ.

But the dogma does not set matters in stone; instead, it uses paradoxes to describe this mysterious junction and intersection of God and human being in Jesus Christ. In Jesus, God did not become another God. He has always remained God, the ungraspable and sole transcendent God. But the Christian faith tells us: This God shows us his visage in the human face of Jesus. In this human being Jesus, the merciful face of God is shining out toward me. In this human being Jesus, God is encountering me in a unique, one-of-a-kind way. In the end, all dogmatic statements about Jesus as the son of God seek only to point us to this mystery: that in Jesus, we are encountering God himself. Despite all dogmatic statements, however, the how will always remain obscure to us.

The God of the Abrahamic religions—the same God Islam invokes—is also a historical God, a God who intervenes in history, unlike in Buddhism, where god is without time and history. God's deeds, for example, are revealed in the exodus from Egypt, which for Israel was an important experience of God. The appearance of Jesus is also a historical event. And the crucifixion of Jesus also occurred within history. To us Christians, theology means interpreting the events of history in the light of faith. We must not develop a theory about the cross of Jesus as though we knew precisely why Jesus died. We can only interpret the fact that he did. Different interpretations of this fact are found already in the Bible. And over the course of Church history, this initially incomprehensible event on the cross has been reinterpreted again and again. Nevertheless, it still remains a thorn for us Christians to have our idea of God and of human beings questioned by the event on the cross. At the same time, reflecting on the event leads us to deep insights into the nature of God, who is a compassionate God, and into human nature, which (as the image of the cross shows) contains many contradictions that must be united in order to become a whole human being. And the cross shows us the depth of human life: it is often suffering that breaks us open to the ungraspable God who is nevertheless always love—an ungraspable love, as Karl Rahner puts it.

So when we Christians speak of God himself becoming human in Jesus, this is an interpretation of the historical event that a child was born to Mary in Bethlehem, that this Jesus spoke wonderfully of God, and that he said of himself: "Whoever has seen me has seen the father" (Jn 14:9) and "the Father and I are one" (Jn 10:30).

3. The "One God," the Theology of the Trinity, and Jesus as God's Son

Christianity teaches that God is a trinity—but does this idea of a trinity not violate the absolute oneness of God? When Christians speak of the mystery of God, are they not undoing this very mystery through the model of the Trinity? And does the doctrine that Jesus is God's son not also contradict faith in the one God?

Like Judaism and Islam, Christianity is a monotheistic religion. We confess the one and only God. The doctrine of the Trinity is an attempt to describe the mystery of God. The Christian conviction is that this God relates to us human beings in three distinct ways: as the creator; as the one who walks beside us; and as the one who is within us, as the spirit. The metaphor of three persons produces a mistaken impression. It is the one God who reveals himself to us in different ways. Judaism speaks of the *shekhinah*, the holiness or wisdom of God. The image of the word of God become flesh must be interpreted in this fashion as well. And certainly in Christianity we have sometimes drawn the mystery of the threefold God too much onto a human level, speaking of three persons as if they were independent persons. Greek theology does not use the word "person" at all, but instead speaks of "hypostasis." Karl Rahner has pointed out that this term means something else than what we today mean by the word "person," and that therefore it can lead to misunderstanding to speak of one God in three persons. It is all too easy to distort the mystery of the one, threefold God into the sense of a tri-theism.

The Church Fathers saw a trinity, a threefold nature, in human beings, as well: humans are body, soul, and spirit, and are still one human being. In the same way, God is a single God, and speaking of the Trinity is only an attempt to describe this one God. God's threefold nature—God's trinity—means that God is a God who is open to us, that he takes us up into his communion, that he is flowing love. Here too, it is important that we leave the mystery open. Of course we cannot know precisely how God is; that is a mystery. But it is clear that he is the one God.

In Hebrew-Judaic thought, the word "son" expresses a special relationship. Jesus is the son of God because he has a special relationship with God. It seems to me that Muslims, too, could accept this Hebrew understanding of Jesus as God's son. The ancient Greek Church Fathers, in dialogue with Hellenic philosophy, interpreted this Hebrew conception in their own way. To theologians of a Hellenic bent, "son of God" meant not just a relationship, but a manner of being: Jesus is God as well. But here again the question is: What exactly does this mean? I believe it means that it is not just my feeling or experience, but that I am truly encountering God in this person. Nevertheless, this person still remains wholly and entirely a human being. Theological statements do not work according to the "either-or" rules of exclusionary logic. Christian dogma is expressing a tension that must be borne: truly God and truly human, undivided and unmixed. God is not mixed with human nature, he is fully human, and at the same time God. To be sure, in the Christian tradition this tension has often been resolved by identifying Jesus as God in ways that no longer correspond to the biblical message. The German writer Heinrich Böll once stated that he found it too romantic to see Jesus as only a human being. It was important to him that through Jesus another dimension breaks into our lives: God himself. All the dogmatic and philosophical statements about Jesus are attempts to understand this mystery of Jesus without setting anything in stone. If I say that Jesus was nothing more than a religiously gifted person, I am adjusting the understanding of Jesus to a level we know and are familiar with. At the same time, I am placing myself above him. On the other hand, when I say that Jesus was the son of God, I am far from knowing what that truly means. But I am facing up to Jesus' claims because in him I recognize God's claims upon me. Paul Tillich once said that God is what ultimately concerns us.[12] When I describe Jesus

---

12. Paul Tillich, *Systematic Theology: Volume One: Reason and Revelation, Being and God* (Chicago: University of Chicago Press, 1951), 12.

as God's son, that means to me that Jesus intimately concerns me, that I must grapple with his words until I understand them. For I believe that in his words, God himself is speaking to me and challenging me.

Many Christians have difficulty with the theological attempts to understand God's incarnation in Jesus Christ and the mystery of the Trinity. Even an educated theologian, in the end, cannot fully understand it. But many Christians have translated this theological doctrine into their own personal spirituality. And there it means to them that they turn not only to God, who is always also the ungraspable and invisible, but also to Jesus Christ, in whom the image of God comes near them in a human manner. Even the simple faithful always know that they cannot "nail down" and "possess" Jesus. They face up to him, they look to the icons, they let Jesus look at and speak to them, and they trust that Jesus will lead them to God and communicate God's love to them. But it is always God's love that they are given to experience in prayer and which they hope will heal their wounds.

4. The Danger of Deifying Humankind

If God becomes human, does that not deify humankind? But human beings are not eternal beings, so isn't the idea of deifying human beings problematic in and of itself? And does the incarnation of God not mean that God changes?

The great problem for Hellenic thinkers was this: Human beings are fallible, mortal, and subject to decay. The good news of the New Testament is that God became human and we are given participation in divine life. The Church Fathers could even say: Man is deified. But this does not mean that we are making ourselves into gods. What these theologians are concerned with is the restitution of humankind as made in the image of God. So when the discussion concerns "deification," it is merely to express the grace that God, in his love, has communicated to us his own divine life, and that this divine life shapes in us the unique image God has made for himself of each of us. Deification means simply that I am not just taken of the earth, but that divine spirit permeates me as well. Nor is this thought foreign to Islam, which also speaks of God's spirit being within us. Nevertheless, we remain wholly human. As human beings, we are the sites of God's presence.

One image that helps me understand the deification of human beings is the burning bush. The bush burns without being burnt up—it remains a bush, dried and without particular value. In the same way, human beings remain entirely human. And yet human beings become the site of God's presence. God's fire burns within us without burning us up. What deification means becomes clear when I listen into myself. There I find not only my own life story, not only my own psychological problems. When I look deep into my soul, I find God's spirit at the bottom of my soul as well. God's spirit, which is within me, is not destroyed even in death. God's spirit is the love of God that permeates me, and this love is stronger than death. In death I will not fall from the love of God. To me, that is the mystery of deification: that in death we dive into the love of God which is already within us. In the end, "deification" means that there is a divine seed within us already; a seed that cannot be destroyed by death. God remains the same. God does not change. But God gives himself to human beings as a gift. He offers them the gift of his grace, his spirit. We can only gratefully accept this gift; we have no claim to it. It is always grace.

5. Original Sin—Salvation by the Cross

Muslims object to the idea that God became human. And the role of Jesus Christ divides the religions just as much as it separates them. According to the Muslim view, people are not born under original sin. And Muslims find the discussion of such a thing as original sin incomprehensible or self-contradictory—along with the idea of salvation by Jesus' death on the cross. It is the Muslim belief that God, with his grace and mercy, is close to human beings. Accordingly, Muslims wonder: Why should human beings need the sacrifice on the cross at all in order to be saved?

In Christianity, too, salvation comes from God. And as for original sin, it does not mean that human beings are born with innate flaws. Rather, the term signifies that we are born into a world which is sinful—which requires no belief at all. A glance at a newspaper is enough to see that it is so. We will immediately recognize that the world is not perfect, but shaped by sin. We are born into a world which is not perfect. To Judaism and ancient Greek philosophy, likewise, human beings require salvation. Human beings become alienated from themselves, let themselves be led by their negative emotions and their passions. They are disoriented, find no meaning in their lives. Education, too, creates many wounds. The result is that human beings are ruled by anxieties and often enough by senseless rage, as well. In the first place, salvation occurs through the teachings of Jesus: through his showing us the path toward a good life and pointing us to the meaning of life. Further, salvation occurs through the healing deeds and lived existence of Jesus. And salvation occurs through his death and his resurrection. This heals human beings' ultimate fear: their fear of death.

In his theology, Anselm of Canterbury related salvation too closely to sin and guilt. These are, of course, also human hardships. Many human beings suffer from the guilt of having sinned, raising the question: how can we experience forgiveness and believe in forgiveness? Islam, too, is familiar with human guilt. When humans err, they are dependent upon the mercy of God. But many people who have become entangled in sin and guilt no longer hope for God's mercy. For such people, Jesus' death on the cross is a powerful help to believing in the forgiveness of God. Truth be told, even today many propagate a theological view of salvation which posits that Christ had to die on the cross in order to atone for our sins. Karl Rahner, instead, has described the connection between Jesus' death on the cross and our need for salvation much more appropriately as follows: When, entangled in our sin and guilt, we look at the cross, on which Jesus forgives even his murderers, then we may trust that there is nothing within us that cannot be forgiven. In looking at the cross, then, we feel unconditionally accepted and loved. We can recognize this same theology at work in the Gospel of Luke, for example.

Luke was Greek. In Jesus, he recognizes the truly just man of whom Plato speaks in his *Republic*. Almost four hundred years before Christ, Plato described the fate that would most likely await a truly just person in our unjust world, predicting that he would be hounded from the city and crucified. Luke identifies Jesus on the cross as this truly just person, as one who would not let himself be moved from his justice—his orientation toward God—even by his murderers. Luke uses the Greek image of mass entertainment to explain salvation: "And when all the crowds who had gathered there for this spectacle saw what had taken place, they returned home, beating their breasts" (Lk 23:48). By looking at the spectacle of the cross, the onlookers are transformed, are once again oriented towards God, are justified, that is, made just. Karl Rahner has clothed this view of Luke's with theological terms: The cross does not cause forgiveness. Rather, it communicates God's forgiving love. God forgives because he is God, not because Jesus died. That idea is the same as in Islam: God forgives because he is merciful. For us as Christians, however, the cross communicates God's forgiving love.

Those who have taken upon themselves great sin and guilt can hardly believe in the forgiveness of God. They need this image of the cross in order to believe in the forgiving mercy of God. Luke strengthens this trust by telling us of the criminal crucified to Jesus' right. This criminal has nothing to show for himself except a wasted life. But because he addresses Jesus with trust and humility, Jesus gives him the wonderful news: "Truly, I tell you, today you will be with me in paradise" (Lk 23:43). This affirmation strengthens our faith in God's forgiving love.

To us Christians, it remains a paradox that this pure person, Jesus, died on the cross. It was a shock to his disciples, who at first did not understand it. The gospel writers also tell us how Jesus himself grappled with the idea in the garden of Gethsemane. Jesus grappled with God that the cup of suffering might pass by him, but could then feel: If I save myself and leave my disciples behind, that does not fit my message. And he could feel: "No one has greater love than this, to lay down one's life for one's friends" (Jn 15:13). To him, that was the motivation for not saving himself but submitting to the suffering.

One cannot say that Jesus' death was "necessary"—it was a historical event. Karl Rahner says that in Jesus, God accepted history, as well. And with history, he accepted the specific circumstances of the time, shaped by Roman occupation and by dissent within Judaism. In a certain sense, Jesus was thus in a double bind. He could have freed himself from it, but by living it to its end, he transformed it.

Mark interprets the passion of Jesus such that, at the beginning, Jesus is the great healer and liberator whom all people follow. In the second part of his account, Jesus makes his way to Jerusalem and instructs his disciples. But they do not understand what he is actually trying to tell them. In the third part, Jesus enters into the realm of darkness and illuminates that darkness from within. Through Jesus' love, evil is transformed from within. Death is the fulfillment of this transformation. The Romans believed that they had vanquished Jesus, but in truth, it was love that vanquished hate on the cross, God who vanquished the enemies, life that vanquished death. In the Bible, we can find many other interpretations of Jesus' death on the cross and his resurrection as the central points of the Christian message. It will always remain a mystery what happened on the cross and what it means for us. But for me, the cross remains a constant thorn to keep thinking anew about the mystery of God and humankind, about the mystery of love and death, of good and evil, of human salvation and liberation.

6. The Social Role of Christianity

Muslims often object to religion being exiled to a separate sphere and limited to the inner realm. On the other hand, is Christianity not in danger of losing its power to shape society—all while still being too close to the state?

Some people may bemoan a general secularization, the increasing worldliness of our society. But the Second Vatican Council pointed out and indeed approved of the fact that the worldly has its own realm and independence. It is true that in my native Germany, the number of people who leave the Church is growing, and that fewer and fewer people are attending services, as well. The larger picture is this: the typically religious concerns—the search for God; the yearning for a community in which faith, hope, and charity are truly lived; a sense of prayer and of stillness—all that is still present in many people. But it is often no longer connected with the Church. This represents a challenge to the Church to once again become the place of spiritual experience. Today, many are suffering because of the failings of the reality of the Church they experience, and often many seekers do not feel at home in their parishes, because they find too little spirituality and perhaps even too little humanity there.

Nevertheless, I believe that in our society, Christianity still has power and vibrancy. In many companies, too, I see leaders wanting to live values rooted in the Christian tradition. And so they do shape society in a Christian spirit. In this context, admittedly, the greatest challenge is passing on faith to children and grandchildren. I am often startled to hear that even Christian parents can no longer motivate their children to go to church and open themselves up to faith. With a view to the future significance of Christianity in our society, we Christians certainly have to develop creativity in how to motivate and move children to an enthusiastic life in faith. Some young people say that they are religious. But it is often a very diffuse, vague religiousness. The challenge is in rediscovering and newly communicating the core of what is Christian without watering down this core in any way. In addition, Christians can see Muslims, who practice their religion openly, as a challenge to stand by their faith in daily life and in public, even if, for example, it is only by saying grace in restaurants.

It is hard to say why Church life is declining to such an extent. There are many attempts to explain the phenomenon. One thesis is that the meaning religions offer has acquired a great deal of competition in our pluralistic and open society. Another thesis refers to Christians' failure to develop creativity, credibility, and persuasiveness in communicating our faith. It is also, then, a matter of speaking of our faith and of living Christianity in such an infectious way that young people feel that their own questions, problems, and longings are being addressed as well. And it is not only Christians who nowadays experience the difficulty of authentically proclaiming and persuasively passing on their faith in a society shaped by secular and material values. The same applies to Muslims as well. Together, we are concerned with the question of how we can communicate our understanding and practice of religion to the younger generation in a convincing and existentially meaningful way. That is particularly relevant with regard to the many people who are what could be called "tone-deaf" in religious matters. Muslims and Christians together have the task of breaking apart the negative view that many people link with their religions and instead drawing a positive image of religions as capable of making an important contribution to humanizing our society. While we are at war with one another or devalue the other religion, we will not succeed in convincing young people. We cannot expect the young to be open to religion if they can see too little of how adults authentically and convincingly live their religion, of how their religion makes them more human, merciful, and sensitive to the needs of the poor and outcast. The mere moral appeal to live religiously will not succeed. The young need role models in whom they can read religion's capacity for transforming people to the good and turning them into valuable members of society.

And as regards the connection to the state: In the history of Christianity there have been many instances in which state and Church were closely linked. Under emperor Constantine,

Christianity was made a state religion. Already then, early monks protested against the concomitant danger that the Christian faith could be lessened by the union of civil and ecclesiastical hierarchy. The Desert Fathers sought to live the original power of Christian faith free of state co-option. The conflict between pope and emperor runs through the Middle Ages: both laid claim to power. Only in the Enlightenment did we properly understand Jesus' instruction to give back to the emperor what is the emperor's and to give back to God what is God's (Mt 22:21). The state needs as its basis the values that Christianity has continued to propagate and which it has to some extent also itself adopted from ancient Greek philosophy. And the state should also remain independent of the churches and offer a space in which people of all religions can live side by side and with the same rights. But this separation does not need to be as strict as it is for example in France. The social engagement of churches in caring for the poor and the elderly shows that a sensible cooperation can be good for both sides.

7. Christianity's History of Violence

Although Christianity set out as a religion of peace—as shown and demanded in the Sermon on the Mount, for example—it has by no means always acted non-violently throughout its history. Again and again, expansive and exclusive power has been aggressively sought in its name. And it is not only the Bible's violent passages that are problematic, but also the acts of violence perpetrated in the Crusades, which have left a lasting scar in the consciousness of Muslims. How can Christianity's message of love be brought into harmony with these acts of violence that continue to resonate into the present?

Over the course of history, religion and politics have always been in a relationship that was reciprocal, as well. Religious feelings were repeatedly made to serve the interests of power, were instrumentalized and misused politically. The political scientist Hans Maier, among others, has pointed out this "double face of the religious": after all, to this day, terrorists, dictators, and nationalists justify their acts by referring to "divine commands." Hans Maier therefore demands the classic distinction between religion and politics and notes that in order to not be open to such misuse, religion must return to its actual purview, must be clarified by reason, and must be institutionally secured. This applies to all religions, and particularly for the impulse toward peace as given in the Sermon on the Mount. Regarding the more violent passages in the Bible, it is first of all important to interpret metaphorically those sections relating wars and acts of violence. Today, after all, it is no longer a question of vanquishing external foes. Already within the Bible, these sections have been interpreted metaphorically as battles against inner foes who are keeping us from opening ourselves up fully to God.

And of course the Church must honestly assess its history of violence and grieve over how many people have been injured by religiously motivated violence. The Church must grieve the suffering created for example by the crusades, by a theologically founded aggressive anti-Judaism, by the violent conquest of Latin America, and by the violent Christianization of the Indigenous peoples. Unfortunately, even today there are fundamentalist Christians who approve of violence against those who hold different views. They argue much like the Islamists.

Together, Christians who understand the message of Jesus and Muslims who interpret the Qur'an according to their tolerant tradition share the task of exposing as false the aggressive tendencies propagated in the name of Christianity and Islam alike and of disempowering these tendencies.

Again and again, we Christians must face up to the message of Jesus anew, to the message he proclaimed in the Sermon on the Mount. Germany's former chancellor Helmut Schmidt once stated brusquely that the Sermon on the Mount was not suitable for making politics. But especially today, Christian politics must be guided by the Sermon on the Mount. Loving your enemy is nothing romantic, but rather the precondition for people who have been enemies for centuries to find their way into a shared community. Not valuing and not judging are suitable ways of carrying a more merciful attitude into our society. We Christians have the message of Jesus, but we do not always live it consistently. That is certainly a justified demand of Muslims to us Christians. Conversely, we of course see the same problem in Islam. Both sides thus require the humility to admit their own mistakes and (on the Christian side) to honestly endeavor to follow Jesus' true intention or (on the Muslim side) to take a tolerant interpretation of Islam as the basis for acting toward those who think differently. We will not make progress simply by tallying the mistakes the other side has made in the history of Christianity or of Islam. What is important is seeking a peaceful future together. And that future is possible only if we listen honestly and humbly to the message of our own religion and then follow it.

Horizons and Fields of Spirituality

Where Do We Come From?

I. The Muslim View of Createdness

Ahmad Milad Karimi

We Are Not Coincidences of Nature

According to a saying of the Prophet Muhammad often quoted in the Sufi tradition, David once asked God: "O Lord, what was your intention when you created the world?" The answer: "I was a hidden treasure, and I wanted to be discovered, so I created the world." Here, God is identified as the yearning of creation. Humanity's createdness must therefore be understood from the perspective of humankind's lasting relatedness to God. Anyone who lives from and in a yearning for God is human. We are no chance product of nature but have sprung from the love and decision of God. The first words revealed to the Prophet Muhammad form the beginning of the Qur'an's surah 96: "Read! In the name of your Lord who created: He created man from a clinging form. Read! Your Lord is the Most Bountiful One who taught by [means of] the pen, who taught man what he did not know."

God as the origin of all creates humankind and remains its companion in life by first giving human beings knowledge and insight, and then a revelation, since they are created weak, as the Qur'an states (4:28). Accordingly, Indian-Pakistani poet and philosopher Muhammad Iqbal (d.1938 CE) has rightly noted that the "main purpose of the Qur'an is to awaken in man the higher consciousness of his manifold relations with God and the universe."[1]

---

1. Muhammad Iqbal, *The Reconstruction of Religious Thought in Islam* (Stanford, CA: Stanford University Press, 2013), 7.

The Creation of Humankind

Islamic tradition does not agree on whether and what humankind was before the creation. One significant place in the Qur'an alludes to a kind of pre-existence of human beings: "When your Lord took out the offspring from the loins of the Children of Adam and made them bear witness about themselves, He said, 'Am I not your Lord?' and they replied, 'Yes, we bear witness.'" (Qur'an 7:172). But the opposing viewpoint, that we were and are nothing, can also be found, for example in the writings of Omar Khayyam. In the Qur'an, the creation of humankind is described at several different times and from many perspectives, and it is always conceived of with regard to the relation to God. First, in the biblical tradition, it is indicated that humanity was created from clay.

Adam is the prototype of humankind in and of itself. That means that to the extent that I am human, my humanity is of the same origin as that of the first human being: "Praise belongs to God who created the heavens and the earth and made darkness and light [...] He is the one who created you from clay and specified a term [for you] and another fixed time" (Qur'an 6:1-2). Human existence is defined by its finiteness. But humankind's Creator does not remain distant and abstract; rather, he reveals himself as the "Lord of People" (Qur'an 114:1). Human beings originated in "dried clay, formed from mud" (Qur'an 15:26), but they do not remain so, taking on shape and reason. Addressed next is the forming of humankind: "We created man from an essence of clay, then We placed him as a drop of fluid in a safe place, then We made that drop into a clinging form, and We made that form into a lump of flesh, and We made that lump into bones, and We clothed those bones with flesh, and later We made him into other forms—glory be to God, the best of creators!" (Qur'an 23:12–14). And we learn from the Qur'an that it is God who created "created the two sexes, male and female, from an ejected drop of sperm" (Qur'an 53:45 f.) and has inspired them with some of his spirit (see Qur'an 32:9): "People, be mindful of your Lord, who created you from a single soul, and from it created its mate, and from the pair of them spread countless men and women far and wide" (Qur'an 4:1). Both sexes are created from one soul.

The Beauty of Creation

It is also significant that humankind's createdness is predicated as beautiful: "He created the heavens and earth for a true purpose; He formed you and made your forms good: you will all return to Him" (Qur'an 64:3). And even more concisely: "We create man in the most beautiful form" (Qur'an 95:4, translated from the German). Not only humankind, but all of God's creation is beautiful, as the Prophet testifies: "Into all things God inscribed beauty."[2] In an Islamic view, the beauty of all creatures and human beings in particular mirrors the beauty of God, since the Prophet says: "Truly, God is beautiful and loves beauty." In beauty, we encounter our own finiteness, and in beauty we see ourselves supported.

Createdness: Beauty as a Calling

But insight into this beauty does not want to remain a mere figure of speech. It is aimed at lived practice. It is recited several times in the Qur'an that "God loves those who do beautiful things" (2:195, translated from the German). A central part of createdness is also the idea that we human beings have a particular calling on Earth. In the Qur'an, humankind is called to act as "steward of God" (Qur'an 2:30) in the world. This gives us human beings the particular responsibility for preserving creation in the long run out of respect for the value God has given it, as well as for preserving life and the living, and for creating peace between human beings. The Qur'an movingly relates the story of how God tells the angels that he is entrusting this responsibility to humankind. The angels are astonished and ask: "'How can You put someone there who will cause damage and bloodshed, when we celebrate Your praise and proclaim Your holiness?'

---

2. Sahih Muslim, hadith no. 1955, 924; Beirut 1427/2007, 1189.

but He said, 'I know things you do not'" (Qur'an 2:30). Being a created human being means trusting in God, and this trust is the foundation for our existence.

The Muslim Understanding of Self: Servants of God and in Need of God

Islam's idea of createdness is outlined clearly by Muslims' self-conception as servants of God. The description "his servant" is used twice in the Qur'an to describe the Prophet Muhammad.[3] This both clearly identifies the Prophet as created and also emphasizes his dignity in being God's servant, of whom it is also said: "Truly you have a strong character" (Qur'an 68:4). Being a servant of God does not devalue the human being; rather it incorporates praise of God into one's very personhood. Muhammad Iqbal writes of a person who could have the world groveling in the dust at his feet, and yet would call himself merely "servant of God."[4] But to be a servant does not mean enslavement, military obedience, blind subservience, or the like. Instead, it means insight into our own createdness and limitation, and hope that we are supported by our creator to whom we devote ourselves. Islam teaches that we human beings are not sufficient to ourselves. To live, we not only need fellow human beings (since we are social animals) and more fundamentally God: "People," the Qur'an says, "it is you who stand in need of God" (35:15). This is not a need in the sense of some economic lack, but a spiritual need expressed in yearning. It is this yearning that orients us toward and opens us up to God. Where are coming and where we are going thus collapse into one: "We belong to God, and to Him shall return" (Qur'an 2:156).

---

3. See Qur'an 17:1 and 53:10.
4. See Annemarie Schimmel, *Muhammad Iqbal: Prophetischer Poet und Philosoph* [Muhammad Iqbal: Prophetic poet and philosopher] (Munich: Diederichs, 1989), 178.

2. The Christian Idea of Creation

Anselm Grün

Gratitude and Responsibility

To us Christians, it is clear that God created humankind. That is a theological statement. Clarifying how humankind developed is the task of researchers in the natural sciences. The theological statement that God created humankind means: only by understanding themselves as creatures of God can human beings do justice to their nature. We owe our being to God. The appropriate human stance therefore is gratitude. Everything that we are and have is received from God, is thanks to his goodness. We are dependent on God's grace. And it is our calling to become one with God, our creator, in contemplation. But as creatures gifted with reason, we are also responsible for creation. That is to say: we must treat it well. The Greek Church Fathers even believed that as beings gifted with reason, humankind was tasked with holding together creation according to God's plan.

Two Biblical Accounts of Creation

The Bible relates two stories of how God created humankind, each of which describes it somewhat differently. Both stories should be understood metaphorically. They still apply today as imagery for the nature of humankind—and they stand in no opposition to scientific insight. The two ways of expressing the truths are each on its own level. The first account states that after creating the world, the Earth and the heavens, the plants and the animals, God created humankind:

> So God created humankind in his image,
>   in the image of God he created them;
>   male and female he created them. (Gn 1:27)

According to the second creation account, God "formed man from the dust of the ground, and breathed into his nostrils the breath of life; and the man became a living being" (Gn 2:7).

God places the man in the Garden of Eden, where he forms the various animals out of earth as well, so that man can give them names. But God recognizes that it is not good for man to be alone. And in the animals man will not find a suitable partner. So God forms a woman from Adam's rib and this woman is called Eve. In her, Adam recognizes that she is flesh of his flesh. This inner connection between man and woman is the reason that a man leaves his father and mother and binds himself to a woman: "and they become one flesh" (Gn 2:24).

In the Image of God

Christian theologians attempted to link the Bible's metaphorical stories with the statements of Greek philosophy. The Septuagint translates the two words that in Hebrew mean one thing— "image"—using two different terms: *eikon*, meaning "image [of God]," and *kat' homoiosin*, meaning "in his likeness." From this distinction, Greek theologians developed the doctrine that each human being in each one's very nature is in the likeness, or image, of God. But it is the task of every human being to continually increase this likeness,to become ever more similar to this image. Throughout human history, sin has darkened the original image of humanity. Jesus is the true image of God: in him, the pure image of God is visible. And so human beings are meant to become ever more like Christ, so as to become ever more alike to the original image of God within that person. As Lars Thunberg has summarized, God's original image only shines through in humankind once Christ has liberated human beings from their enslavement in sin. It is under these circumstance that human beings become capable of fully maturing into and developing the gifts with which they were created.[5]

---

5. See Lars Thunberg, "Der Mensch als Abbild Gottes: Die östliche Christenheit [The human being as likeness of God: Eastern Christianity]", in Bernard McGinn and John Meyendorff (eds.), *Geschichte der christlichen Spiritualität* [History of Christian spirituality], Vol. 1 (Würzburg: Echter, 1993), 306.

In other words, the second account of creation is interpreted theologically to mean on the one hand that humankind is intimately close to God, because it is pervaded by God's breath of life. And on the other hand, it was this account from which an independent theology of man and woman, of sexuality and partnership was developed: man and woman belong together and together are the image of God. The love that man and woman feel for one another takes part in the love of God for humanity. In their sexual love for one another, man and woman experience something of the original unity with God and their inner union.

Beauty as the Touch of God

The idea of beauty that Islam links to humankind's createdness is important to Christian theology as well, even if the aspect of beauty has not always been appropriately discussed in this tradition. The Bible tells us that after God had created the world and humankind, he "saw everything that he had made, and indeed it was very good" (Gn 1:31). But the Septuagint translates the Hebrew word for "good" as *kalos*, which means "beautiful." God, then, saw that all was beautiful. The philosopher Plato is known to have said that everything which is is true and good and beautiful. Beauty, then, is a central aspect of being. In beauty, the original beauty that is God himself shines through. The Bible speaks frequently of God's grandeur and beauty. The psalms praise God's beauty. Beauty is certainly a space in which Christians and Muslims alike can experience God. Human beings are always fascinated by beauty. When we let ourselves be touched by beauty, we let ourselves be touched by God himself. For God is the originally beautiful.

Plato links beauty with love. Beauty calls up love within us, and love enables us to recognize beauty. This is equally true of human beings. If I look at myself lovingly, I am beautiful. And if I look at others with loving eyes, I will recognize their beauty. Only those who hate themselves are ugly, and those around us will appear ugly to us if we hate them. Beauty must be recognized, but it must also be treated with care, which is to say preserved. I can only perceive what is beautiful if I also preserve it. This is true of people as much as of creation. The beauty of creation seeks to be preserved—only then will it shine through in me.

The task of Preserving Creation

According to the second account of creation, human beings are tasked with caring for and preserving the Garden of Eden. We are therefore called to take care of nature. In the first creation account, God instructs humankind to "fill the earth and subdue it; and have dominion over the fish of the sea and over the birds of the air and over every living thing that moves upon the earth" (Gn 1:28). Some Christians of the Industrial Age have misunderstood this command in such a way as to exploit creation for their own ends. But that is not what the biblical quotation means. The Church Fathers and the Middle Ages understood this command to mean that humankind is God's steward on Earth and should preserve the creation as it was meant by God to be. Humankind should therefore take its place in God's order, rather than set itself above creation.

Unity in Adam and Christ

The Bible relates that Adam was created first by God. Adam is the father of the tribe from which all people descend. The Greek Church Fathers developed this idea into the doctrine that all humankind is one according to its beginnings. All human beings thus belong together and have a duty to live together in peace. Salvation through Jesus Christ was understood to mean that by becoming a human being, Christ reconstituted this unity of humankind. The incarnation of Christ is thus a matter that touches all people. Through Christ, all have been put back in touch with the divine spark. And therefore all are meant to be united in Christ, even if they do not know him or confess him. What is crucial is that at the foundation of our humanity we should be in union with one another. It is our task to continually increase the realization of this unity.

Origin and Goal of our Life: God

I. The Muslim Conception of a God

Ahmad Milad Karimi

Faith in God: Islam's Central Element

Before Muhammad is chosen as Prophet, he is familiar with a large number of religious communities and their deities and idols all across the Arabian peninsula of the seventh century. But in the midst of the colorful variety of displays around the Kaaba in Mecca (then the central sacred site for many of the deities revered by the Arab tribes), Muhammad's heart finds no peace. He is a God-seeker who does not know where to seek the unknowable God. And when the Angel Gabriel unexpectedly appears to Muhammad, the angel bids him arise and speak "in the name of God." The question Muhammad asks himself, but does not utter, is clear: In the name of which god? Then, verse by verse, the Prophet is instructed. The Qur'an is therefore a school for understanding what we mean when we say "God." In Arabic, he is called *Allāh*, which means "the God," or "the one God." This does not mean some special God of Muslims: Jews and Christians conversing in Arabic also address God as *Allāh*. And Muslims who cannot write Arabic refer to him in their own language. The great Muslim theologian Muḥammad al-Ghazālī (d. 1111 CE), for example, uses "*Allāh*" when he is writing in Arabic and "*Khūdā*" when writing in Persian. Into the lives of Muslims everywhere is inscribed the insight that God is not merely a word or merely a name. When Muslims speak of God, they predominantly mean that yearning towards which they orient their lives. It is a life that realizes God, who comforts me, supports me, leads me toward the good and guides me towards my truth: "So remember me; I will remember you," in the words of the Qur'an (2:152).

The Prophet Muhammad becomes acquainted with the fact that God, as the creator of all things, also wields justice on the Day of Judgment,[6] since he is the eternally alive[7] and solely lasting,[8] the Lord of life and death. "We belong to God and to Him we shall return," the Qur'an tells us (2:156). Muslims view the fulfillment of their existence as possible only in and through devotion to the one God: "Who could be better in religion than those who direct themselves wholly to God?" (Qur'an 4:125).

A Special Emphasis on Oneness

Above all things, Islam emphasizes the oneness (Arabic: *tauḥīd*) of God. "Say: 'He is God the One, God the eternal. He begot no one nor was He begotten. No one is comparable to Him.'" (Qur'an 112: 1–2). There is only the one God. This is not to speak of numerical entities in the sense that we should imagine that instead of two gods, there is one. Instead, his absolute oneness represents his uniqueness, that is to say, he has no partner or participant, is not subdivided into persons and is above the sexes. In creating the world, God created something other without damaging his absolute oneness. He does not remain independent of the world but affects it—through his messengers, through his revelation, through his guidance—in order to perfect it. God is the incomparable one, wholly pure of all inner relation or categories. "If there had been in the heavens or earth any gods but Him, both heavens and earth would be in ruins," says the Qur'an (21:22). Everything that has ever been, that is in this moment, that will ever be can be traced back to the one God. He is beyond duality or multiplicity. In the Qur'an, however, this reality of God does not occur in opposition to Jewish or Christian notions of God. On the contrary, the Prophet Muhammad recognizes God as the God who has revealed himself to Abraham, Isaac, Noah, Jacob,

---

6. "The praise to God, the Lord of worlds, the merciful and giver of mercy, the ruler on the day of judgment" (Qur'an 1:2–4).
7. "God, no god except him, the alive, the lasting" (Qur'an 2:255).
8. "All is ephemeral: not his visage" (Qur'an 28:88).

Joseph, David, and Solomon[9] and has communicated himself in the Torah as well as in the Gospel. As a result, Muslims believe in one God who has revealed himself to humankind in different ways according to differing historical contexts.

Unimaginable and Unpossessable
—Types of Knowledge along the Path of the Heart

But part of the Islamic conception of God is also that God cannot be conceived of. We cannot imagine God; he is not accessible to us in the way the things of the world are accessible or made accessible to us. The Qur'an, admittedly, does contain a series of anthropomorphic statements about God, such as in metaphors about the hand or face of God. But today the dominant view in Islamic theology is that we may talk about the face of God but will always do so without being able to say what it is like. While God is inaccessible to rational knowledge, the spiritual path of Islam offers a wholly different way of knowing God. This could be called the path of the heart. On the path of the heart, there is a series of different types of knowledge, ranging from inner bolt of insight, inner discovery, and inner vision all the way to ecstasy and the spiritual taste of God.[10] The Prophet Muhammad, accordingly, says: "The paths to God are as numerous as the breaths of human beings."[11]

---

9. "Say: We believe in God and in that which was to us sent down, and which was to Abraham sent down, Ishmael, Isaac, Jacob and the tribes, and which Moses and Jesus received, and which the prophet received from their Lord. Among them we do not distinguish and to him we submit." (Qur'an 2:136)
10. "To believe in the Prophet is to admit that there is above intelligence a sphere in which are revealed to the inner vision truths beyond the grasp of intelligence." (Abu Hamid al-Ghazali, *Confessions, or Deliverance from Error*, trans. Claud Field, ed. Jerome S. Arkenberg). Available online at: https://sourcebooks.fordham.edu/basis/1100ghazali-truth.asp.
11. A. Ibn Taimīya: Majmū' al-fatāwā li Shaikh al-islām Ibn Taimīya, Vol. X, collected and categorized by 'Abd ar-Raḥmān b. Muḥammad, Medina 1424/2004, 454.

God's absolute oneness and complete transcendence—God as the creator of the world is not himself part of the world but is beyond it—is exceeded only by his love and mercy in turning towards human beings, in healing, guiding, and pacifying them. "Say: 'Call to God or call to the merciful, however you call to him, his are the names, the most beautiful'" (Qur'an 17:110, translated from the German). God's names are the most beautiful because God is the most beautiful, the Prophet Muhammad testifies, saying: "He loves beauty."[12] The Qur'an contains a number of characteristics and names of God that are highly significant in Muslim spiritual life: the ruler and king; the majestic; the wise judge; the kind; etc. These are the most beautiful names, revered in the Islamic tradition as the ninety-nine names of God—with the idea that the hundredth name of God is hidden. The Prophet himself is said to have spoken aloud the ninety-nine names of God and whispered the hundredth into the ear of a camel...

Distinction between Characteristics of Deed and Nature

Islamic theology distinguishes between two types of characteristics of God: the characteristics of his deeds, which acquire their significance only with the creation of the world, and the characteristics of his nature, which apply ineluctably to God as God and can have no opposite. Each theological school has classified the characteristics in these categories differently. But what is undisputed is that God has the essential attributes of life, knowledge, power, and will. In Ash'arī theology, hearing, seeing, and speaking are also described as characteristics of God's nature, while Māturīdī theology counts the creation of the world (Arabic: *takwīn*) in addition to the previous seven, for a total of eight. Not only the wonderful but also the terrible in God is discussed. For example, Omar Khayyam and Farīd ud-Dīn 'Aṭṭār both mention the dark side of God in the

---

12. Y. b. Sh. Nawawī: *Riyāḍ aṣ-ṣāliḥīn, bāb taḥrīm al-kibr wa al-i'jāb*, 2nd ed., hadīth no. 617, Cairo 1424/2004, 194.

context of grappling with and accusing God, much like Job did. Here too, the inaccessibility of God is expressed strongly. When Islam speaks of the fear of God, we should not conflate this with worldly fear: worldly fear causes us to run away, whereas fear of God, according to al-Ghazālī, is an awe-filled trembling which draws human beings closer.

Inner Nearness: Taking up the Names of God

In the process, the names of God should not remain external and theoretical but be taken up into one's own self. The Muslim mystic Ibn 'Arabī (d. 1240 CE) even remarked that taking into oneself the names of God was the very essence of Sufism.[13] He reasoned that the adoption of divine attributes created an inner closeness to God. In that way, God's self-revelation in a person can be realized through God's names. This is the approach of a person towards God, and it is in this context that the idea of annihilation of the self arises. The path to God is revealed as a path inward: "We shall show them Our signs in every region of the earth and in themselves, until it becomes clear to them that this is the Truth" (Qur'an 41:53). In the revelation of the Qur'an, the transcendence of God thus gains an unfathomable nearness. Outside the Qur'an, the Prophet Muhammad reveals that "God said: Heaven and earth do not enclose me, but the heart of my faithful servant encloses me."[14] Although in the Islamic view God was not incarnated, he is nevertheless close to humankind. The Persian poet 'Aṭṭār, at the end of his *Conference of the Birds*, writes that though life's journey to God may end, the journey in God begins—but that he can say nothing of this journey and must therefore be silent. This is the context in which one should consider what God said to the Prophet Muhammad: "If My

---

13. M. Ibn 'Arabī: *Al-Futūḥāt al-Makkīya* [The Meccan discourses], Vol. II, 267.
14. I. b. M. al-'Ajlūnī: *Kashf al-khāfā' wa muzīl al-ilbās*, Vol. II, hadīth no 2256, n.p., n.d., 229.

servants ask you about Me, I am near. I respond to those who call Me" (Qur'an 2:186).

Nearness and Distance: "God Is With Us"

To non-Muslims, it often seems that the Muslim conception of God is marked by a great distance to God. But God's distance consists not in his being "up above," which is to say infinitely far away, but rather in his being incredibly close to us: "closer to him [man] than his jugular vein," as the Qur'an (50:16) says. God himself says: "I respond to those who call Me" (Qur'an 2:186). And my personal favorite verse in the entire Qur'an reads: "The East and the West belong to God: wherever you turn, there is His Face" (2:115). Christians might say that God is among us through the person of Jesus of Nazareth. In the terms of Judaism, one could say that God is above us. The corresponding Islamic formula would be: "God is with us." From this point of view, Islam could be considered the reconciliation of the two religions, Judaism and Christianity. But this closeness is still a kind of denial: it denies me the possibility of setting myself above God. If God remained accessible to me, I could live "in his name." Muslims, however, do not actually live in the name of God but in responsibility towards God. If I were to undertake something "in the name of God," I would have God, as it were, right in front of me. And this is a misunderstanding. A justification "in the name of God" can in principle justify anything. In this line of thinking, it could even be "good" to kill someone, the misinterpretation goes, as long as I were to do so in the name of God. In contrast, if I act, live, and love in responsibility towards God, that means that I always also need to cultivate a critical distance to myself and my actions.

2. How Christians Speak of the Threefold God

Anselm Grün

God is Fundamentally Ungraspable and Inaccessible

Many things that the Qur'an says about God we Christians might put similarly. To us Christians too, God is the one God—there is only one God, and the various religions merely have various different names and conceptions of God. No conception is wholly and completely identical with God. Because just as for Muslims, for Christians too God in the end is beyond all imagery and imagination. To us Christians too, God is inaccessible: again and again, he evades our efforts to define him. God, in the end, is unimaginable and ungraspable. And yet, the Bible invites us to think of God in images and to attribute characteristics to God. Just as Islam has the ninety-nine names of God, Christian theology, on the basis of biblical stories, describes important characteristics of God: God is merciful, he is all-powerful, good. He is love. He is power and energy and light. He is spirit. He is the creator of the world and its preserver. And he protects humankind. He loves humankind and cares for human beings. If dogmatics is the art of keeping open the mystery, then even the discussion of the Trinity in Christian dogmatics is a model for speaking of this intangible God without resolving his mystery and his inaccessibility. The image of the Trinity, too, is an effort to express the tension between God and humanity but also the closeness of God to humanity, and to strive for an adequate understanding of the particular significance of Jesus.

What the Christian Idea of Trinity Means

The Christian conception of God as the Trinity is difficult for Muslims to understand. When we speak of the three-personed God, we are speaking not of three gods, but of the one and only God. Speaking of three persons is open to misunderstanding, because that way in the end we do imagine God in three different persons. Greek theology, which developed the doctrine of the Trinity based on biblical imagery, therefore refers not to persons but to "hypostases." This term is difficult to understand but does not subdivide God into three persons. The doctrine of the Trinity seeks to describe that God relates to humankind in three different ways. First, God is the creator who made us and preserves us in being. Second, God has come close to us in Jesus Christ. God descended into our humanity, so that deep in our soul and deep in our body, we can perceive God precisely in our humanity. And in Jesus, God accompanies us, walks our path with us. Thirdly, this closeness of God is heightened in the image of the Holy Spirit. God not only walks with us in Jesus, he is within us. The spirit we breathe is Holy Spirit. God's spirit is within us and inspires us. As Christians, we really do receive divine life, because the Holy Spirit is divine.

Speaking of Human Beings Means Speaking of God

Theologians have tried to describe the Trinity in many images. And they have seen the Trinity in human beings themselves, as well. Marius Victorinus, on the basis of Neoplatonist philosophy, saw the triad of *esse* (being), *vivere* (living), and *intelligere* (understanding) present in both God and in humankind. And thus he described God as being the source (that is, father) of the outpouring of life (the son) and the return through understanding (the Holy Spirit). To him, accordingly, Jesus Christ was universal life which heightened the senses' life and divine insight so that humankind might be led towards God. After the death of Christ, he held, the immanent but hidden Christ continued to act through the Holy Spirit to effect humankind's return to God through understanding.[15] In the end, all statements on the Trinity seek to describe God's closeness to humankind. The Christian God is the God who has opened himself up wholly

---

15. See Mary T. Clark, "Die Dreieinigkeit in der lateinischen Christenheit" [The Trinity in Latin Christendom], in Bernard McGinn and John Meyendorff, eds., *Geschichte der christlichen Spiritualität* [History of Christian spirituality], Vol. 1 (Würzburg: Echter, 1993), 290.

and utterly to humankind, who is open to each human being, who has linked himself indelibly with humankind in Jesus and in the Holy Spirit. We can therefore not speak of God without also speaking of human beings. And we cannot speak of human beings without speaking of God.

God is Love—Approaching the Mystery through Metaphor

According to the First Epistle of John, God is love: "God is love, and those who abide in love abide in God, and God abides in them" (1 Jn 4:16). God's nature is love, and St. Augustine sees this love revealed in three ways: As Father, that is to say, foundation of creation and providence; as Word, that is to say as foundation of conversion and illumination; and as Spirit, which as foundation of love is the principle of return to the Father.[16] There is, then, no end of new images that describe to us this mystery of love. Christian mysticism consists in meditating oneself ever further into this love. But this love leads us not only into the mystery of God, but also from God into society and the world, so that through us the world may become ever more permeated and transformed by God's love.

Ideas of God Are Not Divisive

If we understand the nature of the Trinity as loving closeness to humankind, then Muslims too may be able to sense that our conception of God does not divide us. We all believe in one God. We differ only in how we describe how God opens himself up to and approaches human beings. But our concern is the same: God is not only the distant, unimaginable God. He comes near to humankind. He shows them his face and extends his hand towards them. What the Qur'an describes in imagery of divine nearness, Christian theology narrates in the story of Jesus, who approached humankind, who touched human beings with his healing hands and proclaimed to them

---

16. See Mary T. Clark, 292.

the word of God. For both Christians and Muslims, God always remains transcendent, unimaginable, invisible. But God reveals himself to human beings and wants not only to be believed in but to be experienced, as well. The idea of God as the Trinity wants to guide us to this experience of God. Spiritual tradition teaches us that the conception of God always corresponds to human beings' conception of themselves. The image of the Trinity is meant to mirror itself in the images of persons who open themselves up to God in the depth of their soul and let themselves be sent out into the world so as to shape this world through divine love. To us Christians, the fundamental image of this love is the incarnate word of God. And the power of this love works within us through the Holy Spirit. By our very nature, then, we are oriented towards God. Human beings can only fulfill their nature if they are open to God's love and act in the world out of this love.

Living from the Source: The Holy Scriptures as a Guide

I. The Christian Approach to Holy Scripture

Anselm Grün

Word of God—Norm for Our Lives

Like many other religions, Christianity too has holy writings as norms for our lives. Since the days of the early Church, the Christian Bible has been divided into the Old Testament and the New Testament. The Old Testament is shared by Christians and Jews, and without it, the New Testament cannot be understood. The New Testament adopts the experience of God and the piety described to us in the Old Testament. It simply reinterprets these writings in the light of the story of Jesus Christ, in the light of his death, and in the light of belief in his resurrection.

Christians believe that Holy Scripture is the word of God. But of course we know that the books of the Bible were written by human beings. Even in the Old Testament, we can recognize the different authors, each of whom advocates a slightly different theology. And in the New Testament, we have four Gospels describing the story of Jesus. The author of each Gospel has his own perspective on Jesus. We trust that the different theological perspectives will open our eyes to the mystery of Jesus Christ, which is always greater than all our concepts and imaginings. And the New Testament also includes the epistles of St. Paul and other writers, all of whom interpret Jesus' acts in reference to a concrete situation in a particular congregation, drawing concrete conclusions for Christian life.

Many Genres—Inspiring and Binding

Although we understand Holy Scripture as the word of God, which is binding for us because it is inspired by the Holy Spirit, we nevertheless know that the Bible contains many different genres in which it proclaims God's word for us. There are mythological tales like the accounts of the creation of the world and of humankind. We do not interpret these biblical creation stories as scientific accounts. Instead, they use metaphor to describe the inner core, the beauty and mystery of creation. The Bible also contains historical narratives, parables, stories of being called by God, legal texts, prophetic texts, consolations, and admonitions. There are hymns, songs of praise, and prayers, such as the psalms. Each genre, or form, has its own truth. Some fundamentalists want to interpret the Bible literally. But this does not do justice to what the Bible means to say. Each form has its own truth. And only by doing justice to the form can we recognize the truth of what the Bible means to say. For us Christians, the Bible is normative. The Ten Commandments remain the norms for our behavior as Christians, as well. But many of the specific prescriptions found in the books of Moses we now see as more historical rather than absolute norms for us to follow today.

This kind of interpretation of older texts already occurs in the Bible itself. Within Judaism, for example, the historical narrative of the flight from Egypt became the fundamental metaphor for salvation. Salvation means liberation from imprisonment, from control by others, and journey to the Promised Land, the land of inner freedom where we may be fully ourselves. Particularly the psalms offer no end to new imagery for singing of this liberation from Egyptian bondage. From the point of view of the psalms, that event describes the salvific and liberating acts of God—acts which apply to us today just as much as to the people then.

Different Interpretations

Understanding the Bible as word of God is not in opposition to engaging scientifically with the Bible. Biblical scholarship first examines the authentic text and then its historical circumstances, social environment, and similarity to other religions' accounts. Bible scholarship does not resolve the word of God. But it does help us to interpret the words of the Bible more appropriately.

Already within the Bible we find two types of interpretation: allegory and typology. Paul himself describes the flight from Egypt as the type—that is, as the fundamental image—of baptism. He also reads the two wives of Abraham—Sara and Hagar—allegorically, as metaphors for the Old and New Testaments. The early Church applied the hermeneutic principles of Greek philosophy to biblical exegesis. But it also developed another method of interpretation, which was the spiritual reading of Scripture. The goal of this method is to understand all words of the Bible as statements on the true nature of our being. In contrast with moralizing interpretation (such as was prominent in the last hundred years), spiritual interpretation of the Bible wants to offer us an answer to the questions: "Who am I? How should I look at myself?" Moralizing interpretation, which seeks to answer the question: "What should we do?" is also legitimate, of course. But it should not be seen as central. Our primary experience is that of a new way of being. Today, there are many kinds of interpretation of the Bible, all with their justification, but none able to lay claim to being the only or definitive form of interpretation. There is interpretation from depth psychology, which mostly takes the metaphorical texts of the Bible as archetypal imagery. Then there are liberation theology, political interpretations, ecclesiastical readings, and personal-spiritual interpretation. All these interpretive methods reveal the openness of biblical language, along with the treasures that lie within these divinely inspired words for all human beings of all eras.

Biblical scholarship shows us that the books of the Bible did not simply fall from the sky fully formed. They were written over many centuries by many different authors. And alongside the writings authorized by the Church, there were many others, known as apocryphal writings, that the Church has not recognized. Since the third century, therefore, a canon has developed that is binding for us today. We therefore see Scripture and tradition in conjunction.

Existential Engagement with the Bible: A Guide for Successful Living

We Christians read the Bible and meditate on it. Every day, we monks pray the psalms that the Old Testament has handed down to us as a school of prayer. The stories of the Old Testament describe the relationship between God and humankind. They reveal to us our own truth. The New Testament is a book that, on the one hand, we meditate on through prayer. On the other hand, we develop our theology in a perpetual dialog with the Bible. Dogmatics must never stand in contrast to the Bible. It can only ever be an interpretation of the Bible. The Bible is and always will be the standard of our theology, our faith, and our prayer. But we must engage with it creatively.

Augustine gave a beautiful description of what such engagement looks like:

> [The word of God is] the adversary of your will, until it can become the author of your salvation. O what a good adversary, what a useful adversary! It's an adversary to us, just as long as we are so to ourselves. As long as you are your own enemy, you also have God's word as your enemy; be a friend to yourself, and you agree with it.[17]

This to say: whenever we are irritated by a word in the Bible, it is a sign that we are not at one with ourselves. Reading the Bible means grappling with its words until we understand them. And we understand them correctly when we deal with ourselves as friends, when we become a friend to ourselves. Then we will also experience the word of God as our friend, showing us how our life can be successful. We are never finished meditating on the Bible. And every age must interpret it anew. Because the words that were written then interpret our

---

17. Augustine of Hippo, "Sermon 109," Edmund Hill O.P., trans., John E. Rotelle O.S.A, ed., in *Sermons, III/ 4 (94A – 147A) on the New Testament* (Brooklyn, New York: New City Press, 1992), 133-34.

lives now and seek to show us new ways in which our life can succeed out of God and out of Jesus Christ. What matters is that the words of the Bible are always words of life, words that lead to an authentic life in the spirit of Jesus. And whenever those words make us afraid or when we interpret those words in a way that we make others afraid, we are not understanding them in the spirit of Jesus, but are using them to strengthen our own prejudices.

2. The Qur'an as Divine, Aesthetic Event

Ahmad Milad Karimi

Meant for All People: God's Revelation to Muhammad

Muslims believe that Islam's holy text, the Qur'an (literally: reading, recitation), contains the literal revelation of God to the Prophet Muhammad. The idea that Islam as a "religion of the book" bases itself on an orally revealed source seems paradoxical only at first glance. The Prophet did not receive a piece of writing; rather, the Qur'an, a text of poetic beauty, was inscribed into his life in musical recitation. The Qur'an itself, admittedly, describes itself as written (see the opening of surah 2), and all of Islamic calligraphy is inspired by the fact that the Qur'an is available in writing. Islam sees itself as a religion endowed by God, and the Qur'an as God's revealed gift is directed not at a particular people or a particular community, but is meant for all people.

In the Muslim view, the revelation of the Qur'an occurs in the life of the Prophet Muhammad in the seventh century on the Arabian Peninsula. It was the habit of the Prophet to retreat to solitude for a certain time to find quiet. One of these times, when he had retreated from city life into a mountain cave, the Angel Gabriel appeared to him unexpectedly. The angel is said to have communicated the Qur'an to him. When the Prophet Muhammad received the qur'anic revelation for the first time, this first divine spark occurred not as an external instruction, as some sort of dictation from above. Rather, he reports, "It was as though these words were written on my heart."[18] As the Qur'an puts it, his heart is opened to the revelation of God.[19] With the Qur'an, God is revealing his presence to Muhammad. And this revelation existentially touches and spiritually fills the Prophet. Peace pervades his heart and it pulses for God as never before. The Prophet Muhammad is transformed. This revelation, meanwhile, does not occur as a single event; rather, the qur'anic revelation takes place over twenty-three years.

The Structure and Transcription of the Qur'an

The Qur'an neither narrates Muhammad's life, nor is it structured thematically or chronologically. The individual chapters, known as surahs, are instead organized by length, so that the longer surahs occur at the beginning and the shorter at the end. Each surah is composed of at least three verses (Arabic: *āya*). The titles of the individual surahs are later editorial editions and not part of the original message. Except for the ninth, all surahs begin with the words: "In the name of God, the Lord of Mercy, the Giver of Mercy." It is indicated at the beginning of each surah whether it was sent down in Mecca or in Medina. Especially the longer surahs are composed of many different themes and layers of meaning. What is more, the Qur'an is not a narrative prose text. Some themes remain fragmentary, others are discussed only briefly or even just alluded to, and some sections of the text are obscure and enigmatic. This complex nature of the Qur'an means it cannot be easily condensed or simplified.

Today, the Qur'an is available to us in writing, but it was only after the death of the Prophet that the text was written down by the third calif, 'Uthmān ibn 'Affān, between 644 and 656 CE. Although the Prophet Muhammad had ordered that

---

18. Alfred Guillaume, *The Life of the Prophet: A Translation of Isḥāq's Sīrat Rasūl Allāh.* (Karachi: Oxford University Press, 1967), 106.
19. See Qur'an 94:1.

parts of the Qur'an be written down on palm stalks, papyrus, and bone, the entirety of the Qur'an was at first preserved in people's memories. Even the first complete compilation of the Qur'an in writing, to which vowel markings were added only much later, was intended primarily as a mnemonic aid. The Qur'an, then, is preserved in people. Those who hold the entirety of the Qur'an in their memories are given the cognomen "Hafiz," which literally means "Preserver." The important Persian poet and mystic Shams ad-Dīn Shīrāzī, for example, who inspired Goethe's *West-East Divan*, is known by the name Hafiz. Hadith, sayings of the Prophet inspired by God, also contain normative statements. But the normative nature of the Qur'an as direct word of God is different. The "sacrosanct" and normative nature of the Qur'an consists not in its physical manifestation as writing or book, but in its significance as message of God to humankind.

Recitation and Interpretation as Paths to the Qur'an

The Qur'an can therefore be accessed in two ways that are distinct but belong together: One, with reference to the form, is the melodious, sonorous, and rhythmic recitation of the Qur'an in Arabic. The other is the necessity of taking in the content and meaning through interpretation. This second path has its own constitutive exegetical tradition. Since the beginning of theological engagement with the Qur'an in Islam, a large number of massive volumes of qur'anic exegesis have been created, interpreting the Qur'an with different methods. Some prefer philological interpretation, others genuinely historical readings, and yet again others a spiritual interpretation of the individual verses.

The text of the Qur'an has not changed over the centuries, but the understanding of it certainly has. To that extent, the different interpretive works are not by their nature normative, because they merely present a particular approach to interpretation for their own era. Those who want to understand the Qur'an thus inescapably need a historical understanding of the time in which the Qur'an was revealed. Only this context allows one to make sense of the Qur'an as a whole. In their historical context, for example, the violent passages of the Qur'an can be read, understood, and put into perspective. The same is true of statements that at first seem to contradict other passages of the Qur'an. They too are easily explained with reference to the correct historical context. This is why scholars consider the different occasions for the revelations.

That means there were reasons why certain verses of the Qur'an were revealed. But the occasions are not always recorded in the Qur'an itself. Therefore, engaging with the Qur'an requires an extremely sensitive and knowledgeable academic and hermeneutic practice. This seems to be where the extreme and fundamentalist groups have misunderstood matters: they assume that in their lives they can follow the Qur'an to the letter. But those who want to follow the Qur'an in such a way are holding on to a very specific interpretation of the Qur'an. And to speak of an "interpretation" is to acknowledge implicitly that another person might have a different interpretation. Between me and the Qur'an, in other words, there is always a third space: the space of interpretation. This interpretation can vary and might even be wrong. Admittedly, there is not only room for misunderstanding: a new interpretation can also improve, can deepen understanding, etc.

Humility as the Appropriate Stance:
God's Word in Human Words

What the Qur'an therefore demands is a decidedly religious attitude: humility. Those who think they know with absolute certainty what God wants of them are setting themselves above the Qur'an, and precisely by doing so, they are missing the core of the message they try to proclaim. Receiving and interpreting the Qur'an is thus a never-ending task, one which needs to be undertaken anew again and again. That also means that not a single verse of the Qur'an can be taken literally, because each word must first be understood—which is to say interpreted. To Muslims, the Qur'an is the unadulterated word of God. But it is also the eternal word of God throughout history, which is to say, in time. One could, then, describe the Qur'an as God's word in human words without detracting from its nature as God's word. In this context, the question of the Qur'an's createdness (Arabic: *khalq al-qur'ān*) or non-createdness (Arabic: *ghair makhlūq*) is highly significant and has been hotly debated within Islamic theology since the eighth century CE. Since God alone is eternal and uncreated, there can be nothing else uncreated beside him. But the Qur'an itself speaks of a Qur'an on a "preserved tablet" (Arabic: *lauḥ maḥfūẓ*)[20] While particularly the theological school of the Muʿtazila sought argumentatively and at times politically to define as doctrinal the createdness of the Qur'an, the Hanbali school—going back to the theologian and legal scholar Aḥmad ibn Ḥanbal (d. 855 CE)—held vehemently that the Qur'an was not created. In between these two, especially the schools of the Ashʿarīya and Māturīdīya have, within the Sunni tradition, carved out a moderate position distinguishing between God's "speaking inwardly" (Arabic: *kalām nafsī*) and his "speaking aloud" (Arabic: *kalām lafẓī*). Since both schools view God's speech as an attribute of his nature—i.e., God's speech is an eternal part of God—the Qur'an as God's speech is at once "eternal" (Arabic: *qadīm*) but "created" with respect to its revealed form—that is, both in view of its recitation and in its written form (as ink on paper, etc.).

Reference to Jewish and Christian Scripture

The Scriptures of Judaism and Christianity play a significant and self-evident role in the Qur'an's understanding of itself, because the Qur'an is written in an allusive (that is, in a referential, implicative) style. Both the Torah and the Gospels are mentioned in the Qur'an and dignified highly: "We revealed the Torah with guidance and light. […] We gave him [Jesus, son of Mary] the Gospel with guidance, light, and confirmation of the Torah already revealed–a guide and lesson for those who take heed of God" (Qur'an 5:44–46). Nevertheless, some

---

20. Qur'an 85:22; see. however Qur'an 42:52 and 43:1 ff.

critical voices discount these passages, technically known as *isrā'īlīyāt*, as foreign content and reject consulting or referring to this material. But classical exegetical literature has largely valued this connection and accounted for it in the commentaries.

Inexhaustible Source of Spirituality

To Muslims, the Qur'an represents the inexhaustible source of spirituality. "Say, 'If the whole ocean were ink for writing the words of my Lord, it would run dry before those words were exhausted'– even if We were to add another ocean to it" (Qur'an 18:109). The Qur'an is not, for Muslims, an everyday object. Instead, it is a divine, aesthetic event. The Qur'an lives in recitation. Only when it is sounded aloud can one speak of the Qur'an. This recitational nature makes the Qur'an a spiritual and aesthetic event in the lives of Muslims. It is recited again and again and gets under our skin, it comforts, it calls to our minds the presence of God, it endows the hearts of the faithful with peace, it affirms life, and it demands that we work towards the healing and the good. Additionally, the Qur'an as a concrete book also has a spiritual significance in the life of Muslims. The book is usually kept wrapped in cloth and touched and recited from only after ritual ablutions. Particularly in the month of Ramadan, when the Qur'an was first sent down, it is read in its entirety. Each day of Ramadan, the month of fasting, is accorded to a particular part of the Qur'an. But the Qur'an is also recited at significant events in a person's life, such as birth, naming, and on one's deathbed. Since parts of the Qur'an are also spoken in ritual prayer, the Qur'an is a constant companion in the everyday life of Muslims.

The Prophet: Testimony of One Called by God

I. How Do Christians Conceive of Prophecy?

Anselm Grün

Called and Caller

The Hebrew word for prophet—much like the Arabic word used in Islam, *nabī*—comes from a verb meaning "to call" or "called." To biblical authors too, a prophet is one called by God, but also one who calls God's message out to humankind. In the Old Testament, prophets are also called men of God or seers. God calls a prophet to proclaim, at God's behest, God's reaction to the deeds of humankind. This proclamation is both judgment and the annunciation of salvation. The prophet proclaims the judgment of God upon humankind's misdeeds. But he also proclaims salvation, addressing not only the people of Israel, but all peoples. God's salvation is accorded to all people, with all their different religions. Prophets, then, see beyond the boundaries of their own religion. Prophets proclaims to all people—Christians, Jews, Muslims, Buddhists, and Hindus—God's gift of salvation. But they also point out: before salvation must come judgment, must come repentance.

Different Types of Prophecy

The Old Testament distinguishes between different types of prophets. There are the cult prophets, who serve at a particular shrine or altar. Then there are prophets working at the royal court, such as Nathan, who continually re-orients King David to the will of God. And there are those known as scriptural prophets, most prominently Isaiah, Jeremiah, Ezekiel, and Daniel. And then there are also the so-called twelve lesser prophets, including

Hosea, Amos, Zechariah, Micah, Malachi, and others. Just like Islam, the Old Testament also recognizes prophets as preachers of law. Examples of this conception of prophecy are particularly Moses, Elijah, Elisha, and Hosea. There are also women who are explicitly described prophetesses, such as Deborah (Jgs 4:4), Miriam (Ex 15:20), and Huldah (2 Kgs 22:14–20). In the New Testament, prophets are seen primarily as soothsayers, telling us the future.

Serving God

Each prophet is called by God and taken wholly into his service. Often enough, the prophet will rebel against this calling. Jonah runs away because he suspects that he will not succeed in the task God has given him. Jeremiah, too, resists his calling: "Ah, Lord GOD! Truly I do not know how to speak, for I am only a boy" (Jer 1:6). But God tells him: "You shall go to all to whom I send you, and you shall speak whatever I command you. Do not be afraid of them, for I am with you to deliver you" (Jer 1:7 f). Sometimes Jeremiah laments his mission: "O LORD, you have enticed me, and I was enticed; you have overpowered me, and you have prevailed. I have become a laughingstock all day long; everyone mocks me" (Jer 20:7). Being a prophet, then, can also mean letting oneself be taken over by God and being obedient to God even in the face of ridicule and taunts that his words will never come true.

The Office of Critical Observer

The Greek word "prophet" actually means someone who speaks openly and bindingly. In this sense, we can apply "prophetic speech" not just to significant religious figures of the past. Instead, it refers to something topical and common. In baptism, we Christians have all been anointed prophets and prophetesses, and thus sent out. Each of us has the task of expressing something of God in this world—something that can be expressed by that individual alone. But if we speak of prophetic service to the Church today, we generally mean men and women in the

Church who are speaking out against problems in the Church or society. Prophets direct their protest at unjust structures, against politicians, but also the Church, for disadvantaging the poor. In this way, prophets have a critical role in society. They fulfill the office of guardian, holding up a mirror of criticism to society and indicating God's reaction to the various situations in society.

Jesus as Prophet—and More Than Prophet

In the Christian tradition too, Jesus is a prophet. He is announced by John the Baptist, whom Jesus himself calls more than a prophet. John is the voice of God in the wilderness of which Isaiah has spoken (Lk 7:26-27). Jesus himself fulfills all that the Old Testament prophets have said of him. When the evangelists describe Jesus himself as a prophet, they describe him as one who essentially outdoes the prophets of the Old Testament, fulfilling their message in a way that cannot be surpassed.

Jesus describes himself as a prophet as well: "Yet today, tomorrow, and the next day I must be on my way, because it is impossible for a prophet to be killed outside of Jerusalem" (Lk 13:33). In other words, criticism of and objection to the powerful—criticism and objection that are spoken at the behest of God's liberating message—involves accepting the danger such speech poses to the prophet's own life. And in the death of Jesus, this fate of the prophet is indeed fulfilled.

Jesus' deeds also show: prophets are empowered and affirmed through God's signs. When Jesus raises from the dead the son of the widow of Nain, bystanders react with the words: "A great prophet has risen among us . . . God has looked favorably on his people!" (Lk 7:16). Jesus as a prophet works healing miracles as the Old Testament records several prophets doing.

In Jesus, God himself has looked favorably on his people— or, as the Greek text has it, has visited his people. God himself works in the prophet Jesus. And so Jesus outdoes all prophets of the Old Testament. In Jesus, God himself comes to the people. In Jesus, God himself is present among his people. It is in this sense that Jesus is both prophet and more than a prophet. In him we are encountering God himself.

All Christians' Gift of Prophecy

In the First Epistle to the Corinthians, Paul discusses the varieties of spiritual gifts that Christians may receive. Among these is the gift of prophecy (1 Cor 12:28). Paul defends the task of the prophets in the face of the charismatic gift of speaking in tongues that so fascinated the occultist Corinthians. He sees the task of the prophet as follows: "Those who prophesy speak to other people for their upbuilding and encouragement and consolation" (1 Cor 14:3). Paul takes for granted that even in the present there will continue to be prophets in the Church whom God grants special gifts—in particular the gift of building up the congregation. Prophets have the capacity to bring the congregation together and build it up, to encourage individual Christians and offer them comfort and new strength.

Admonishing and Proclaiming the Absolute Truth of God

Considering the Old Testament and Pauline conceptions of prophecy, we Christians can apply the label of prophet to people outside of Christianity as well. That is, we can understand Mohammed in this sense as well: as a critic pointing us to the absolute reality of God. The Christian tradition holds that God keeps instituting prophets among us who admonish us when we depart from God's will and who proclaim to us how near God is. Significant figures of church history, such as Hildegard of Bingen or, more recently, Oscar Romero, have been described as prophets because their deeds and their lives demonstrate or represent to us that God's nearness is not just an affirmation of our lives, but often also a criticism of our behavior. In either case, however, it is always simultaneously comfort, admonition, and encouragement, as well as the affirmation that after his judgment, God always offers his salvation as well. Today, there are surely also individuals whom God chooses as his prophets. Admittedly, in this context it is important that those persons not identify themselves too fully with this task or role. Otherwise there is a danger that they might set themselves above others or live out their own craving for recognition in the idea of the prophet. The prophet can only humbly accept his mission and listen closely to what God is sending as message to pass on.

The Christian tradition also speaks of the prophetic mission of the Church as a whole. The Church is meant to raise its voice on behalf of the poor and disenfranchised, is meant to point out—like prophets—the injustice which is present everywhere in our world. And like the prophets, the Church is meant to stand up for a more just world, for a world shaped according to God's will.

2. Muhammad as "Seal of Prophecy"

Ahmad Milad Karimi

Prophets: Spiritually Singled Out

The Qur'an speaks frequently of prophets, that is to say, persons who are spiritually singled out, called upon by God to proclaim his message to the people and to ensure that his message is obeyed, perhaps in the face of resistance. The Arabic term for a prophet is *nabī* (plural: *nabīyūn* or *anbiyā'*), and the word occurs seventy-five times in the Qur'an. Special mention is made, among others, of the prophets Noah, Abraham, Moses, David, Solomon, Jesus, and finally Muhammad. There are, generally speaking, no distinctions in rank or hierarchy among the prophets, but each prophet is accorded particular recognition in the Qur'an: Abraham as the forefather of pure faith; Moses as the one to whom God speaks directly; Jesus as the prophet God created through his spirit, etc. The "seal" of prophecy—in the sense of final definitiveness—refers to prophetic figures, rather than to the nature of prophecy in itself.

Muhammad as Prophet—Connected with All Religious Communities

Muhammad's understanding of himself as a prophet must be interpreted through the lens of an understanding of the Qur'an. Furthermore, the contents of his prophecy suggest that Muhammad stands within a particular tradition. According to the Qur'an, prophecy arises from a genealogical calling (see Qur'an 29:27, among others). God, then, does not select one prophet and then another, but chooses a line of prophets who are genealogically linked. The Qur'an names three such groups as chosen in a prophetic sense: the line of Abraham (pre-Mosaic Judaism), the children of Israel (Mosaic Judaism), and the line of Imran (post-Jesus Judaism and Judeo-Christianity). Another characteristic of prophecy lies in the fact that it is God who chooses and thus singles out each prophet. This is why the outdated term "Mohammedan" as a descriptor of Muslims points to a fundamental misunderstanding: the idea that Muhammad actually created any new religious community at all.

Rather, Muhammad sees the revelation vouchsafed to him as an affirmation and at the same time reformulation of an old covenant made new, since it is now a universal covenant of God with all humankind. Muhammad felt connected not only to the aforementioned other prophets, but to their religious communities as well, to the extent that they do not undercut what he saw as the central truth of God's absolute oneness and universal devotion. This central truth was of the utmost importance to Muhammad. He saw the mission given to him by God as destined for all humankind, in order to end infighting between religions. In truth, Muhammad is convinced, what matters is not the denomination, but pure faith. Accordingly, the Qur'an reads: "They say, 'Become Jews or Christians, and you will be rightly guided.' Say [Prophet], 'No, [ours is] the religion of Abraham, the upright, who did not worship any god besides God'" (Qur'an 2:135). This means: Muhammad, do not lose yourself in terms such as "Jew" or "Christian" and the concomitant disagreements, but turn instead to the pure faith of Abraham, for he is the one seen as a founding father to both the Jewish and the Christian communities too.

Prophecy in the Qur'an: Honor and Responsibility

When Muhammad knows himself to be deeply connected with the prophets who have gone before him, what this means is: like they were, he sees himself bound most intimately by God to do a duty (Arabic: *mīthāq*). Prophecy, to him, is not only being singled out by God, but also a responsibility. His prophesying is marked by two characteristics: In the first place, he is passive—pure and receptive as a vessel of divine revelation. Second, he is active, shaping the world by trying to realize God's message in it. A further significant characteristic of prophecy in the Qur'an is contained in the aforementioned thought that prophets are not elected by their community but chosen by God. God singles out a prophet from the midst of a community, as described in the Old Testament book of Deuteronomy (18:15). But they are chosen not just for a particular people, but for all of humankind.

To Muslims, the Prophet is both a normative role model to be emulated, but also an institution never to be equaled. It is impossible to anoint oneself prophet; God alone selects his prophets, for they are his messengers. This is the sense in which Muslims see the Prophet Muhammad as the "messenger of God and seal of the prophets" (Arabic: *rasūl Allāh wa-khātam an-nabīyīn*). The Qur'an, then, precludes that any other prophets, with new revelations or wonders, will be chosen after Muhammad (see Qur'an 33:40). Whether there can nevertheless still be prophetic voices and deeds today is a different question. According to the Islamic view, this is indeed possible, and not only in Islam, but in any tradition. The decisive criterion is not the origin of the message—that is, its belonging to a particular religion or culture—but only its content and nature—that is, whether it is in harmony with qur'anic revelation.

The Islamic understanding of prophecy has an ethical aspect as well, and this aspect goes hand in hand with the idea of refining character. The prophet is entrusted with the purpose of using his noble character to lead people to their best. A saying of the Prophet Muhammad is: "I have been sent to perfect your character."[21] Prophetic deeds can be encountered where people have internalized the contents of prophecy. What matters here are the virtues that mark the inner core of Muhammad's prophecy and the person of the prophet. Its most prominent pillars are peacefulness, justice, mercy, love, humility, mildness, patience, and moderation.

What Makes Muhammad Unsurpassable

On principle, Islam rules out the possibility of a hierarchy of prophets, given that the prophets are all chosen by God. The difference between Jesus and Muhammad is therefore only in their distinct historical situation, not in the message they proclaimed. According to the Muslim view, however, the Qur'an in particular is a definitive divine event in the life of the Prophet. It is the yardstick by which and in reference to which prophecy, which crucially consists of mission, must be measured. The revelation of the Qur'an as the message of God, at its core, represents God's universal devotion. This living event of divine presence is inscribed in all of Muhammad's life.

When his wife Aisha was asked about his character, she responded: "His character was the Qur'an—what pleased the Qur'an well pleased him well, and he was wrathful where the Qur'an was wrathful."[22] What Muslims see as the "added value," as the unsurpassable quality expressed in the figure of the Prophet Muhammad, then, is his attitude towards life of subjugating his own will to the will of God. As the Qur'an encapsulates, he was sent out as "as a mercy . . . to all people" (Qur'an 21:107). When he was asked what the best Islam might be, the Prophet answered: "The best Islam is to feed the hungry and spread peace among those known to you and unknown to

---

21. Mālik b. Anas: *Muwaṭṭaʾ, Kitāb ḥusn al-khulq*, Ḥadīth no. 1677, Mecca 1425/2005, 443.
22. An-Nasāʾī, *Sunan, Kitāb qiyām al-lail*, Ḥadīth no. 1601, Cairo 1431/2010, 281-82.

you."²³ To that extent, his prophecy particularly consists in being a "servant of God."

The Difference between Jesus and Muhammad

Although Islamic tradition has arrived at the position that Muhammad was without sin—because God protects his beloved prophets from sin and error—this veneration of the Prophet in Islam cannot be compared with the elevation of the historical Jesus to the Christ of Christian faith. Muhammad has never been seen as God or as the son of God. Even when he is described as the perfected human being, his perfection is revealed most of all in his humility before God. While miracles are ascribed to him, he can dispose of these powers only because God wills it. That is why he is instructed: "Say, 'I do not have the treasures of God, nor do I know the unseen, nor do I tell you that I am an angel. I only follow what is revealed to me'" (Qur'an 6:50). Again and again, the Qur'an states that Muhammad is only a human being—but in him, Muslims see humankind ennobled "as a ruby among stones." Accordingly, the Islamic mystical tradition speaks of the Prophet as the "light of right guidance" (Arabic: *nūr al-hudā*), since the mystery of God is both hidden and revealed in him: "If you did not exist, if you did not exist, I would not have created the spheres," as a famous extra-qur'anic word of God records.²⁴

Muhammad: Not Just Messenger, But Message of God

To Muslims, Muhammad as prophet is not merely the messenger and proclaimer in—as one might say—an instrumental sense. Rather, he himself is considered the message of God. In him we recognize what he proclaims: "The Messenger of God is an

---

23. Ṣaḥīḥ al-Bukhārī, Vol. I, *Kitāb al-īmān*, Ḥadīth no. 12, Cairo 1428/2008, 19.
24. I. M. al-'Ajlūnī: *Kashf al-khāfā' wa muzīl al-ilbās*, Vol. II, Ḥadīth no. 2123, n.d., n.p., 191.

excellent model for those of you who put your hope in God" (Qur'an 33:21). To that extent, the Prophet as person plays a significant role in piety. For example, the Prophet's birthday has been celebrated since the twelfth century CE. Similar to the celebration of the birth of Jesus in the Christian holiday of Christmas, this is a day for memorializing the message of the Prophet and extolling his virtues and ideals. The giving of alms, recitations from the Qur'an, and songs of praise mark the festivities. Despite numerous attempts to construct as precise as possible a picture of the historical Muhammad from biographies, written testimony, and historical reports, the person of the Prophet was interpreted spiritually from a very early date onward, specifically as a doctor (*ṭabīb*) and friend (*ḥabīb*). In the lives of the faithful, the "Muhammad of faith" has gained a power all his own, regardless of whether one is referring to his name, birth, or moral character. The Turkish mystic Yunus Emre writes: "The world was wholly bathed in light in the night of Muhammad's birth!"

Muhammad as "Living Qur'an"

As prophet, Muhammad clearly has a spiritual mission: what matters to him is the spirit and spirituality of humankind. Muslims accord him normative character not merely because he proclaimed the Qur'an as divine message, but also because of the way in which he himself appeared as the "living Qur'an" by interpreting the Qur'an and—through divine inspiration—advocating a life in the spirit of Islam. What matters for Muslims in this context is not imitating his actions in blind literalism. Instead, it is about the principles from which his actions arose. Accordingly, his political decisions for the early Muslim community—some of which also had violent implications, for example—can be understood only from within the context of his own time, and can be considered legitimate only in that context, as well.

When it comes to social, political, economic, intercultural, and interreligious matters, it is obvious that we today live in a completely different time, with completely different challenges, questions, and problems. But this self-evidence demands specific criteria for the practical realization of general principles (such as justice) that may transcend different contexts but nevertheless require a different interpretation and implementation for each different historical and societal instance. The spirit of prophecy is not affected by this concern. On the contrary: its significance and its value lie in the fact that it is duty-bound to dynamic, mutable life, independently of the temporal circumstances or societal context.

Jesus—Prophet or Savior?

I. My Prophet Jesus

Ahmad Milad Karimi

Honored in the Qur'an: A Prophet Like No Other

Jesus, son of Mary, is mentioned numerous times in the Qur'an. And the Qur'an finds the most beautiful words to describe him: "The angels said, 'Mary, God gives you news of a Word from Him, whose name will be the Messiah, Jesus, son of Mary, who will be held in honour in this world and the next, who will be one of those brought near to God'" (Qur'an 3:45). And Mary is the only woman—pious, faithful, and honorable—mentioned by name in the Qur'an (Qur'an 3:36): "Her Lord graciously accepted her and made her grow in goodness" (Qur'an 3:37). The divine message that, untouched by any man, she will bear a son, will overwhelm her. And we take part in this overwhelmed feeling: Mary, after all, is somewhat uncertain and devoted to God, but she is also more. Humbly, she accepts that over which she has no control and which overwhelms her. Jesus overwhelms us because he cannot be. And yet he is, and his being is filled with love and kindness. In the Qur'an, Jesus, son of Mary, is honored as a prophet like no other. It is not only his existence itself that carries within it the mystery of God. Everything about him seems to be a miracle as well. How can we speak of him, how grasp his nature?

The Qur'an records his words: "I am a servant of God. He has granted me the Scripture; made me a prophet; made me blessed wherever I may be. He commanded me to pray, to give alms as long as I live, to cherish my mother. He did not make me domineering or graceless. Peace was on me the day I was born, and will be on me the day I die and the day I am raised to life again" (Qur'an 19:30–33). When Mary asks how it can be that Jesus exists at all, the Angel Gabriel tells her: "This is how God creates what He will: when He has ordained something, He only says, 'Be,' and it is" (Qur'an 3.47). The "breath of the merciful"—to quote Islamic mystic Ibn 'Arabī in description of this decision by God—lets Jesus breathe the mercy as spirit and word of God so that, on the basis of this own act of creation, he is set as equal to Adam (Qur'an 3:59).

Jesus is not the prophet of others. He becomes my prophet. The Qur'an states categorically that God does not distinguish between his messengers (Qur'an 2:285). And so we Muslims encounter the prophet Jesus, son of Mary, with the greatest respect. The "good news" entrusted to him—the Gospel—is seen by the Qur'an as a source offering light and right guidance (Qur'an 5:46). Jesus, son of Mary, who in his abstention and surrender opens our eyes to what is essential, is a constant presence and role model in Islam. Abū Ḥāmid al-Ghazālī records a thought attributed to Jesus: "The world is a bridge: cross it, but do not build a house upon it." In our journey to God, Jesus is a stop that is highly significant, as it liberates us from all material things, even up to the liberation from our ego. Jesus' way of life, his purity, his poverty, his itinerancy, his love—all these ideas that he personified are deeply inscribed in Islamic intellectual history. The path of Islam leads to Jesus; without him, an Islamic spiritual path is unthinkable.

Jesus as an Example of Islam's Mystic Path

Islamic tradition is filled with statements, legends, and motifs from the life of Jesus. The Prophet Muhammad speaks of Jesus, son of Mary, with great respect. For example, the earliest biographer of Muhammad reports that on his journey through heaven, Muhammad encountered Jesus as well. The purity of Jesus has become a trope and exemplar for the mystical path of Islam, going back to a story told by the Prophet Muhammad: Satan is said to have touched every child at birth, but not Jesus or Mary. Therefore, Jesus not only remained pure, but his purity in fact shaped his character and thus his way of seeing the world. Of particular importance is his goodness, which still moves and teaches Muslims. Ahmad Ghazālī (d. 1126 CE) writes that Jesus said: "A single tear wept by a sinner extinguishes the fire of God's wrath." In Islamic mysticism and in the life of the Muslim faithful Jesus therefore occupies an outstanding position. His breath is like the living morning wind that gives life to everything. The Muslim mystic Saʻdī (d. 1238 CE) is said to have written: "Friend, make use of the breath of Jesus in the morning / whether it may waken your dead heart, because it is from Him that this breath comes." At the same time, Jesus is seen as the prayerful one who has fully become prayer. Held in the hand of God, he heals the blind and the deaf. Jesus as a healer personifies the faith that, in its simplicity and humility, can transform people, lead them to the good, and heal them. In words attributed to the Muslim mystic Maulānā Rūmī (d. 1273 CE): "We are skillful healers, for we are students of Christ."

Distancing from Deification—Denial of the Crucifixion

In contrast to the Christian view, the Islamic understanding is that Jesus remains the son of Mary alone. His divinity—that is, the idea that he is fully God and fully man—is untenable according to Islam. It is not only the Qur'an that distances itself from deification of Jesus. The Islamic tradition, too, sees in the face of Jesus an outstanding servant of God, but nothing more. Although the Qur'an does go into considerable detail on his birth and the special circumstances of his life, it remains remarkably laconic on the topic of his death. The Qur'an denies Jesus' death on the cross. A relevant passage reads: "They did not kill him, nor did they crucify him" (Qur'an 4:157).

A reason is given for this denial: *"wa-lākin shubbiha lahum"* (Qur'an 4:157). It is not easy to translate this passage; indeed, it is among the most obscure in the Qur'an. It can be understood as saying either "it appeared so unto them" (Pickthall translation) or "for them, he merely appeared similar to him" (Karimi translation). Both variants unmistakably state that a crucifixion took place. In other words, the Qur'an does not dispute the occurrence of a crucifixion. All the Qur'an disputes is that it was indeed Jesus who was crucified. In this context, it should be remembered that in early Christianity, too, there were those who denied the crucifixion of Jesus. One such was the Alexandrian gnostic Basilides (d. 145 CE), who stated that it was not Jesus but Simon of Cyrene who died on the cross. In this regard, the Qur'an formulates a clear thesis: In truth, it was not Jesus who was crucified. Rather, God preserved Jesus from crucifixion. But the Qur'an does not tell us precisely how God saved Jesus from being crucified. Jesus, in any event, is not immortal (Qur'an 19:33). And yet the Qur'an is silent on the question of where, how, and at what age Jesus died. It is plain to see that the Qur'an practically provokes the question: So what really did happen to Jesus? The Qur'an says that "God raised him up to Himself" (Qur'an 2:158). Jesus, then, did not die a violent death.

In any case, apart from the historical circumstances, the rejection of the theology of the cross seems to be a simultaneous rejection of salvation theology, which aims to locate the salvation of humankind precisely in Jesus' death on the cross. The qur'anic distancing from the death on the cross and its concomitant denial of the crucifixion as salvation are meant to open up the possibility that human salvation is based in human beings themselves, since humankind is in its essence oriented towards God. In Islam, human beings are neither weighted with original sin, nor is it theologically necessary to pass through the cross to salvation.

Faithful Awe

Undoubtedly, the cross is not Christianity's last word. To Christians, an essential aspect of Jesus' death on the cross is his resurrection; the great sign that death itself is conquered. To us Muslims, this interpretation of the life of Jesus can be somewhat disgraceful, but it is nevertheless educative. However impossible I as a Muslim may find it to see God in the face of a human being who wore the mantle of mortality, I am nevertheless touched by the idea of God taking on my suffering, my pain, and my lament in order to support me, comfort me, and heal me—that it was not another but God himself who became human among human beings; that in the person of Jesus, God walked the path to the cross. I cannot believe that, and yet it is not unbelief that rises in me. Instead, it is a faithful awe that moves me as a Muslim, while also leaving me behind in reverence.

2. Jesus, Son of God

Anselm Grün

The Concrete Face of God—a Challenge

To me as a Christian, Jesus is the concrete face of God. In him I see God's human heart. I am never done with Jesus. I face up to his words and grapple with them until I understand them. I admire how he approaches people, how he heals the sick, how he raises up sinners. Jesus shapes my praying, too. Like Muslims, of course, I pray to God. But the Prayer of the Heart, which I link with my breath—"Lord Jesus Christ, Son of God, have mercy upon me"—brings something tender, something loving into my prayer. In this prayer addressed to him, I allow Jesus' love as I encounter it in the Bible to flow into my heart—and from my heart to flow into my entire body, so that the spirit of Jesus can permeate and transform everything within me.

As a Christian, I am pleased when I read that the Qur'an treats Jesus so positively as a prophet. Many qur'anic statements on Jesus I can affirm from a Christian perspective: Jesus is a prophet called by God. And when the Qur'an describes the birth of Jesus as something special and relates that Jesus was self-evidently not touched by sin, this is also in line with Christian theology of Jesus' freedom from sin.

The Divinity of Jesus

I would like to look more closely at two subjects that were already mentioned in our appraisal of "stumbling blocks" and with which the Qur'an has difficulty. In the first place there is Jesus' divine nature. Here, we must distinguish between the Jewish and the Greek view of Jesus. For the Jews, Jesus' description of himself as God's son indicates his special relationship with God. Just as the king is son of God, Jesus also has a particular closeness to God and therefore describes himself as the son of God. The content of such a statement might well be acceptable in the eyes of the Qur'an. But in dialogue with ancient Greek philosophy, Greek theologians understood God's fatherhood of Jesus ontologically. That is to say, Jesus not only has a special relationship with God, but furthermore is in essence not merely human, but divine as well. The way in which humanity is connected with divinity must in the end remain a mystery. Greek theology, which came to be adopted by Christianity, sees not only a special relationship between God and Jesus, but a fundamental unity of God and Jesus. This dogmatic phrasing is another attempt to understand and express the mystery of Jesus. To me as a theologian it is clear that dogma does not mean that I can explain everything with the utmost precision. To me, rather, dogma is the art of keeping open the mystery. In the end, dogmas are another metaphorical approach to the mystery of God and the mystery of Jesus. No one can therefore fully understand and exhaustively describe the actual meaning of the dogmatic statement that God and human are one in Jesus.

What we say remains open to the mystery. I also bridle at reductionist statements. If I were to say that Jesus was just a person who was especially skilled in religion, that would allow me to distance myself from him and set myself above him. But if I instead say: Jesus is the son of God—then I may be far from knowing what that truly means, but the way of putting it tells me that Jesus has a claim on me that is equal to the claim God has on me. Recall Paul Tillich's statement that God "is what concerns us ultimately."[25] When I say that Jesus is the son of God, then Jesus concerns me. I take his words seriously. I grapple with them. I do not set myself above his

---

25. Paul Tillich, *Systematic Theology*, 12.

words. I do not criticize him as a historically contingent and limited personality, but instead face up to his divine claim. Perhaps mutual understanding between Muslims and Christians is possible from this perspective. The differing interpretations will remain. But dialogue will then be about openness for the other's point of view, not about proving that one is right.

The idea that God descended to us in Jesus is precious to us Christians. It expresses the special closeness God has to us human beings. God linked himself to the human being Jesus in an unprecedented way. Wolfgang Amadeus Mozart, in his settings of the Credo in the Latin Mass, always emphasizes the *descendit*: in Jesus, God descended to us so that we might find the courage to descend into the depths of our own souls and let everything within us be illuminated by God's light. And if God sometimes seems distant from us, then it can help us to look at Jesus. In such moments, I imagine how in the person of Jesus, I am encountering God's love. In other words: Jesus speaks to me in a way that opens me up to God utterly.

Jesus' Death on the Cross and the Mystery of Resurrection

The second topic I want to discuss in the context of the Muslim position is Jesus' death on the cross and the mystery of resurrection. To us Christians, the cross is indeed the thorn that makes us question our view of God. For Jesus' disciples, his death on the cross was a shock. And only after the resurrection did they recognize that this death of Jesus on the cross was not a failure, but rather reveals a mystery of God's love, which is stronger than death. Jesus' death on the cross is not necessarily linked to the doctrine of salvation. The cross is not a theological necessity for salvation. In the Bible, the cross is interpreted in very different ways, and all of these interpretations arose after the resurrection. Luke, as the Greek, does not see the cross as atonement for our sins. To him, the death of Jesus on the cross is theater. By watching this performance, we are transformed. As already mentioned, in his death on the cross, Jesus appears as the truly just person of whom Plato wrote in his *Republic*. To the question of how a truly just man would fare in our unjust world, Plato responds that "the just man will have to endure the lash, the rack, chains, the branding-iron in his eyes, and finally, after every extremity of suffering, he will be crucified."[26] In Jesus, we see this truly just man. That is why the Roman captain in the Gospel of Luke does not say: "He was God's son," but "Certainly this man was innocent"—in an alternative reading, "righteous" (Lk 23:47). The Greek Septuagint is even clearer, stating: "Truly, this man was just."

Sin, Atonement, and Salvation

According to the Gospel of Luke, Jesus' death does not effect salvation—not even redemption from sin. God forgives our sins because he is a kind and merciful God, not because Jesus died on the cross. But Jesus' death on the cross can show us God's forgiving love. When we see how Jesus, on the cross, forgives even his murderers, we can trust that there is nothing in us that God will not forgive. Looking at the cross can strengthen our faith in forgiveness, can resolve our deep, unconscious resistance to forgiveness. For when persons have sinned, they reject themselves so strongly that they can no longer believe in forgiveness.

The Gospel of John likewise contains no theology of atonement. To John, the cross is the consummation of love: "No one has greater love than this, to lay down one's life for one's friends" (Jn 15:13). And Jesus says of himself: "And I, when I am lifted up from the earth, will draw all people to myself" (Jn 12:32). The cross, in other words, is a gesture of embrace. To us Christians, the paradox consists precisely in the fact that on the cross—the point where the sins of the world, the cowardice of Pilate, the envy of the Sadducees, and the cruelty of the soldiers all did their worst—love was stronger than all hate. For that

---

26. Plato, *The Republic*, trans. by James Adam (Cambridge: Cambridge University Press, 1902), 361 ff. Accessed online through http://www.perseus.tufts.edu/hopper/text?doc=Perseus%3atext%3a1999.04.0094.

reason, the cross is a symbol of hope to us. When we look at the world, there is enough cruelty and suffering and evil that seek to harm us. The cross shows us that it is not cruelty that has the last word, but love. And the resurrection affirms that this love, which is stronger than hate and enmity, is stronger than death as well.

To us Christians, original sin is not a flaw that clings to us and is canceled out by the cross. Original sin is simply a way of describing our world. Original sin refers not to some abstract doctrine of faith, but to the reality we find before us. We need only look at the world, and we will see enough evil. And what we see in the world seeks to infect us. To us, salvation means that Jesus' love, which was revealed in its fullness on the cross, enables us to love in a way that is stronger than this evil. Salvation means that we are placed in a space of love into which evil cannot penetrate.

The Lasting Challenge of the Cross

What Milad Karimi writes at the end of his section touches me as well, and to me, it is the lasting challenge of the cross: what kind of a God is it who does not protect Jesus, his prophet, his son, from death on the cross, who rather goes through all suffering with him, who suffers with us in Jesus and thus transforms our suffering from within? But I can look upon this God only in the light of the resurrection. In me, the resurrection as answer to Jesus' death on the cross strengthens my hope that there is nothing God will not transform. There is no darkness not lit by the light of God. There is no failure that God cannot transform into a new beginning. There is no petrification that God will not crack open into new liveliness. There is no death that God will not transform into new life. There is no grave in which life is not resurrected. So the cross, for us Christians, is not a dark sign but a sign of hope.

That is why the early Christians always understood the cross as a sign of victory. They decorated crucifixes with gems and sang: "Through the wood of the cross, joy came to all the world." The images that Christian poets developed to describe the mystery of the cross are truly wonderful. They do not breathe sacrificial theology. An old Lenten hymn runs:

> You are the secure ladder
> upon which one ascends to life
> which God wants to grant eternally.
>
> You are the sturdy bridge
> across which all pious
> come safely through the torrents.
>
> You are the banner of victory
> before which the enemy takes fright
> when he but looks at it.
>
> You are the pilgrims' staff
> on which we can lean securely,
> neither swaying nor falling.
>
> You are the key to heaven,
> you unlock life
> which was given to through you.

Sacrifice and Devotion

We never finish meditating on the mystery of the cross and deepening our grasp of it. Perhaps Islam rejected the cross because it saw the cross as too deeply linked to sacrificial theology. Of course, the Christian tradition does have such a sacrificial theology. And often it has unfortunately been proclaimed in such a way that we as faithful theologians cannot accept it today. After all, what kind of conception of God is it to say that God must sacrifice his own son in order to be able to forgive our sins? When Paul speaks of atonement and the Epistle to the Hebrews speaks of sacrifice, we must understand these terms correctly. If we say that Jesus sacrificed himself for us on the cross, what we mean is: he gave himself for us. Sacrifice is devotion, and this devotion—that someone gave his life for us out of love—gives us a new worth, shows us how important we are to God. On the one hand, we should reinterpret sacrificial theology in new ways; on the other, the Bible also allows us to interpret the cross in various ways. And perhaps some of these interpretations could be held by a Muslim too and could reveal the mystery of a love that is stronger than death.

Understanding Different Perspectives

And so, even in good-faith dialogue, some different perspectives will certainly remain. To me, however, much is already gained if we simply try to understand others and their perspective. And to me, another's perspective is always a challenge to question my own and perhaps expand it. So I will see Jesus with new eyes. And I am grateful if Muslim conversation partners can gain a new perspective on Jesus through my representation, as well.

Mary: A Special Woman

I. The Muslim View of Mary

Ahmad Milad Karimi

Unique as a Role Model of Devotion

Her breath must have caught when the Angel Gabriel appeared and spoke to her: "Mary, God has chosen you and made you pure: He has truly chosen you above all women" (Qur'an 3:42). At any rate, the Muslim mystic Jalāl ad-Dīn Rūmī has written about this scene: "A shaking took hold of Mary's limbs, for she was naked" when the angel revealed himself to her: "Mary stood in her washroom, when a form, enchanting and graceful, arose out of the floor before her: Gabriel." And in Rūmī's account, Mary answers: "I give myself into the protection of God!" The Angel Gabriel then reveals himself to be a messenger of God and affirms that God is with her "wherever she may flee to." Mary does not ask for proof, but believes the words of the angel. It is Mary's humility that the Qur'an expresses with particular dignity. Mary (in the Arabic form, Maryam) is the only woman explicitly named in the Qur'an, a full thirty-four times, and these mentions are not offhand: the nineteenth surah of the Qur'an is devoted to her.

Significance in the Qur'an and Islamic Mysticism

Mary plays such an outstanding role in the Islamic spiritual world and particularly Islamic mysticism because the Qur'an accords her such high status. It is recorded that the Prophet Muhammad reckoned Mary among the four best women in the world, next to Asija (Pharaoh's wife, who mercifully took in Moses when he was a child), Fatima (the daughter of the Prophet), and Khadija (the Prophet's wife and the first Muslim).

Just like her son Jesus, Mary is considered the quintessence of a pure human being, a pure soul, untouched by evil. The Muslim mystic Farīd ad-Dīn 'Aṭṭār writes that on the Day of Judgment God will let humankind into the garden of paradise, and the first person to enter will be Mary, as she is above all other human beings.

Whenever the Qur'an discusses Mary, she is surrounded by an aura of spirituality, borne up by God's hand. Her birth is described in the Qur'an as follows:

> Imran's wife said, "Lord, I have dedicated what is growing in my womb entirely to You; so accept this from me. You are the One who hears and knows all," but when she gave birth, she said, "My Lord! I have given birth to a girl"—God knew best what she had given birth to: the male is not like the female—"I name her Mary and I commend her and her offspring to Your protection from the rejected Satan.' Her Lord graciously accepted her and made her grow in goodness, and entrusted her to the charge of Zachariah. Whenever Zachariah went in to see her in her sanctuary, he found her supplied with provisions. He said, "Mary, how is it you have these provisions?" and she said, "They are from God: God provides limitlessly for whoever He will." (Qur'an 3:35–37)

God has chosen Mary and is close to her; he lets her be nourished by his own hand. Mary grows up in a niche in the Jerusalem Temple, as tradition has it. For that reason, these verses from the Qur'an are often seen as calligraphic decorations of prayer rooms in mosques. Mary's devotion is immeasurable, and in that she is a role model for Muslims.

Mary represents the unsurpassable subordination of her own will in the face of the will of her Lord. Untouched by a man, Mary becomes pregnant with Jesus through the spirit of God. And so it says in the Qur'an: "The angels said, 'Mary, God gives you news of a Word from Him, whose name will be the Messiah, Jesus, son of Mary, who will be held in honour in this world and the next, who will be one of those brought near to God'" (Qur'an 3:45). Mary is overwhelmed by this news which she can hardly believe. "She said: 'My Lord, how can I have a son when no man has touched me?'" (Qur'an 3:47). And she is informed of what awaits her: "This is how God creates what He will: when He has ordained something, He only says, "Be", and it is" (Qur'an 3:47). But Mary does not quarrel with God. In humility, she takes upon herself that over which she has no control. This attitude of Mary's is accorded special dignity in Islamic mysticism. Mary is therefore seen as a symbol of devotion. In particular, as Islamic tradition has it, she bore Jesus in great pain; Mary's contractions take her over fully: "And so it was ordained: she conceived him. She withdrew to a distant place and, when the pains of childbirth drove her to [cling to] the trunk of a palm tree, she exclaimed, 'I wish I had been dead and forgotten long before all this!' but a voice [the Angel Gabriel —A.M.K.] cried to her from below, 'Do not worry: your Lord has provided a stream at your feet and, if you shake the trunk of the palm tree towards you, it will deliver fresh ripe dates for you, so eat, drink, be glad'" (Qur'an 19:22–25). Mary's pain, the record tells us, is showered with sweet dates.

Creative Power: the Impossible Becomes Reality

But Mary is also seen as a counterpoint to Eve—for example in the works of the Muslim mystic Ibn 'Arabī. While Eve proceeded from the purely male, Mary as the quintessence of pure femininity brings forth the masculine. As such, Mary is considered a creative force who lets life thrive within her. Jalāl ad-Dīn Rūmī shows the rich significance and symbolic power of Mary by writing: "The body is like Mary. Each of us has a Jesus, but before pain is not revealed in us, our Jesus cannot be born. If the pain never comes, Jesus returns to his origins along the same path along which he had come, and we remain behind, bereft and without any part in him."[27] Mary suffers

---

27. Jalāl ad-Dīn Rūmī, *Von Allem und von Einem* [Of all and of the

through the bitter pains of birth and thus lets the impossible become reality: Jesus.

Symbol of Steadfastness and Patience

But the Virgin Mary is simultaneously a symbol of steadfastness and patience. In his *Divan*, Jalāl ad-Dīn Rūmī writes: "If the treasure 'sorrow for His sake' is in your heart, then the heart will become 'light beyond light,' just as the lovely Mary, who carries Jesus within her body."[28] And Jesus, who wakes unto life from the spirit of God himself, affirms the purity of his mother: "She went back to her people carrying the child, and they said, 'Mary! You have done something terrible! [...] She pointed at him. They said, 'How can we converse with an infant?'[But] he said: 'I am a servant of God. He has granted me the Scripture; made me a prophet; made me blessed wherever I may be. He commanded me to pray, to give alms as long as I live, to cherish my mother" (Qur'an 19:27–32). While Jesus speaks, blessed by God, in the cradle, Mary has silence imposed upon her for a while: "Say to anyone you may see: 'I have vowed to the Lord of Mercy to abstain from conversation, and I will not talk to anyone today'" (Qur'an 19:26). Mary, who "guarded her chastity" and was "truly devout" (Qur'an 66:12) embodies silence as a stillness with God. Jalāl ad-Dīn Rūmī writes: "Sometimes I am become all tongue, as Jesus; sometimes I have a silent heart."[29]

Role Model for Muslims—but without Veneration

Nevertheless, Islam has no veneration of Mary as Christianity developed not only in the theological discipline of dogmatic

---

One]. Translated and prefaced by Annemarie. Schimmel. (Munich: Diederichs, 2020), 84. Translated from the German.
28. Annemarie Schimmel, *Jesus und Maria in der islamischen Mystik* [Jesus and Mary in Islamic mysticism] (Munich: Kösel, 1996), 149. Translated from the German.
29. Schimmel, *Jesus und Maria*, 153. Translated from the German.

Mariology, but also in a rich store of iconographic and symbolic imagery. The Qur'an, for example, expressly distances itself from any exaggeration of Mary's significance in the sense of deification (see Qur'an 5:116–17). Rather, the image of Mary is to be seen in her exemplary attitude in life as a devoted, pure soul, as a mother, as a woman filled with pain and blessed with grace, as a steadfast and humble sign for us human beings who hold her as a role model in life, and simultaneously as a spiritual and creative source for memorializing the mercy and mildness of God. In these characteristics, she is a role model for all Muslims, regardless of her sex.

2. The Christian View of Mary

Anselm Grün

Role Model and Archetype of Faith

The ideas and interpretations that the Qur'an offers with regard to Mary correspond to the reading handed down to us in the Gospel of Luke. And some of the individual points of Mary's life as related in Islamic tradition are similar to the stories about Mary found in some apocryphal Gospels. Because it is also found in the Christian tradition, what connects us is this: Mary's birth is something special. She is pure from the beginning. She is the virgin mother of Jesus.

In Islam, Mary is primarily a role model of devotion and of subjugating her own will in order to give herself over fully to the will of God. In Christianity, Mary is predominantly a role model and archetype of faith. Mary opens herself up to the promises God makes to her through the Angel Gabriel. Unlike Zechariah, she does not doubt what the angel says to her. She speaks with the angel and lets him explain to her how the birth of Jesus will occur. At the end of the conversation, she tells the angel: "Here am I, the servant of the Lord; let it be with me according to your word" (Lk 1:38). Mary does not know what to expect, but she opens herself up to God's word.

She has faith in this word. And she devotes herself to the will of God. In this respect, the Islamic view corresponds to the Christian view, as well.

Archetype of Contemplation

But another thing is important about Mary's faith. When the shepherds told her what the angel had said about the birth of the child in the stable in Bethlehem, she "treasured all these words and pondered them in her heart" (Lk 2:19). That, at least, is the New Revised Standard translation. The Greek Septuagint has the two verbs *synterein* and *symballein*. The first means "to see together"—Mary sees the words of the shepherds together—that is, in context—with the poor and helpless child in the manger. And she understands what she sees to be a symbol of God's deeds. She is therefore the archetypal image of contemplation. She meditates on the word of God and lets it drop into her heart in order to interpret her outward experience from the perspective of God's word.

Marian Imagery—Depictions of Longing

The rich store of iconography—both in Eastern Christianity as well as in the West—does not seek to deify Mary. Rather, the artists tend to depict Mary as a role model for us Christians. The depiction of Mary as a queen reminds us of our own royal dignity. She is the Madonna, the beautiful woman in whom as in a mirror we recognize our own beauty and dignity. She is the mother who recalls to us the maternal within us. Of course, archetypal longings flowed into Marian depictions in art as well, just as they were expressed in depictions of ancient mother goddesses. Images are always open, and one must be wary of turning images into dogmatic claims. For example, depictions of Mary as Madonna with a cloak of protection do not mean that she preserves us from all danger. Rather, this image points to the maternal God. Protestant piety came to reject such Marian depictions. Catholic spirituality, meanwhile, was always willing to be catholic—in the sense of "all-encompassing." It integrated the longings expressed in other religions into the Christian faith.

The Christianized Indigenous people in South America certainly saw Mary as the fulfillment of all the longings that they associated with the "Earth Mother." Of course, whenever we direct at Mary our primeval human longings, such as are expressed in other religions, then there always remains the danger—especially among simpler people—that Mary will be set on too high a pedestal and have divine characteristics ascribed to her.

Tasks for a Critical Religious Dialogue

In order to separate clear-sighted theology from populist exaggeration, then, we will always also need critical dialogue between faiths and between religious confessions. Theology has always clearly understood that Mary is a human being, a simple woman of Nazareth, chosen by God to become the Mother of Jesus—and as defined later by the Council of Ephesus, God-bearer. The title "Mother of God," however, was not conferred by the Council and arose out of popular piety. This title, too, requires the clear theological statement that will preserve us from exaggeration, or else we may misunderstand it.

A Mirror in which We See Ourselves

But aside from Mary's character as role model, the artists' renderings and theological statements about Mary also reveal something else: Mary is wholly and entirely human. She is not deified, but rather is the archetype of the saved human being. For this reason, all theological statements about Mary are statements about us as human beings who are saved. Just like Islamic mystics, Christian mystics see Mary as the archetype for the birth of Jesus in humankind. Each of us is to become the mother of Jesus. Christian mystics, however, speak not only of the birth of Jesus in our hearts, but of the birth of God within us.

But what does "birth of God" mean? This expression is a metaphor for a reality that we can discuss only in metaphor.

"Birth of God" means that we come into contact with the fundamental, undistorted, and pure image that God has made himself of each one of us. Mary, in other words, is a mirror in which we see ourselves. And in the end, the praise of Mary that resounds in numerous songs and hymns is always praise of God, who dignified Mary that she might bear his son. And it is a song of thanks to God for the great things he has done for us. That is why every day the Church sings the song in which Mary praises God:

> My soul magnifies the Lord,
>   and my spirit rejoices in God my Savior,
> for he has looked with favor on the lowliness of his servant.
> [...]
> for the Mighty One has done great things for me.
> (Lk 1:46–49)

When we Christians sing this hymn, then together with Mary we are praising what great things God has done for each of us. We connect with Mary's faith and trust, and in her words, we recognize what God does for us. For us Christians, then, Mary is a challenge to us to say "Let it be so!" and give ourselves up to the will of God. But this devotion also involves the praise of God and gratitude for what God has done for us and continues to do.

The Meaning of Marian Dogmas

Not only Muslims ask on what basis the Church has the right to make dogmatic statements about Mary not explicitly made in the Bible. In particular, the question often concerns the dogma that Mary was "taken up body and soul to the glory of heaven" (*Munificentissimus Deus*, 1950)[30] and the dogma of the

---

30. Pope Pius XII, *Munificentissimus deus*. Accessed online at: https://www.vatican.va/content/pius-xii/en/apost_constitutions/documents/hf_p-xii_apc_19501101_munificentissimus-deus.html.

Immaculate Conception, meaning that Mary was "conceived without the stain of original sin" (*Ineffabilis Deus*, 1854).[31] Again and again, the Church has reflected anew on the mystery of Mary and then made dogmatic claims about her in accordance with the Bible and spiritual tradition. Even within the Catholic Church, there has been resistance to such dogmatization. The Swiss psychologist C. G. Jung, on the other hand, is said to have welcomed the dogma of the assumption, calling the inscription in dogma the Church's "ingenious answer" to the "human disdain and valuelessness of life in the last World War." Understood in this way, the Church's more recent dogmatic statements have always been answers to questions of the times.

Accordingly, the dogmas say nothing about the special role of Mary, but something about us as saved human beings. In death, we are taken up into heaven with body and soul. Naturally our body will decay. But in this context, the expression "body" is a metaphor for the unique person expressed in the body. We as unique persons will be saved into God. What the dogma of the Immaculate Conception states, meanwhile, is believed similarly in Islam when Islam speaks of Mary as the quintessence of a pure person and a pure soul. To us Christians, Mary is an archetype expressing that—despite all the sins we heap upon ourselves again and again—there is within every one of us something that is exempted from sin, something that is pure and clear, not dirtied by sin. In the end, then, what we associate with Mary are positive images. The dogma of the Immaculate Conception was the Church's answer to pessimistic views of humanity such as had already been common, for example, in the morally rigorous Jansenism of the seventeenth and eighteenth centuries and in other movements of the time period.

Necessary Clarifications in Dialogue

Muslims find it difficult that we Christians address prayers to Mary. But here we must distinguish to whom we are actually

---

31. Pope Pius IX, *Ineffabilis deus*. Accessed online at: https://www.newadvent.org/library/docs_pi09id.htm.

praying: We pray only to God. Mary is not prayed to. Rather, we ask Mary to be our intercessor with God. We ask this not only of Mary, but also of the saints and indeed the deceased who have known us and whom we believe to be with God now. It is a human faith that we know ourselves to be in the communion of all those who have had faith before us and who are now with God in his glory. In prayer, it is as though we were contacting them so that they might stand by our side. This is an idea in the Catholic practice of piety with which Protestants, too, have difficulty. Certainly there have been many exaggerations in the Christian tradition, especially in the tradition of the recent centuries. In theology, however, it has always been clear that Mary is not prayed to. She is seen as the model of faith, as archetype of the saved human being, and as intercessor.

Feminist theology views Mary as the archetype of the strong and independent woman not defined by her relationship to a man. For feminist theologians, the veneration of Mary is a way to experience the feminine dimension of God, and Catholic Marian piety is an attempt to counteract the deficit in femininity that was inherent in the male Church, which to this day ordains only men. Mary is not a goddess but merely a prism through which we can see the maternal God. By praising the great things God has done for Mary, we come to see God's maternal face. But we must always remember that Mary is a human being, not a goddess. Dialogue with Islam, then, can also help us more clearly elucidate authentic Church teaching on Mary. In our Marian teachings that we share with the Islamic interpretation of Mary, what becomes especially clear is that Christian and Islamic mystics speak a similar language and understand Mary in an almost identical way.

The Spiritual Challenge: Life as a Battle of the Spirit

I. The Spiritual Battle as Path toward God

Anselm Grün

The Enemy Is Inside Us, Not Outside

In the prologue to his *Rule*, St. Benedict addresses all those ready "to enlist under Christ, who is Lord of all, by following him through taking to yourself that strong and blessed armor of obedience."[32] And somewhat later, he says: "We must ... prepare our heart and bodies to serve him ... conscious in this undertaking of our own weakness."[33] The enemy against which the monk must fight is not outside but within himself. The goal of the battle is obedience to God, or obedience to Christ, who is called the Lord of all. When we enlist under Christ—that is, serve Christ as a soldier—we become truly free of our own egotism and become open to God. This is the sense in which Benedict speaks of the *militia Christi*, of military service for Christ. He does not mean a fight against others, but a battle against everything that prevents us from opening ourselves to God. The later, more literal reading of this phrase as a military battle—such as in the battle of Charlemagne against the Saxons, or in the Crusades—does not correspond to the intention of Christianity's spiritual tradition. Unfortunately, throughout the history of the Christian Church, too, faith has often been taken as an argument for military engagement. Every religion

---

32. Benedict of Nursia, *Saint Benedict's Rule*. Translated and introduced by Patrick Barry, OSB (Mahwah, NJ: HiddenSpring, 2004), 45.
33. Benedict, *Rule*, 48.

is inherently in danger of distorting religious thoughts and mixing them with political action.

The Meaning of "Spiritual Battle"

The spiritual image of a battle or struggle goes back at least to the Epistle to the Ephesians. Its author writes: "Put on the whole armor of God, so that you may be able to stand against the wiles of the devil. For our struggle is not against enemies of blood and flesh, but against the rulers, against the authorities, against the cosmic powers of this present darkness, against the spiritual forces of evil in the heavenly places" (Eph 6:11–12). Early monks viewed the struggle against the devil not as the fight against a person, but as a battle against forces within us keeping us from our true self and seeking to cut us off from God. It is a spiritual struggle, which the monks called "battle against the demons." Demons, too, are not people but powers that keep us from inner freedom. For the monks, indeed, spiritual life consisted largely of such a battle against our demons. But the monks also use the term to describe our struggle with our own passions, the *logismoi*. These are emotionally based thoughts, thought constructs that arise within us and keep us from devoting ourselves entirely to God. In a sense, the monks go back and forth in the language they use: sometimes they speak of thoughts and passions that overcome us, and then again of demons who give us such thoughts.

The "demons" are a metaphor for the power of these passionate thoughts, which are frequently inimical to us. In his book *Praktikos*, Evagrius Ponticus, the most significant monastic author of the fourth century, details this battle against one's own passions. He also refers to these passions as vices. Monks, he writes, have to confront eight such vices. The term "vice" sounds moralistic, but Evagrius simply means certain dangers to human beings, and these still occupy us today. A person who succumbs to these dangers, to these eight vices, is then ruled by them. In the battle (the monks often phrase it as struggle rather than battle) with these vices, or passions, the goal is to conquer but not to eradicate them. For the passions also contain great power. If I cut myself off from the passions, I lose strength. But if I am ruled by them, they harm me. The goal of the spiritual fight, or battle, is therefore *apatheia*. Unlike its cognate "apathy," this term does not mean absence of feeling or interest. Rather it means freedom from the tyranny of passions: a state in which the passions are integrated into my spiritual life. To Evagrius, *apatheia* means the health of the soul and the capacity for pure love.

Asceticism: Training for Inner Freedom

Another word the monks use for this inner battle is asceticism. Asceticism is actually practice, training for inner freedom. It is about becoming free of the rule of the passions, but without eradicating them. In the parable of the weeds among the wheat (Mt 13:24–30), Jesus explains how in trying to uproot the bad, we would also uproot the good, since the roots of the weeds are interlocked with the roots of the wheat. If we want to be wholly free of imperfections, without any weeds, then no wheat will grow within us, either. We will bear no fruit. But we must cut back the weeds, so that the field of the soul can bear rich fruit.

Monks described themselves as athletes wrestling with the passions. And often they went too far in their wrestling. For example, they sometimes fasted so much that they sickened. Or they battled against sleep. But when we read the writings of the early monks, we can feel the power behind their struggle. Their goal was to be wholly and utterly permeated by the spirit and the love of God. On the path to God, however, they encountered dangers: the passions, thoughts, and emotions that sometimes threatened to darken their entire thinking. The monks' life thus remained a constant battle to the last. This battle kept them alive, and it kept them humble. For even in the last moment, they were wary of dangers. Especially when a monk thought that he was now completely disciplined, the demon of pride appeared and cut that monk off from God. To the last, a monk must be ready to fight these dangers and wrestle with these passions. It is meekness that shows whether a monk is wrestling with these passions in the right way. Those whom their battle makes hard-hearted towards others have misunderstood the main purpose: the capacity for true love and meekness.

Two Ways to Deal with Passions

However, there are also some thoughts, emotions, and passions that cannot be transformed. One must avoid these, or, as the spiritual tradition has it: one must kill them. The Christian tradition knows two ways for dealing with the passions. In some hagiographies, the fight with one's passions is described as a fight with a dragon. There are two options: I can either tame the dragon without killing it, as is described in the story of St. Margaret of Antioch. In Christian iconography, Margaret is therefore often shown leading the dragon on a chain. The dragon serves her, in a sense giving her more power. In the terms of Jungian psychoanalysis, this would be called the integration of the shadow. Our shadow contains those aggressions that we have repressed. When they are made conscious, they can be integrated into my life.

But there is also the other option: St. George slays the dragon. There are some inimical powers within me that I must simply kill or excise from myself. This requires strength and also the anger we use to fight against these powers. Among the tools of the spiritual art, Benedict lists the following ability: "Whenever evil thoughts occur to your mind, cast them down at the feet of Christ and talk about them frankly to your spiritual father or mother."[34]

The image of the spiritual battle shows us that individuals must overcome many obstacles on their path to God. Those persons want to open themselves up to God, while some powers seek to cut them off from God. But the image of the spiritual fight also reveals the passion with which the monks followed their path to God. They wanted God to rule within them. And so they battled against the rule of their own inner demons. The monks' spiritual battle is a challenge to us today to follow in

---

34. Benedict, *Rule*, 61.

their footsteps: to set out on the spiritual path with strength and to open all within us to God so that God's spirit can permeate and transform everything within us.

2. Spiritual Battle as the Great Jihād

Ahmad Milad Karimi

Exertion on the Path of God

At their core, the reflections on the spiritual battle that Anselm Grün has unfolded from a Christian perspective correspond to the interpretation we find in Islam, as well. In spite of all misunderstandings that may arise from the term "battle," it must be stated categorically: in Islam, this battle is not one against others, and in fact is not a military engagement at all. Instead, it is the attempt to exert oneself on the path to God. This exertion is mentioned many times in the Qur'an. Here, human beings are focal points of God's mercy.[35] In the Qur'an, God challenges human beings to exert themselves in life, because it is only this exertion that opens us human beings to God. And only when we are open to God can we find our true, noble nature. Under these circumstances, the battle is a spiritual one because it is directed inward.

"Strive hard for God as is His due: He has chosen you and placed no hardship in your religion" (Qur'an 22:78). This inner battle is not meant to enslave or lower human beings, nor to overwhelm or isolate them. Instead, it is meant to uplift human beings to the dignity of attaining their own true self. The Muslim poet-philosopher Muhammad Iqbal writes: "Reaching the place of the self, that is to live!"[36] The image of an inner battle shows

---

35. See Qur'an 2:218.
36. Annemarie Schimmel (ed.), *Die Botschaft des Ostens: Ausgewählte Werke* [The message of the East: Selected works]. (Tübingen: Edition Erdmann, 1977), 324-25 Translated from the German.

us that in the Islamic view, a person is not a fixed but an open, dynamic being. The idea of a person's true self thus does not mean some point at which we arrive in life. Instead, contact with one's own self is conceived of as a path on which we must exert ourselves. In his *Javid Nama* [Book of Eternity], Iqbal writes:

> Life is not a mere repetition of the breath,
> its origin is from the Living, Eternal God.
> The soul near to Him who said "Lo, I am nigh"—
> that is to take one's share of everlasting life.
> The individual through the Unity becomes Divine.[37]

On the Difficult Path to Oneself—a Qur'anic View

We may fail on this path, and we are allowed to. But every time, we are supposed to dare to return to the path, to keep exerting ourselves. For this reason, exerting oneself always also means being on a path toward oneself. In his treatise *The Alchemy of Happiness*, Abū Hāmid al-Ghazālī writes: "But real self-knowledge consists in knowing the following things: What art thou in thyself, and from whence hast thou come? Whither art thou going, and for what purpose hast thou come to tarry here awhile, and in what does thy real happiness and misery consist?"[38] This path is not free of hindrance. It is marked by difficulty and effort and can be walked only with patience.[39] Al-Ghazālī is said to have thought that exertion is the foremost path of the religion of Islam: "Without first completing [one's] exertion," it is said, one "is not allowed . . . to speak of the nature of the spirit." To al-Ghazālī, the inner path is thus a path of spiritualization, albeit one that does not remain purely spiritual. It is transformed into action—towards one's neighbor, others, strangers. In the Qur'an, the fruit of this

---

37. Muhammad Iqbal, *Javid Nama* [Book of eternity], translated by Arthur J. Arberry (n.p., n.d.), line 3575 ff., accessed online at: http://www.allamaiqbal.com/works/poetry/persian/javidnama/translation/index.htm.
38. Abū Hāmid al-Ghazālī, *The Alchemy of Happiness*, 19-20.
39. See Qur'an 47:31 and 3:142.

effort is viewed as lying in good, beautiful deeds: "And those who exert themselves for us—we will surely guide them rightly on our paths. Truly, God is with those who act beautifully" (Qur'an 29:69, translated from the German).

The Path to Freedom, the Right Measure, and the Middle Road

I as a Muslim feel touched when I read how the Christian monks understood themselves as "athletes" who "wrestle with their passions." It reminds me of the Prophet Muhammad, who used similar terms to describe wrestling with the desires, passions, and especially anger in human beings. According to one source, the Prophet said: "Strong is not the one who conquers his enemy in a struggle, but who conquers his own ire."[40] Not being captive to one's own passions and desires outlines the path of freedom that is essential to living a successful life. In Islam, too, the goal in this respect is not to eradicate the desires, but to find the right measure, the middle path. It is about the spiritual battle, about wrestling with ourselves for the sake of gentleness, but also for the sake of greater justice. In Islam, we are encouraged to seek and ask for this justice, which is why the passions have been created in us. Al-Ghazālī is said to have asked of our passions: "Are they created in you to take you prisoner, so that you languish in them day and night?" The spiritual battle, then, develops inner freedom in dealing with ourselves and with all the inadequacies, weaknesses, desires, and passions we carry within us.

Greater and Lesser Jihād

But frequently, this battle is misunderstood: as a fight against others, as disdain and destruction. As already established, the term for this battle is *jihād*. But in its qur'anic origin, *jihād*

---

40. Ṣaḥīḥ Muslim, *Kitāb al-birr*, 2nd edition, hadīth no. 107, 1189, Beirut 1427/2007, 1189; Ṣaḥīḥ al-Bukhārī, Kitāb al-adab, Vol. 4, hadīth no. 6114, Cairo 1428/2008, 185. Translated from the German.

means nothing like "war," much less "holy war." The Arabic word for "war" is *harb*, and in Islam the term "holy" is unquestionably reserved for God alone. But in outside interpretations, *jihād* is often understood or described as a religiously justified war. This perception is not entirely unreasonable: it correctly describes how *jihād* is misused on the part of some Muslims. But it remains a misuse and at its core a perversion of the religion of Islam.

Understood spiritually, *jihād* is the individual's exertion on the path of God, that is, in responsibility to God and his creation. Moreover, the Islamic spiritual tradition explicitly distinguishes between the "greater" and "lesser" *jihād*. In this context, the "greater *jihād*" is considered the inner, spiritual battle of persons with themselves, with their own demons. It is the "greater" of the two because it represents the battle for God within a person. In contrast, the "lesser *jihād*" means outward engagement. But even the lesser *jihād* does not in any way mean or legitimize active, aggressively injurious force. All that Islamic tradition legitimizes is a defensive, parrying force—which incidentally is also permitted by international law. Not until the present has active, injurious force (that is, violence) been referred to as *jihād* and perpetrated in the name of Islam. This perversion turns the idea of Islam on its head and must never find legitimization in the religious sense. It can be called only one thing: a crime. The fact that the history of Islam contains examples of this dehumanizing interpretation of *jihād* justifies nothing. It merely shows how liable religions are to being abused, in the past and still today, by the political interests of power and rule. The core of Islam's spiritual tradition is as follows: Those who, instead of looking for "infidels" outside themselves, look for un-faith inside themselves, those who turn the battle inward, strive to create inside themselves a place which is not ruled by anger and passions, but in which the fiery heart becomes a metaphor for humans' openness to God. As Rūmī has been quoted: "My heart is an oven; it loves the fire. The oven is satisfied to be the fire's home. Love, like an oven, always has something to burn. If you cannot see it, you are no fiery oven."

On the Significance and Meaning of Prayer

I. Christian Prayer as Personal Encounter with God

Anselm Grün

Talking with and Encountering God

Prayer is talking with God, and prayer is encounter with God. Such an understanding always presupposes a personal relationship with God and a view of God as a person. For us Christians, indeed, God is always both: personal and super-personal. When I pray to God, I not only pray to a personal being looking at and speaking to me. I also pray to the creator and fall down before him because he is God: greater than and unlike anything we know. Prayer as talking with God does indeed differ from talking with a human being who answers us. God gives us an answer not in clear, distinguishable words. Sometimes he answers in silence. We can then feel within us that God has given us instruction. And God is not a clear other in the sense that a human being I talk to can be seen, heard, or perceived with all my senses. He remains an ungraspable mystery. God is a Thou with whom I speak; and I can feel myself facing a Thou who leads me into my own truth. But this Thou often disappears and lies hidden behind the invisible and intangible.

A Transformative Encounter

So what should prayer look like, and what happens in prayer? A prayer to God need not be "pious." Most of all, it should be honest. I should open up to God everything that is within me. That is why to me, the comprehensive term for prayer is encounter. In prayer, I encounter God. I offer up to him everything that is within me: my powerlessness, my doubts, my inner emptiness, my longing, my guilt, my needs, my indecision and internal conflict, all the unknown things within my soul. By holding my entire truth up to God, I imagine God's love streaming into my soul, particularly into my powerlessness and loneliness, into the dark chasms in me. Then everything is filled with God's love.

In his Epistle to the Ephesians, Paul says that "everything exposed by the light becomes visible, for everything that becomes visible is light" (Eph 5:13–14). My encounter with God in prayer transforms me. Everything in me is permeated with God's love. Because of that, I can experience and feel myself differently.

God Does Not Do Magic: Unanswered Prayers

Many people lament that their prayers go unanswered. But what does that mean exactly? Some people who pray imagine that God must hear their pleas and therefore grant their wishes. For example, if I were to ask God to take away my anxiety, I might then expect God—like a magician—to liberate me from my anxiety. But by thinking in such a way, I would be using God to get rid of negative symptoms while still wanting to stay my same old self. True prayer is different. I offer myself up to God along with my anxiety. I speak to God about my anxiety. And then I imagine God's love flowing into my anxiety. My anxiety is transformed. But I am transformed as well: such prayer shows me that I cannot continue to hold on to my perfectionism and still let go of my anxiety. Instead, something within me has to change. I must let go of my perfectionism. Then God will transform not only my anxiety, but also me as a person.

Praying to Jesus, Addressing the Saints

When we pray, we pray to God. As Christians, we can also pray to Jesus, because we trust that as Jesus Christ, he is now in God. But Jesus is not a rival to God. Rather, in Jesus we see the face of God. Jesus points us to God. The same is true of the saints. We do not pray to the saints; rather, we ask the saints to intercede with God on our behalf. When I go on a journey, I ask friends to pray for me. I feel supported by my friends' prayers. In the same way, I can feel supported by the intercession of the saints. I am not alone before God. I stand within a large communion of the faithful who support and comfort me.

The Different Forms of Prayer

Prayer can take different forms: plea and intercessory prayer, praise and thanks, lament or remonstrance. I can ask God to help me or someone else. In intercessory prayer, I hold my own powerlessness up to God and ask him to work in me and in others with his grace. But prayer is just as much praise and adoration. In praise, our well-being is not the point. The point is simply God. We look up to God, who is at the center. But by centering God in praise, we find our own center as well. Lament and remonstrance are also forms of prayer. I remonstrate with God when my life seems too much for me to take. But I never stay mired in the lament. The lament should always turn to trust that God will take care of me and all the other unfortunates of the world. And the lament, finally, should end with gratitude for all the things God has already given me. When I thank God, my trust grows that God will transform this situation as well.

Listening into the Silence of God

If prayer, by its nature, is encounter, then it is not only a matter of speaking, but of listening, as well. In silence, I listen to God.

Sometimes God answers with nothing more than silence. Then I listen into the silence of God for what God is trying to tell me. God's silence forces me to free myself even further of my own ideas of God. And another part of encounter is openness. I sit down before God and observe, in the face of God, all the things that surface in my soul. And I hold all these things up to the love of God. In this loving encounter with God, healing can occur.

Diving into the Riches of Traditional Prayers

Of course, in addition to personal prayer in our own words, we Christians have a rich store of pre-formulated texts, often in poetic language, that are collected in prayer books, have been transmitted by practice or liturgy, and can act as guide to our own personal prayer. Jesus himself taught us the Lord's Prayer, which we are supposed to recite daily. In this preformed prayer, we encounter the spirit of Jesus and take part in his prayer. But the words are also enriched by the many Christians who have prayed these words for two thousand years, using them to get through their lives. And, like Jews, we also pray the Psalms. The Psalms are the quintessential school of prayer. In them, all manner of human emotion is brought before God, but always in the faith that God will transform our suffering and fulfill our deepest longing.

Not Only in the Head: Bodily Expressions of Prayer

Prayer, finally, is something holistic. It happens not only in the head, touches not only our spirit and soul, but also expresses itself in our body, including in particular gestures and postures. We kneel down before God, whose greatness we sense. We stand before him who uplifts us and before whom we may experience our dignity. We lift our hands in prayer. Or we gather ourselves before God and orient ourselves fully and entirely toward him by folding our hands. We lift our hands in blessing and let God's blessing flow to others. And we cup our hands in a bowl to offer up everything within us to God. These gestures not only support our prayers, they also guide us to very different experiences of God and of ourselves.

Daily Prayers

In Islam, daily prayers are among the duties of a faithful Muslim. In Christianity, too, there is a tradition of daily prayer. Many Christians pray in the mornings and evenings. A popular historical prayer was the *Angelus*, said three times a day. Benedict invites monks to pray seven times each day and once at night. Today, monks—like Muslims—pray five times a day, together in church. Praying together supports us and bears up our faith. We immerse ourselves in the faith of others and feel them support us. And by praying five times, we acknowledge that we live and work everywhere and always in God's presence, that God is the actual center of our life.

Transforming Our Selves

We do not pray in order to feel good. Rather, we pray to God because God is the center of our life. But that does not mean we cannot feel how prayer transforms us. There have been medical studies showing that prayer can improve our inner strength and heal illnesses more quickly. These effects, however, are secondary. More decisive and fundamental is this: We may trust in the fact that prayer transforms us. It transforms us from human beings alienated from themselves and immersed in worldly matters into people of God, into people who recognize their center in God and who through prayer become ever more permeable to the spirit of God and the spirit of Jesus Christ.

2. Bringing God to Mind
—a Muslim Understanding of Prayer

Ahmad Milad Karimi

Forms and Purpose of Prayer in Islam

In Islam, prayer takes place various forms, extending from the remembrance of God (Arabic: *dhīkr*) and petitionary prayer (Arabic: *du'ā'*) to ritual prayer (Arabic: *ṣalāt*). But each form of prayer has its own specific charm, its own particular existential significance. At the same time, whether verbally or non-verbally, a prayer articulates all the things that intimately concern us as human beings: our gratitude, but also our pain; our praise and adoration, but also our lament; our hope, but also our ruefulness. What purpose, then, does prayer serve? Prayer is turning to God, and prayer is the most intimate form of opening the borders of one's self.

What does it mean to open up the borders of one's own self? In prayer, the self is transcended. When we turn towards God, our particular concern is no longer a matter primarily for ourselves. Instead, the creator is at the center of our prayer. He is praised. The Qur'an opens with this praise: "In the name of God, the Lord of Mercy, the Giver of Mercy." Prayer, then, demands a particular conception of God. Even if we do not assume God as an other in dialogue in the same way as a person, then God is nevertheless still present in all his fullness: as the one who has created me, permeates my life in goodness and mercy, and finally perfects me and "leads me into my own truth," as Anselm Grün puts it.

Often, however, we instrumentalize prayer by seeing it as something through which our expectations and wishes should be fulfilled. That is already a misunderstanding, even if only because in doing so we objectify God and reduce him to a function, linking him to preconditions centered around us alone. But as Anselm Grün has also emphasized, the essence of prayer is encounter. In prayer, the relationship between God and human being is translated into the language of the personal and existential. Furthermore, prayer is not rigid, not something that a pre-programmed machine could do just as well. Because prayer occurs in one's very own, deeply human act of praying. And so prayer also remains in its essence a question.

Praying with the Prophet

This demonstrates a central stance of Muslims: Muslims are those who perceive themselves as questioners. To not let our lives be ruled by definitive, immutable dogmas but rather seek yearningly for what supports, comforts, and uplifts us—such, in all its brevity, is the description of the religious life of Muslims. Accordingly, it is as one who prays that the Prophet Muhammad enters the life of the faithful. So we Muslims do not pray to the Prophet, but with him, since he himself is reported to have said: "I have found in prayer the comfort of my eyes." Even if we pray to God exclusively, our prayer can nevertheless include prophets and saints in the sense that we pray for them to intercede for us. Especially in the mystical tradition, Islam knows numerous saints, that is, people whose deeds and insights have reached a spiritual, soul-felt depth that we honor. But turning to these saints must not be understood as competing with our relationship to God. All we are doing, in this context, is praying for their intercession.

Infinite Distance Becomes Closeness

Those who devote themselves to God and who long for God, their emptiness is as if lifted away. Self-distancing is turned inside out, infinite distance becomes closeness, becomes a gift, becomes grace. It is existential fullness, rather than material riches, that arrive when we bring God to mind: "those who have faith and whose hearts find peace in the remembrance of God—truly it is in the remembrance of God that hearts find peace" (Qur'an 13:28) Prayer is not a communication, it is an event. Nor is it persons talking to themselves and in the process designing a God in order to be able to stomach their ephemeral loneliness. In prayer, God is made present not as an other, but as an infinite gift.

The encounter with God is unlike any worldly encounter. Prayer is the attempt to encounter the Extraordinary in an extraordinary way. Bringing God to mind means that we know ourselves protected in the face of God. When we pray, we lift ourselves up toward the Absolute.

Ritual Prayer as Religious Duty

At the same time, ritual prayer is an Islamic religious duty. But this prayer, too, is not an external imposition. The prayer is an intentional act: in it, human beings orient themselves towards God, but not because God in some way needs the prayer. God wants human beings to pray, but for their own selves. That is why the Qur'an states: "Whoever purifies himself does so for his own benefit" (Qur'an 35:18). Prayer, then, gains a subtle "anthropological twist" in that those who are praying return to themselves through a prayer addressed to God. It is in this sense that Muhammad Iqbal writes of individual or communal prayer as the "expression of man's inner yearning for response in the awful silence of the universe."[41] In those praying occurs the presence of God, who is closer to the praying persons than their own jugular, as the Qur'an states (see Qur'an 50:16). And yet prayer remains a question, an existential question, since the attitude of those praying is shaped by humility and gratitude. Accordingly, prayer becomes their inner call, expressing that they have become a question to themselves. In this very act of questioning or even lamenting, the presence of God occurs simultaneously: "I am near. I respond to those who call Me" (Qur'an 2:186), as God resounds in the Qur'an. In prayer, then, the most intimate expression of the relationship between human being and God can be witnessed. Iqbal writes: "The truth is that all search for knowledge is essentially a form of prayer."[42] Prayer never goes without effect, at least not unless the prayer has been made merely outwardly. Rather, the prayer transforms the person who prays. Whether ritual prayer, petitionary prayer, or simple silence with God, in prayer we open ourselves up to a reality that extends beyond us. This opening, which uplifts me, transforms my loneliness into encounter, my emptiness into fullness, my fear into hope.

The Sensuousness of Prayer Engages the Entire Person

In this context, it is significant that prayer in Islam is not an act of reason but a deeply aesthetic event. This means that prayer remains not merely in the spirit but involves the entire person. Our entire being is directed toward God. Just as in the Prophet's

---

41. Muhammad Iqbal, *The Reconstruction of Religious Thought in Islam*, (Stanford, CA: Stanford University Press, 2013), 74.
42. Iqbal, *Reconstruction*, 73.

lifetime, the ritual and communal prayer is an expression of this sensuous act in which those praying, in the moment of their devotion, understand themselves as one, without any distinction even according to sex. (Segregation of men and women—to this day not observed at the Kaaba—developed only gradually over time, and there are different stances regarding it.) Especially communal prayer has a social and inter-human significance in Islam. Prayer can be performed ritually, meaning rhythmically and with recurring elements that are repeated prayer by prayer. This creates an uplifting feeling, a sense of the permanent, as if time, our own ephemeral nature, had been interrupted. The quality of ritual, the repetition in this turning toward God, interrupts the ephemeral. Each prayer, particularly in its ritualized structuring, as Muslims pray it five times a day—in the morning, at midday, in the afternoon, in the evening, and at night—is prefigured by a spiritual act: ritual ablution.

It is the running water flowing over the individual parts of the body; both hands touch, then touch the body, while the cold, enlivening water takes away everything mundane, all noise, all stress, and all worry. The water touches the body and cleanses the worldly vessel before the divine touches the soul. The prayer is performed on a cloth or carpet. We feel our naked feet touch the floor. Just like Moses before his encounter with the Eternal in the burning bush, Muslims take off their shoes and let the ground beneath them become hallowed. If life itself—as already the Prophet Muhammad had encouraged—is experienced in devotion to God, then in this act the entire Earth is hallowed ground, is a mosque, a place of prostration. The one who prays then stands erect, recites from the Qur'an—sometimes loud and sometimes soft, but always with reverence and mindfulness—bows, prostrates, wilts, and awakens. The prayer is concluded with a greeting of peace to the right and to the left, the hands uplifted like a vessel symbolizing the person who prays, and that person has become question. The sense of the prayer is thus represented in the sensuousness of praying. There are obligatory prayer texts that must be recited in prayer, most of them from the Qur'an. One of these, for example, is the first surah of the Qur'an, which is comparable to the Lord's Prayer.

In addition to this, the Qur'an itself contains numerous other prayers: prayers of the prophets, the angels, and the faithful in gratitude and in hardship.

Problems in Secular Society

In our secular society, it is not always easy for us Muslims to fulfill our ritual prayers. That can be seen as an obstacle to our religious duties, but it is also entirely understandable that we cannot make any claim to preferential treatment in order to precisely follow the prayer times or even to pray wherever we like. In this respect Islam is a highly dynamic religion. According to most legal schools, the prayers can be combined, and not every prayer need be held communally if the circumstances do not allow it. The purpose of prayer is not fulfilled if it is externally compelled. Technically speaking, a person does not pray only during particular times or in particular places; rather, if the person is anchored in faith, that one's entire life can be performed as a prayer. It is in this sense that Maulānā Rūmī is reported to have said: "I was become all a prayer."

Spiritual Sites—Church and Mosque

I. The Christian House of God

Anselm Grün

Gathering Place for the Faithful and Site of Liturgy

The word "church" (*ecclesia*) often also means "house of God," that is, the place where Christians gather for services. And today it still refers to the community of all faithful. Originally, the term was used solely to describe the Christians of a particular place—or the community of the faithful and the saints with Christ. Only in the Middle Ages did it also come to be used to describe church buildings, as well. Over the course of history, it is true that these buildings have always become imbued with symbolic meaning and have also been expressions of how the community of the faithful saw itself.

Like the Jews, the earliest Christians continued to pray in the Temple and synagogues daily. But they celebrated the Eucharist at home. "Day by day, as they spent much time together in the temple, they broke bread at home and ate their food with glad and generous hearts" (Acts 2:46). The togetherness of community was more important than the space in which they prayed or held their meal. In community, Christ was present. Only when the congregations grew did they start to emulate the architectural style of Roman antiquity and build great halls: the basilicas. Churches served the liturgy. Therefore the altar was placed at their center.

Church Construction: Sermons in Stone

Many different styles of church building developed over the course of ecclesiastical history, each as a symbolic outgrowth of ideas of faith. The eastward orientation of places of worship as practiced in the building of Christian churches corresponded to the pagan custom of facing the rising sun to pray. The Christians, seeing Christ as the "dawn from on high" (Lk 1:78), adopted this old practice. In Romanesque and Gothic architecture, it was common to lay out the church in the shape of a cross. Romanesque churches are more squat; they often symbolize the womb. They are used not only for services: one goes into the church to sit in solemn prayer and feels enveloped by God's love. In Gothic churches, the stones themselves preach. They speak of the beauty of God and lift the human heart toward heaven. In prayer, those in church are meant to lift their hearts toward God. The Gothic buildings are thus prayers given shape, heaven cast in stone. The towers reaching up into the sky were, to the people of their time, signs of the sermon. And the stained glass windows symbolize Scripture, which passes on the light of God. Later, in the Baroque period, the variety of life is brought into the church, with God's glory depicted in rich ceiling paintings.

These churches, as it were, open up heaven above earthly reality. In the nineteenth century, the rapid growth of the population caused the construction of many new churches. They were often built in Romanesque Revival or Gothic Revival styles, rather than departing significantly from past stylistic epochs. Only before and after the Second World War did a new form of church gain a foothold: the church as the tent of God among the people, or the church as the congregation's gathering place around the altar.

A Spatial Expression of Faith

Every church expresses the faith of the people who designed and built it. The people of the Middle Ages were consciously seeking to visualize the beauty and grandeur of God for all people. Today, when we sit down in a Romanesque or Gothic church, that church becomes a space of silent prayer and for experiencing the sacred. Such a sacred space surrounds us with stillness, but with beauty as well. It opens our spirit to God. Of course, one can also pray in nature or in a room at home. But people love to sit down in a church or to kneel before an altar and pray. Many go into churches to bring before God their prayers for family or their own health. Others sit in a church when they want to find stillness. A church can calm an unquiet mind. And churches are where the liturgy is celebrated. The beauty of the space, the beauty of the music made audible by the organ or even an orchestra, and the beauty of the liturgy lift our hearts toward God. And the liturgy opens a window to heaven. We take part in the heavenly liturgy being celebrated by all those already with God. In this way, the liturgy links heaven and earth.

Public Testaments of Faith

Today, the churches in our towns and cities are living testaments to faith. Their very presence does something to a city, regardless of whether the cityscape is marked by skyscrapers or the churches form visible focal points. Churches open even a secularized city toward God. They speak of God whether people want them to or not, whether people perceive it or not. As a result, churches transform a city. They testify to the Christian spirit of the city, even if few people in the city still go to church. One can say that these churches do what Max Horkheimer said that religions in general do: they keep alive our society's longing for the utterly different. Churches open heaven above people. And thus they speak to human beings' deepest longing that there should be something that is greater than themselves, something that moves their hearts more than mere money or power. Churches are places of "stillness surrounded by walls"; they offer people a place of stillness. This stillness is already there, even if people are internally full of disquiet. But when they sit down in a place of stillness, they come into contact with the stillness at the base of their own soul.

In this way, churches offer a space where people can come into contact with themselves, where they can rediscover their own center. Churches thus have a healing effect on their surroundings. And these sacred buildings put us in touch with the roots of our faith. They express the faith of our forebears. When we sit down in a church where people have prayed for centuries, we partake in this faith. And the very architecture of the church puts us in touch with the faith expressed in these stones. The faith and the hope of many people long ago built this church with a great deal of effort, but a great deal of love as well. And so we take part in their love of God and of beauty, and in the faith with which they worked to construct this church, forgoing many superficial comforts.

2. The Mosque as House of Prayer

Ahmad Milad Karimi

Place of Prayer, Memorializing the Kaaba

In Islam, it is the Kaaba in Mecca that is considered the house of God (Arabic: *bayt Allāh*). The word "mosque," on the other hand, does not mean "house of God." Instead, it is a loanword from the Arabic *masjid*, which means "place of prostration" and thus refers to the site of prayer. But every mosque is also oriented towards the Kaaba. The mosque is thus a memorialization, a bringing to mind of the Kaaba as house of God. What Anselm Grün says of churches is true of every mosque, as well: it is an expression of people's faith. In the first place, mosques have a significance dictated by their function: they refer to a space dedicated to Islamic ritual prayer. This space need not be an independent building. It might be a simple room which is clearly bounded and above all clean. Ideally, the wall opposite the entrance should be oriented towards Mecca (Arabic: *qibla*, meaning "direction of prayer"). In addition to the covered room, another part of the mosque is an open courtyard (Arabic: *muṣallā*), which can also serve as a place of prayer. This is so because particularly in Islam's beginnings, believers gathered in an open space to stand up before God. Since the eighth century, other constitutive parts of the mosque have been a prayer niche (Arabic: *mihrāb*) and a pulpit (Arabic: *minbar*), both on the main (that is, Mecca-facing) wall of the mosque. The prayer niche, with its semi-circular shape, marks the place of the prayer leader, who has the central role within the recitation of the liturgy. Often, a lamp is hung above the prayer niche. The lamp refers to the qur'anic Verse of Light—"God is the light of the heavens and earth. His Light is like this: there is a niche, and in it a lamp, the lamp inside a glass, a glass like a glittering star . . . light upon light" (Qur'an 24:35)—and shows the prayer niche as the actual center of the mosque, the place from which blessing and light are to flow forth.

A Symbol of the Presence of Islam

The prayer leader stands at the head of the congregation with his back to them. He looks to the Kaaba, standing in the prayer niche one step in front of the first row of those praying. The pulpit to the right of the prayer niche serves as the place where the leader holds the sermon (Arabic: *khuṭba*) during Friday prayers. Generally, the pulpit has at least three steps, with the third representing the Prophet's step, so that the leader always holds his sermon from the second.

Also part of the larger mosque is a separate washroom, in which the ritual ablution before prayer is performed. Generally, there is an antechamber before the entrance to the mosque so that those praying can remove their shoes. Another early addition to mosque architecture was the minaret—likewise a loanword from the Arabic *manār*, meaning "lighthouse." The minaret is first and foremost the place from which the prayer caller (Arabic: *mu'adhdhin*, the origin of our word muezzin) calls the faithful to prayer, but it also represents how those praying are uplifted to God.

Place of Encounter, Place of Community

The first mosque was most likely built in Qubā' near the city of Yathrib, known today as Medina. But the first significant, large-scale mosque was built in Medina itself during the Prophet's lifetime. The Prophet himself is said to have participated in its construction. Known today as the "Mosque of the Prophet" (Arabic: *masjid an-nabī*), this large mosque was more than merely a place of prayer. It was also a place of encounter, a place of community, a place where the poor were fed, a place of learning and spirituality. In the mosque, the Prophet received emissaries from foreign countries, and community meetings were held there as well. Indeed, mosques generally are understood as a social space where the faithful can share their worries and problems and offer them up to God in communal prayer. Ever since that first mosque was built, mosques have been considered the heart of a city and to this day remain important, especially for the communal Friday prayers.

Very early in Islamic history, the mosque developed into a symbol of living faith, a symbol that shaped and continues to shape the nature of cities. The mosque thus has not only a religious but also a cultural significance. The resistance to the construction of mosques and minarets clearly reveals the tensions that arise when religious identity translates into culture. The minaret is not the quintessential part of a mosque, but whenever a minaret is seen as a symbol of the presence of Muslims it is extremely important for both sides to engage in respectful and precise dialogue without wholesale denunciations. Because to Muslims, the minaret as a lighthouse is originally a symbol of reverence and light.

What Architecture and Design Represent

Mosque architecture did not develop along a straightforward linear progression. Rather, the forms in which mosques were constructed adapted to the various cultural spaces where mosques arose. Depending on these cultural spaces, the styles and designs of mosques can therefore vary considerably. The cupola, often executed as a three-fold structure; the spacious open courtyards; the colonnades and interior spaces shaped as columned halls with large pillars—all are elements of different types of mosque architecture. In general, mosque interiors rarely make use of pictures, so that there is no fixed iconographic program that developed over time. Instead, in addition to calligraphy as a formal aesthetic of Islamic art, ornamentation became the dominant form of decorative design for surfaces, so that mosque walls, cupolas, and even entrances are often decorated with it. This ornamentation took both geometric and botanically inspired forms. Almost as a rule, the interlacing geometric and floral designs practically weave the viewer's gaze into their own pattern, until it becomes difficult to distinguish different levels. Every ornamentation is an infinite pattern in and of itself and never fully depictable. Accordingly, the ornamentation represents human beings' longing for the representation of the unrepresentable. It opens a space of perception that visualizes prayer as humans' turning to God.

"Earth Is a Mosque"

Friday prayers, which are performed in the mosque at midday, are considered the high point of ritual prayer, since those praying share with one another the power of prayer and jointly (as Anselm Grün has put it) "lift our hearts toward God." "No ritual prayer is valid," the Prophet Muhammad says, "if the heart is not present." In this sense, the mosque is a spiritual place, a place of peace and of mindfulness. The mosque represents Earth itself, earth which we Muslims touch with our foreheads when we pray. The Earth is hallowed ground, a spiritual place, because God is present everywhere, because we can remember him everywhere. In responsibility toward God's creation, the Prophet Muhammad said that "Earth is a mosque"—as quintessence of peace, as place of stillness. And the mosque reminds us of this peace with God.

Pilgrimage and the Journey of Life

I. The Christian View of Faith as a Pilgrimage

Anselm Grün

"Pilgrimage for the Sake of Christ": Wandering Monks

The evangelist Luke describes Jesus himself as a wanderer. In Jesus, God himself visits human beings. Jesus walks with them and, again and again, breaks bread with them, giving them divine guest gifts: the gift of forgiveness and love precisely to those who feel ostracized by society. In the monastic tradition, this wandering Jesus became a role model. There were monks who did not settle down in one place but spent all their lives wandering, in pilgrimage. They understood their wandering as *peregrinari propter Christum,* "pilgrimage for the sake of Christ." They were trying to fulfill the words of the Epistle to the Hebrews "that they were strangers and foreigners on the earth" (Heb 11:13).

Letting Go of the World: Silence as Pilgrimage

Benedict of Nursia was somewhat skeptical of these wandering monks. In his *Rule* he criticizes the "gyrovages" who wander from one monastery to another without any discipline. He wanted his monks to swear *stabilitas*, remaining steadfastly in the community and in one place. Benedict internalized the idea of pilgrimage that was so important to the monks. To him—as well as to many Desert Fathers who remained in their cells—the true pilgrimage was remaining silent. As one apothegm (a patristic saying) has it: "Pilgrimage is silence." And another states: "If you do not master your tongue, you are not a stranger wherever you go. Therefore master your tongue, and you are a stranger."[43]

---

43. *Apophthegmata Patrum,* saying 449. Translated from the German.

The Latin word for "pilgrimage," *peregrinatio*, always also means living in foreign lands, or living as a stranger. In silence, the monk emigrates from this world. He refrains from commenting on everything. When I speak, I affect the events of the world, become active, comment, criticize, or guide in a particular direction by ordering or commanding. In silence, the monk lets go of the world. He refrains from changing or improving it. He does not presume to judge it, because he knows it is directed by God. So he lets the world be and walks his path to God through the world as if it were a foreign land in which he must not settle down. Pilgrims cannot settle down. They must keep wandering.

Abraham: Archetype of Faith, Role Model for all Pilgrimage

In the same way, Abraham followed the call of God, leaving his home, his homeland, his hometown. Abraham is considered an archetype of faith and a role model for all pilgrimage. God says to Abraham: "Go from your country and your kindred and your father's house to the land that I will show you" (Gn 12:1). The Church Fathers interpreted this threefold departure as follows:

> We are to depart from all things that make us dependent, all our old habits, all our bonds that rob us of freedom.
> We are to depart from all feelings of the past—both the painful feelings due to injuries we have experienced and the nostalgia, as if the past had been a golden age.
> We are to depart from the visible and make our way towards the invisible.

The Epistle to the Hebrews sees Abraham as an archetype of faith. Like Abraham, we are always on a journey to seek a new homeland. We do not want to return to the old homeland but "desire a better country, that is, a heavenly one" (Heb 11:16).

Faith as a Journey to God

To us Christians, then, the archetype of a pilgrim is Abraham. Accordingly, faith itself means setting out from the familiar, from the merely earthly, and making one's way toward God. Our path to God is a path of pilgrimage. That is also how mystics have often understood it, viewing our life as a pilgrimage to God. It is in this light that Augustine interprets a line from the pilgrimage psalm 122: "I was glad when they said to me, 'Let us go into the house of the LORD'" (Ps 122:1). Augustine concludes: "We are going to the Lord's house! Let us run and not weary, because we shall reach a place where fatigue will never touch us. Let's run to the Lord's house, and let our soul be gladdened by those who tell us these things; for those who cheer us on have seen our homeland before we have, and they shout from afar to us latecomers, 'We are going to the Lord's house! Walk! Run!'"[44]

Many mystics have understood our path to God as a path of pilgrimage. Bonaventure, for example, titles one of his tracts *Itinerarium mentis in Deum* ("The soul's journey to God"). Mystics understand our path of pilgrimage as an ascent to God. A classic formulation of this theme is *Ascent to Mount Carmel*, the great work of the Spanish mystic John of the Cross. The goal of the ascent to God is, in the end, to become one with God; and in a sense the ascent occurs in every single prayer. In prayer, we ascend out of this world to God. But just like pilgrimage itself, the ascent is not first and foremost our achievement. Rather, God's love moves us to set out, to go more and more towards God. In pilgrimage, we are freed from all attachments of the world. We are expressing the nature of our life as always on a journey to God, and God as the goal of all our journeys.

Traditional Pilgrimage Paths and Sites

There have been many paths of pilgrimage in the Christian tradition. The Church adopted them as a phenomenon present

---

44. Augustine, *Expositions of the Psalms, Volume 6, Psalms 121–150,* ed. Boniface Ramsey, trans. Maria Boulding OSB, 2.

in all religions. The biblical Israelites made a pilgrimage to Jerusalem each year to celebrate the most important feasts in the temple there. In ancient Greece, pilgrimages were made to the oracles, which in the end were places of healing. Convinced that only the holy can truly heal, the ancient Greeks traveled to holy sites in order to sleep in the temple and be visited by Asclepius, the god of healing, in their dreams.

The Christians adopted this practice of pilgrimage. To them, the graves of martyrs became holy places where they hoped for healing. By standing at the grave of a person who had died for his or her faith, they were strengthened in their own faith. Later, the Holy Land became a popular destination of pilgrimage. People would journey there to walk on the paths that Jesus walked and to meditate deeper into the mystery of his healing and salvific deeds. The Middle Ages saw the rising popularity of pilgrimages to Rome or to the grave of the apostle St. James in Santiago de Compostela, which today once again draws countless people. In the Middle Ages, when the pilgrimage to Santiago took nine months, the journey was like a rebirth. Pilgrimage transformed people.

The Enlightenment, which championed rational approaches to faith and had little sensitivity to pilgrimage or holy sites, also saw a rise in sites of Marian pilgrimage, particularly in Catholic areas. This was evidently a protest against a view of faith felt to be overly rationalist, since veneration of Mary is particularly shaped by emotion, not by purely rational arguments.

Today, many paths and sites of pilgrimage are experiencing a new revival. The Way of St. James now draws not only Christians but seekers from all religions. Evidently, people are looking to experience inner transformation along a path of pilgrimage.

A Special Experience of God's Nearness

As Christians, of course, we know that God is everywhere. But pilgrimage to a holy site is nevertheless a concrete practice of faith. We are setting out to leave behind us everything that keeps us chained in our day-to-day life. We are leaving behind the conceptions others have imposed on us. The destination of such wandering is God himself. But such wandering always also has something to do with us, as well. We are journeying into the true form that God has conceived of for all of us. Pilgrimage always has a religious significance. We undertake a pilgrimage when something concerns us deeply. We pilgrimage in order to experience healing from illness, resolution of a conflict, or clarity ahead of an important decision. At the same time, such joint pilgrimage is a way of experiencing a deeper community. Wandering connects people. We walk together, feel motivated to keep going, not to stand still on our inner path. There is also an old tradition of pilgrimage for another. When I go on a pilgrimage for someone else, that transforms my path as well, turning it into a path of healing, into a blessing not just for me, but for others as well.

Pilgrimage always has as its destination a place, a holy site. Arriving at such a place after long wandering is always special. We experience God's nearness in a special way.

The Catholic Church has many Marian pilgrimage sites. Mary is one of us who had faith. At such a site, we can see Mary as a role model in faith. She opened herself up to God's word and gave herself to God. At the same time, Mary embodies God's maternal aspect to us. At Marian places of pilgrimage, we experience God as the gentle, maternal God who cares for us like a mother. Mary points us to this maternal God. That is why at Marian sites of pilgrimage, we feel held by God. And we can trust that God has understood us and taken our concerns seriously.

The Church as the wandering people of God

The Second Vatican Council described the Church as the people of God, wandering on a pilgrimage. It adopted this imagery from the Epistle to the Hebrews.[45] As a pilgrim, the Church views itself as connected with all pilgrims of the world. We all are on our way to God, on our way to heavenly fulfill-

---

45. Pope Paul VI, *Lumen Gentium*. Accessed online at: https://www.vatican.va/archive/hist_councils/ii_vatican_council/documents/vat-ii_const_19641121_lumen-gentium_en.html.

ment. And we all must keep leaving behind us too restrictive ideas of humankind, of human society, and of God. God is beyond all our conceptions. That is why we are always on a path—towards the invisible God who will dawn on us in his clarity only when we die. But as pilgrims at a holy site, we may already sense something of the nearness of the loving God, the maternal and paternal God who gives us the wisdom that as pilgrims we will find the eternal home in which we will be one with all people in God.

2. On a Journey to the Near-far God: Pilgrimage in a Muslim Framework

Ahmad Milad Karimi

Pilgrimage to Mecca—Spiritual Pillar of Islam

The pilgrimage to Mecca (Arabic: ḥajj) represents the utmost spiritual pillar of Islam. Understanding it therefore leads us deep into understanding the religion itself. At the center of the pilgrimage stands the Kaaba, a cubic structure in the center of the large mosque of Mecca. Inside the Kaaba there is a black stone that accounts for the Kaaba's true significance. This stone (it is likely a meteorite, but its origin is not ascertained) was given to Abraham by the Angel Gabriel, as legend has it. The stone symbolizes faith as a heavenly gift. Today the stone is kept in a silver frame, as it is so fragile. The Kaaba itself, whose four corners are oriented to the four points of the compass, has a height of over thirteen meters, is opened only twice a year for ritual cleaning, and is veiled with a cloth of black brocade on which calligraphies of Qur'an verses are embroidered in gold thread. The pilgrimage traditionally occurs once a year, in the twelfth month (Arabic: *dhū l-ḥijja*) of the Arabic lunar calendar. But Muslims can also visit Mecca at any other time as well; this journey is called *'umra* and is considered the "little pilgrimage."

The Significance of the Kaaba as House of God

Already before the development of Islam, the Kaaba was a site of pilgrimage and religious cult worship, home to many idols and statues of gods venerated in Arabic tribal society. The steady stream of pilgrims had a particularly attractive economic significance for Meccan traders (which is evident even today among Saudi Wahhabis). Only in the year 632 CE did the Prophet Muhammad lay claim to the Kaaba and the according pilgrimage as Islamic, placing it in the context of this particular religion for all time. Accordingly, the Qur'an reads: "Complete the pilgrimages, major and minor,[46] for the sake of God." (Qur'an 2:196). Muhammad too completed the ritual of the pilgrimage, and ever since his death shortly thereafter, it has been considered a duty for Muslims. His final pilgrimage began by entering the ritual state of sacredness known as *iḥrām*. This state begins with the ritual cleansing; pilgrims wear a simple garment of two white cotton cloths. One cloth is wrapped around the hips, the second covers the back, the left shoulder, and the chest. Pilgrims in this state are to abstain not only from intercourse, but also from hunting and especially from bloodshed of any kind. In the house of God, peace and an atmosphere of the utmost mindfulness reign: not even the smallest insects may be killed. Various different symbolic actions and rituals the Prophet himself performed are still models today. Male pilgrims shave the hair on their heads; female pilgrims cut off a strand of their hair to symbolize their own purification.

Circling the Kaaba

The pilgrimage culminates in circling the Kaaba (Arabic: *ṭawāf*). Pilgrims walk around the Kaaba seven times counterclockwise. Another constitutive part of the pilgrim's journey is remembrance of events in the history of salvation, such as the story of Hagar and Ishmael (Abraham's first son): pilgrims walk

---

46. Translator's note: This refers to the *'umra*, the "little pilgrimage."

back and forth between the two hills Safa and Marwa seven times in order to emulate Hagar's search for water. Hagar, almost dead from thirst, is thought to have walked back and forth between the hills seven times, only to finally find a small spring (Arabic: *zamzam*) bubbling forth under the feet of young Ishmael. It is around this spring that the city of Mecca and the Kaaba in it are said to have been built, founded by Abraham himself. The Qur'an reads: "We showed Abraham the site of the House, saying, 'Do not assign partners to Me. Purify My House for those who circle around it, those who stand to pray, and those who bow and prostrate themselves'" (Qur'an 22:26). The spring, which is felt to be healing water, today is located inside the great mosque in Mecca.

Pilgrimage as a Symbol: Life as Circling God

In the life of faithful Muslims, the Kaaba is predominantly a place of longing, and the pilgrimage symbolizes human life as such. Just as the Second Vatican Council (in its constitution *Lumen Gentium*) had all of humanity in view when it spoke of the "wandering people of God,"[47] Islam too understands all people as beings on a life's journey toward God. That also means that in truth, our life's journey is made together. This is ritually expressed in the fact that Muslims, regardless of sex, origins, confessional differences, or social distinctions all circle the Kaaba together, shrouded in white cloths that symbolize the equality of all pilgrims. In Islamic mysticism, this motif of circling has also frequently been seen as a metaphoric answer to the question of the meaning or our life's journey. From an existential and spiritual point of view, it means: God as the object of our lasting longing is the origin of our journey, and the devotion of the heart is its destination, as well. Symbolically speaking, life is a circling of God, whom we keep approaching but whom we cannot touch or rule over, just as—in another mystic image—a moth circles the candle flame. Incidentally, the description of the Kaaba as "house of God" should not be understood literally, because God "is" not

---

47. Pope Paul VI, *Lumen Gentium*, heading V.

there or at any other location. The idea of effortful, intensive pilgrimage is rooted in the crucial idea that we must set out on a path—toward this near-far God.

The Path Leads Inward: The Heart as the True Kaaba

Throughout Islamic history, the spiritual practice of the "major" pilgrimage to Mecca (the *ḥajj*) has frequently been accorded a healing power, and the Kaaba spiritually always also represents the hope and the succor of yearning hearts. In fact, the actual journey does not occur outside of us and is not directed elsewhere. It happens inside each one of us. When we undertake a pilgrimage, we do not let ourselves go. God cannot be found among external things or in foreign lands, however distant. The path leads inward, into our heart. Our heart is the house of God, the true Kaaba. If we come into contact with our heart, then devotion (Arabic: *islam*) is kindled.

Not all Muslims make a pilgrimage to Mecca. Many cannot do so for economic or health reasons. And the journey is not meant to be a commandment imposing a hardship on them. Nevertheless, their hearts long for the true Kaaba. That being the case, there are many holy sites that can likewise be felt as places of religious longing without being seen as rivals of the Meccan Kaaba—be they Jerusalem, Medina, Karbala, Mashhad, or Mazār-i-Sharīf. Such holy sites are often the graves of saints or spiritual people who in their lifetimes won over the hearts of others through their purity, profundity, and spirituality.

Current Perspectives

What is more, nowadays pilgrimage differs from earlier pilgrimages because of a pilgrimage tourism encouraged by more comfortable modern mass transit flows. Once, the pilgrimage began in one's home town, where people made long preparations to undertake an effortful journey to Mecca. The journey to Mecca is considered pilgrimage to the extent that the pilgrims were changed along the way, were shaped by unexpected and unpredictable encounters and events. In addition, each pilgrimage is understood as a caesura in one's life, meant to change people. In order not to lose this deeper significance entirely, Muslims today must take care to understand the pilgrimage not as an unspiritual trip with all amenities included.

To this day, the Kaaba as a sacred site of prayer to God is inaccessible to non-Muslims. On the one hand, that is lamentable, since holy sites in particular should be autonomous, open places for all. But on the other hand, the Kaaba should not become a tourist attraction but remain a place where people can turn intimately toward God without onlookers.

Part of what makes such a spiritual site still relevant today is that—especially in times when many, even violent global conflicts between Islamic groups and sects are endangering peaceful coexistence—pilgrimage gains a particular significance: Whether Shiite or Sunni, we stand shoulder to shoulder as Muslims. Together, we jointly circle the Kaaba, which was entrusted to us jointly, in the longing for peace.

A Path to Freedom: Fasting

I. On the Meaning of Fasting in Christianity

Anselm Grün

Internalized Expression of Piety

Just like Islam and Judaism, but also like other religions such as Hinduism, Christianity has a tradition of fasting. In Judaism, almsgiving, fasting, and prayer were all considered expressions of piety. In the Sermon on the Mount, Jesus takes up these three forms of piety, but he internalizes them. In each of these expressions, we are in danger of focusing too much on ourselves, of boasting or being proud of our charity, fasting, or praying. Jesus therefore tells us to pray in private, not to give alms and fast openly. And he makes another essential point about the attitude of fasting: We should not look downcast but anoint our hair with oil and wash our face (see Mt 6:16). Fasting, then, is nothing dismal but something to be done with joy. Fasting wants to purify us, body and soul. It wants to express the beauty of the body and the soul. Jesus sees an inner connection of the three forms of piety: fasting allows us to give alms to the poor. That is why the largest church collections are still held during Lent. And fasting also intensifies prayer. This is true of personal prayer—it becomes more wakeful, more alive during fasting—and especially for intercessory prayer, as well. For this reason, Christianity has a tradition of purposely praying and fasting for others. When we combine prayer for others with fasting, that prayer happens not only in our head but involves our entire body. By personally weakening myself in the fast, I am trusting in God, from whom alone help comes.

Understood in this way, fasting in Christianity is a spiritual path that has nothing to do with today's craze for healthful or slimming fasts. It is essentially a path to inner freedom. By abstaining from certain foods, by consciously eating less, I am testing my freedom. Through discipline, I am proving to myself that I need not immediately give in to every need, but that I can purposely abstain from them, as well. This experience of inner freedom does us good and is appropriate to our dignity.

The Gospel of Matthew also recalls a question that John's disciples asked Jesus: "Why do we and the Pharisees fast often, but your disciples do not fast?" Jesus answers them: "The wedding guests cannot mourn as long as the bridegroom is with them, can they? The days will come when the bridegroom is taken away from them, and then they will fast" (Mt 9:14–15). In his lifetime, Jesus was not seen as one who would typically fast. In fact, he was even called a "glutton and drunkard" (Mt. 11:19). But the early Church did fast, and it understood Jesus' words to mean that fasting was a way of awaiting the coming of the bridegroom. In fasting, Christians reach out to the coming Messiah. And when the Messiah arrives, Christians will celebrate eternal union with God.

The traditional Jewish fast days were Tuesday and Thursday. The early Christians therefore chose Wednesday and Friday as their fast days to distinguish themselves from Judaism. On Wednesdays they commemorated the persecution of Jesus and on Fridays they commemorated his death on the cross. Baptismal preparations, too, involved a fast. And before the disciples ordained those among them called to ministry, they also prayed and fasted (Acts 13:1–3). This is why bishops were supposed to fast for a day before ordaining priests. Fasting was also how early Christians prepared for the celebration of Easter. This tradition developed into the forty-day period of Lent as a response to the forty days that Jesus fasted, which in turn had antecedents in the forty-day fasts of Moses and Elijah. Early monks, too, followed a strict regimen of fasting, with many eating only every other day and some only on weekends.

The major fasts in the Church calendar, which traditionally come before Easter and before Christmas, have a Christological motivation—that is, they refer to the suffering and resurrection of Christ and to the waiting for the birth of Christ.

Purification and Repentance

One important aspect of fasting—aside from the experience of inner freedom as the result of purposeful abstention—is purification. Fasting is meant to purify the body of toxins. But even more, it is about cleansing the spirit. A fourth-century monk is said to have told another: "It does not help when you do not eat meat. For you are constantly eating the meat of your brothers by speaking ill of them." In the same way, a time of fasting is meant to cleanse the spirit of all value judgments and apprehensions about our fellow human beings. A purposeful abstention from talking about others might be a good exercise for fasting that would give a bodily fast spiritual meaning.

For Christians, fasting is always an expression of repentance: I acknowledge that my life is not in order, that I have strayed from God. In fasting, we bodily profess our will to repent. The Greek word for turning away in this manner is *metanoia*, which—translated literally—means a change in our thinking. So we are to examine our thinking. Does our thinking correspond to the spirit of God, to the spirit of Jesus? Or has the egotistical desire for possession wormed its way into our thoughts?

Opening Ourselves for Prayer

The ultimate goal of fasting, however, is to open our spirit for prayer. Bernard of Clairvaux describes the connection between fasting and prayer by saying that fasting lends confidence and fervency to prayer. It was the early monks' experience that fasting opened the human spirit to God. Philoxenus of Mabbug is said to have called for fasting with the following reason: "Fast that you may see!" Fasting makes human beings more open to divine visions. On the second Sunday of Lent, the reading is always the Transfiguration of Jesus. This shows us the aim of Lent, the most significant fast within the Catholic Church: fasting is supposed to cleanse our spirit of all the things that cloud it, of negative thoughts, guilty deeds, superficiality. All those things fasting is meant to purge so that the true glory of God can shine out in us. Accordingly, fasting has a positive meaning for Christians. Augustine holds that it is the joy of the spirit which drives one to fast, and that fasting prepares the body for resurrection. Fasting leads us to a life oriented wholly and solely towards God.

The Social Dimension: Fasting for Others

One important aspect of fasting is fasting for others. The early monks fasted when a brother had fallen into sin. They hoped that through their fasting and prayer, their brother would repent and be healed. However, fasting for others must not be confused with prisoners' hunger strikes. In a hunger strike, fasting acquires an aggressive element. Gandhi, too, often used fasts as a political act, as a protest against structures of injustice. He wrote: "My religion teaches me that, whenever there is distress which one cannot remove, one must fast and pray."[48] Gandhi sought to cleanse the atmosphere with his fasting. But for Gandhi, this cleansing effect can only arise if the fast is linked with prayer and if I show love and understanding for the person for or against whom I am fasting. When fasting is filled with thoughts of aggression and hatred, it is no longer fasting but a hunger strike.

A New Sensitivity to the Importance of Fasting

Over the course of the last century or so, the emphasis on fasting had been reduced further and further. But more recently the idea of fasting has attracted renewed interest, including in Christian circles. And there is greater understanding of the purpose of undertaking a communal fast for forty days. Much like Ramadan, Lent too is meant as a time of purification, a time in which we purposely think back on the actual goals of our life. There are attempts to fill this time of Lent with new meaning.

---

48. Mohandas K. Gandhi, *The Mind of Mahatma Gandhi*, R K. Prabhu & U. R. Rao (eds.), chapter 6. Accessed at: https://www.mkgandhi.org/momgandhi/chap06.htm.

In the Protestant church, Lent is understood as a time in which to "live differently," as "seven weeks without": without meat, without alcohol, without television, without online gaming, etc. But also as a time for positive impulses: seven weeks in which one departs from old habits, practices new attitudes, and tries to give space to the Holy Spirit.

The Spiritual Goal: Purity of the Heart

Like some Islamic scholars, Benedict sees fasts as an invitation to live consciously with and before God in essentially every moment. He therefore starts his chapter on fasting: "There can be no doubt that monastic life should always have a Lenten character about it, but there are not many today who have the strength for that. Therefore, we urge that all in the monastery during these holy days of Lent should guard conscientiously the integrity of their lives and in this holy season get rid of any negligence and compromise which may have crept in at other times."[49] The important aspect is the purity of the heart (*puritas cordis*), the goal of the ascetic path of monastic life. Working towards purity of the heart together is also the purpose of Lent, which reminds us all that our life must be oriented toward God so that we can become healed and whole.

2. Fasting: A Central Pillar of Islam

Ahmad Milad Karimi

An Interruption for What is Essential:
The Meaning of Ramadan

Fasting is one of the central pillars of Islam. The Arabic word for fasting in the month of Ramadan is *ṣaum*, which roughly means "resting" or "finding stillness." In the Arabic lunar

---

49. Benedict, *Rule*, 119-20.

calendar, Ramadan, the month of fasting, is the ninth month. It finds special religious commemoration in particular because it is the month in which the Qur'an was sent down (see Qur'an 2:185). The Qur'an also states: "You who believe, fasting is prescribed for you" (Qur'an 2:183). Accordingly, in this month all Muslims, if their health allows and they are not traveling, are supposed to fast from sunrise to sunset: primarily, this means that they must abstain from food, drink, and sexual activity as well. Children and pregnant or nursing women are also exempt from the duty to fast.

But the month in which all Muslims are enjoined to fast has greater significance than a mere rule to abstain from this or that. Fasting in the month of Ramadan can be most succinctly described as a break, an interruption. Not stasis, but stillness. Our everyday routine, stress, the entanglements between life and surroundings, the striving for more and ever more, for progress and optimization; the constant wanting and desire, consumerism, meaningless communication, gossiping—in short, all our tendencies to live as if we would live forever—are what we interrupt in Ramadan. Suddenly everything is different, turned on its head. Our abstention becomes real not because we abstain from this or that, but because we are essentially abstaining from all those things that supposedly sustain and give life. Ramadan is a month like no other, but it is actually supposed to be exactly what it is not: a month like any other. It should not be understood as an exception in the year but rather be present in our entire life. If there was a single question that concerns all the fasters through Ramadan, it would be: What is it that actually keeps me alive? It is not bread and water, nor any of the other delights we yearn for. So what happiness, what kind of welfare, what good do we seek most in our lives? What does our true happiness consist of? What are the joys that uplift us, the joys we seek at our deepest level? How should I view my own welfare in the context of others and their suffering? What is it worth? What has worth?

A Critical Appraisal of the Self, and New Freedom

Fasting during Ramadan is also a subtle criticism of our usual attitude towards life. This criticism is not theoretical: one could say that Muslims practice it on their own body. Waste, greed, and selfishness are only some of the ideas focused on here. Those who feel at home in Islam use this time to examine themselves critically. Doing so does not devalue the life we live here and now, but instead puts it in proper perspective. Fasting and abstention are like an existential correction, so that in Ramadan Muslims come closer to themselves by distancing themselves from the self.

At first glance, fasting seems to be the epitome of a kind of negative freedom: by giving up and as it were untying ourselves from everything, we become free from this and that. But strangely, this negative freedom is transmuted into positive freedom by revealing itself as the potential for the good, the valuable, and the sustainable. We become more open to others. That is the sense in which fasting during Ramadan can be seen as granting freedom: it gives and preserves personal autonomy by centering the experience at one's limits, in living devotion to God. Fasting is therefore revealed as an attitude in life that leads to reflection on what is truly essential. Ramadan interrupts the uniform, the appearance that everything is the same. The time between sunrise and sunset has a great significance. Usually, we ignore the rising and setting of the sun because we have lost some of our connection with nature. Fasting therefore becomes a whetstone for our senses, sharpening them by exercising the ability to abstain.

Opening toward God: Abstaining with Hand and Heart

In the Islamic mystic tradition, abstention as a fundamental attitude of life is linked with two concepts that exemplify what abstaining really means. These two concepts are the hand and the heart: the heart should become empty of what the hands are empty of. It is no one-time act to free ourselves from the things we hold in our hand, but that actually have a hold on us because we have bound our heart to them. Rather, the heart has to practice abstention—practice abstaining, and abstaining, and abstaining over and over. Practicing abstention in this way turns abstemiousness into a character trait, an attitude. Now, abstaining does not mean turning away from all that the world around us has to offer. But those who do not tie their heart to what they hold in their hand will have a free heart. Abstention does not mean simply refusing something, taking a negative attitude towards it. Instead, this kind of abstention has a positive quality: it opens our heart to God, the rightful object of our devoted desire. If one's heart is centered on God, then the hand will receive everything that it holds as a gift—a gift that we do not possess, that does not fulfill us, and that does not serve to fulfill our desire. Being borne by this abstention means for my heart to desire the poverty I carry in my hand. This experience of inner poverty opens the heart too, makes the heart sensitive to the needs of others. For this reason, Ramadan is also a time of encounter, of sharing, and of justice.

During Ramadan, it is common to read the entire Qur'an once through. The Qur'an is subdivided into thirty parts, so that each day is linked to a part of the Qur'an. There are also special prayers (Arabic: *tarāwīḥ*) that are completed after the evening prayer in the mosque. Ramadan, moreover, fosters community: one shares one's abstention—something that is hardly sharable—and walks the path of abstemiousness together.

Breaking the Fast: A Special Moment

But fasting would not be complete without the breaking of the fast (Arabic: *ifṭār*), which is celebrated each evening. A special moment during the fast occurs when, in breaking the fast, one first takes a sip of water. Ordinary water suddenly tastes sweet, and one can feel the body absorbing it. Gratitude and appreciation of the ordinary is present within Ramadan. We share with one another this appreciation for the world in which we live and all its gifts we may enjoy day after day. Above all, this has a social significance, for families and friends visit one another to break the fast. They share food and encounter one another in a time shaped by mindfulness. And so it is not surprising that the mystic Maulānā Rūmī should write: "Though faith rests on pillars, fasting—by God!—is the greatest pillar!"[50] Fasting in the month of Ramadan, therefore, encapsulates Islam as a whole: in a subtle way being in the world while simultaneously being beyond the world.

---

50. Annemarie Schimmel, *Das islamische Jahr: Zeiten und Feste* [The Islamic year: Seasons and celebrations] (Munich: C. H. Beck, 2002), 98. Translated from the German.

Mercy: Core of Spirituality

I. God has Mercy on the Merciful

Ahmad Milad Karimi

God as the Most Merciful

According to the common outside view, Islam seems to speak of a God who is above all strict and authoritarian, who punishes, threatens, and reigns in anger. But in Muslims' self-conception, and especially in the history of Islamic piety, an entirely different idea of God prevails. Undoubtedly, as the strong universal ruler, he is also always the sublime God upon whom we human beings can have no claim. But in line with the qur'anic revelation, another image of God has inscribed itself deep into the hearts of the faithful, and that image is characterized by the motif of mercy.

The Qur'an reads: "Say, 'Call on God, or on the Lord of Mercy– whatever names you call Him, the best names belong to Him'" (Qur'an 17:110). God has many names, many attributes. But the name with which he identifies himself to human beings in his creation is that of mercy. "Your Lord has taken it on Himself to be merciful" (Qur'an 6:54). Almost every surah of the Qur'an begins with this memorialization: "In the name of God, the Lord of Mercy, the Giver of Mercy." What is more, God's self-identification with mercy is among the most frequently mentioned attributes of God, so that mercy occurs over six hundred times in the Qur'an. The fifty-fifth surah, which has this special name of God in its title, begins with the words: "It is the Lord of Mercy who taught the Qur'an. He created man and taught him to communicate" (Qur'an 55:1–4). The central message of the Qur'an is that God's actions in his creation, his care, his revelation are supported by his mercy.

According to Ibn 'Arabī, therefore, the entire world is in "the breath of the merciful." The Arabic word for mercy is *raḥma*. Unlike the English word, which comes from the Latin cognate for "reward," "wares," and "merchandise," etymologically the Arabic root *r-ḥ-m* resonates with the meaning of "womb." The merciful, then, is the one who expresses a fundamental, undistorted, peaceful connection. The Qur'an, in this context, speaks of God as "the Most Merciful of the merciful" (Qur'an 21:83) and as the "the most merciful of all" (Qur'an 23:118). Conversely, this means that God is near me in mercy, and in the experience and the attitude of mercy I am supported by God and held as in my mother's womb.

Absolute Justice and Boundless Mercy Are Not Opposites

Seen from this perspective, God's mercy is in no opposition to his absolute justice. Justice and mercy are not opposites. Rather, God's mercy is a constant companion in life, since unlike God's punishment, his mercy is boundless, as the Qur'an says: "I bring My punishment on whoever I will, but My mercy encompasses all things" (Qur'an 7:156). Even when we stray, when we choose wrong, make a mistake and rue it, he is with us in mercy. The following idea, central to the inner understanding of Islam, is related as written into Muhammad's heart by the eternal one: "Truly, my mercy surpasses my anger."[51] In the heart of the faithful, God's visage is defined by—indeed the very experience of God is permeated with—this mercy. In the Qur'an, human beings are again and again reminded to trust in God's mercy: "Say, 'My servants who have harmed yourselves by your own excess, do not despair of God's mercy. God forgives all sins: He is truly the Most Forgiving, the Most Merciful'" (Qur'an 39:53). Accordingly, the Prophet once said: "In the West there is a gate that stands open to remorse; its width is seventy years, and it will not be closed before the sun does not rise in the West."[52]

---

51. After al-Bukhārī, hadīth no. 3194. Translated from the German.
52. Ibn Māja: *Sunan, Kitāb al-Fitan, bāb ṭulū' ash-shams min mashriqihā*, hadīth no. 4070, Cairo 1424/2004, 212. Translated from the German.

Lived Religion: Mercy as a Mission for Life

The spiritual dimension of mercy has a crucial significance in how we live religion: divine mercy is meant to be realized in practice by our just dealings with one another. God's explicit turn towards humankind in the revelation of the Qur'an is understood in Islam as an act of mercy itself. For in mercy, God creates the world, in mercy he supports it, and in mercy he leads human beings to their truth. That means that the Qur'an as right guidance for human beings should be understood simultaneously as God's mercy towards human beings, so that fourteen times in the Qur'an, the reason for its revelation is given as God's mercy.[53] But it is not only sending the Qur'an that is understood as an act of mercy. A central thought is also that the Prophet Muhammad was sent as prophet of mercy, since he is addressed in the Qur'an with the following unmistakable words: "It was only as a mercy that We sent you [Prophet] to all people" (Qur'an 21:107). The life of the Prophet, his normative significance, and his spiritual power for the life of Muslims is measured in the category of mercy. On this point, the Qur'an is decisive: it is not merely for Muslims, but for the entire world. Accordingly, seeing in the deeds and work of Muhammad a mercy that applies to the entire world is to understand and shape Islam as a religious force in the service of humankind. A mercy that excludes other people and applies only to one's own community does not do justice to this comprehensive view. That is why the Prophet is sent not out of mercy merely for Muslims, but for the entire world. Specifically, this is to say that mercy amounts to a mission for life. To call oneself Muslim, one must stand in the service of humanity.

Not Merely Within

At its core, Islamic spirituality means: divine mercy fills the hearts of the faithful, but it does not remain merely within. Rather, it simultaneously affects our relationships, determines our relation to our neighbors. How human beings deal with one

---

53. See Qur'an 6:157; 7:203; 27:77; 28:43; 45:20; and others.

another should be borne by mercy—since according to a saying of the Prophet, "the hearts of the people are between two fingers of the merciful." What matters in Islam is this: We all are on a journey, and every believer shares their life with others. The path of each of us is a joint, a shared path together. When Islam speaks of a shared path, this once again means that it is Muslims' duty to shape this path together in humility and mercy. This duty is derived from the mercy of God himself. By practicing mercy so that it becomes their fundamental attitude, Muslims are realizing an attribute of God in their lives. The account of the Prophet's life illustrates this vividly: when Muhammad receives the news that his daughter's child is dying, he runs to her, takes the boy onto his lap and holds him in his arms during his last breaths. When a companion of the Prophet sees his tears, he asks: "What is that, O emissary of God?" Muhammad answers: "That is a mercy God lays into the hearts of some of his servants whom he has chosen. And God has mercy for only those of his servants who are themselves merciful."[54]

2. Mercy: Attribute of God and Command for Human Beings

Anselm Grün

An Impulse Anchored to the Conception of God

Pope Francis has described mercy as a Christian impulse relevant for the entire world today: "Both the Church and the world today particularly need Mercy so that the unity willed by God in Christ may prevail over the negative action of the evil one."[55]

---

54. After al-Bukhārī, Ḥadīth no. 5556. Translated from the German.
55. Pope Francis, "Homily", *Holy Mass for the meeting of the missionaries of mercy with the Pope*, April 10, 2018. Accessed at: https://www.vatican.va/content/francesco/en/homilies/2018/documents/papa-francesco_20180410_omelia-missionari-divinamisericordia.html

In so saying, he centered a perspective that is an essential part of the biblical Christian faith and aims far beyond the churches in both its claims and its significance. According to the Christian conviction of faith, mercy is the fundamental attribute of God. But human beings are to practice mercy as well. Already in the Old Testament, God describes himself as the merciful:

> The LORD, the LORD,
> [is] a God merciful and gracious,
> slow to anger,
> and abounding in steadfast love and faithfulness.
> (Ex 34:6)

Human beings' answer to this mercy is their merciful behavior to their neighbors. According to the Book of Tobit, those who show mercy and justice will live long lives (see Tb 12:9). The biblical prophets repeatedly emphasize God's merciful love towards humankind, and the existence of human beings in God's eyes is described by saying that he loves goodness (see Mi 6:8). The Hebrew word for mercy, *raham*, corresponds to the Arabic word *raḥma* and likewise means "womb." God's mercy is like a womb in which we can feel secure and accepted.

Walking with Sinners and Abstaining from Judgment

The New Testament has three terms for mercy. One is the Greek verb *splanchnizomai*, which actually means "to be gripped in the gut"—that is, an empathy, a fellow-feeling. The word is used to describe Jesus' feeling of pity for the lepers (Mk 1:41). But we too are enjoined to act out of this feeling, just as the Good Samaritan does (Lk 10:33). The second term for mercy is the noun *eleos*, which means acting mercifully: I do deeds of mercy, and my speech is merciful. This is the root of the Christian tradition's seven works of mercy, which for a long time shaped our social climate. Jesus often speaks of *eleos*. In the Gospel of Matthew, Jesus twice says: "I desire mercy, [and] not sacrifice" (Mt. 9:13 and 12:7). Both times, he is quoting a saying of the prophet Hosea. The first time, he says: "Go and learn," a typical Jewish phrase of instruction. In other words: go home, sit down, and learn what is truly important. The central element of faith is mercy. It is not a matter of sacrifices, of demonstrating achievement before God, or of sacrificing money or animals. Rather, what matters is dealing mercifully with people, not judging them. Here, mercy means above all not to judge the sinners but to go to them in order to show them a new path.

The Connective Nature of Mercy

The third Greek term for mercy is the adjective *oiktirmon*, meaning "empathetic," "having fellow-feeling." This is the word Luke uses when he records Jesus as saying: "Be merciful, just as your Father is merciful" (Lk 6:36). Mercy, in the sense of feeling for other human beings, is an attribute of God's being. But human beings are meant to empathize not only with all other human beings, but with nature, plants, and animals, as well. By empathizing, we are connected with others. We do not place ourselves above them but walk a shared path with them together. And in empathy, we take part in God himself. By feeling for others, we feel at one with God, recognize the nature of God.

God Acts in Mercy

Luke sees mercy as the true motivator out of which God acts. In the *Magnificat*, for example, Mary praises the mercy of God with which he looked down upon her and did great things to her (Lk 1:50). And the mercy of God is the reason for the salvific and liberating acts of God throughout history (Lk 1:54). In the *Benedictus*, Luke describes God's mercy as the reason for God's incarnation in Jesus. He uses a strange expression to describe God's mercy here: *dia splanchna eleous*, literally, "through the bowels of mercy," meaning heartfelt mercy (Lk 1:78). In the New Revised Standard translation, this is rendered as "by the tender mercy of our God." Through this heartfelt, tender mercy, God lets the light from on high shine out to us in Jesus.

Indeed, God's mercy visits us in Jesus, so that this mercy can come before our eyes concretely.

God's nature is mercy, and God acts mercifully toward us. He does not judge us but accepts us in his merciful love, forgives our sins and liberates us from self-recrimination and self-doubt. But Christians should answer the mercy of God by becoming merciful themselves and letting their actions be shaped by mercy. Part of the nature of mercy is that we do not judge or disdain others. Mercy is a maternal attitude. And the nature of a mother is not to judge her child but to care for it, to foster and cherish it.

With an Eye to All People, not just Fellow Christians

But the Christian understanding of mercy has a societal and political dimension as well. Mercy must take the form of dealing mercifully with the individual and with groups. The seven works of mercy, which are based on the words of Jesus in the Gospel of Matthew, refer to all people. Jesus identifies himself with all human beings, no matter what culture or religion they belong to: "For I was hungry and you gave me food, I was thirsty and you gave me something to drink, I was a stranger and you welcomed me, I was naked and you gave me clothing, I was sick and you took care of me, I was in prison and you visited me" (Mt 25:35–36). In other words, Christians are meant to show mercy not only to their own brothers in faith, and what is more, they are meant to care particularly for those who are suffering. Jesus' parable of the Samaritan, who even as a non-Jew is the only one to spontaneously and actively help the injured man on the road to Jericho (see Lk 10:25–37), has become emblematic and influential in this context. Jesus has in mind all the people to whom we should mercifully give help. Although Christians have not always implemented this idea according to Jesus' intent, it must still be said that the words of Jesus have had an effect throughout history and have made society more humane and merciful through hospitals, homes for the handicapped, and care for the poor and ostracized, for foreigners and refugees. Throughout ecclesiastical history, ways of doing merciful deeds have also developed outside the institutional framework of the Church, in private foundations and associations as well as large-scale efforts in social causes and social welfare. To see suffering and to help, regardless of religion, status, or sex: that is the fundamental impulse. Today, Christian care in my native Germany has also become institutionalized in the form of associations within the framework of the welfare state (which itself goes back to Christian impulses as well), organized as the Protestant *Diakonisches Werk* and the Catholic *Caritas* associations, both of which are active with their mission internationally and world-wide. According to the constitution about the Church in the modern world (*Lumen Gentium*, see in particular paragraph 1), the Church is meant to recognize in the poor and the suffering the image of him who founded it and was himself poor and suffering.

Having an Open Heart

Unlike Greek, Latin has only one word for mercy: *misericordia*. It means having a heart for the poor, orphaned, weak, and wounded parts within myself, and for the poor, orphaned, weak, and wounded people around me. Merciful persons do not act purely rationally but look at all people with their heart. And in the heart, merciful persons feel with others. When we open our hearts to the poor and weak, we will approach them not heartlessly and coldly, but with heartfelt mercy, showing them our open heart.

Love: Longing and Fulfillment

I. Love: The Foundation of Christian Faith

Anselm Grün

Biblical Testimony: God is Love

To us Christians, God is not only the God who loves us but also the God who is love. In the Book of Jeremiah, we read: "I have loved you with an everlasting love" (Jer 31:3). God loves his people and he loves each individual human being. This love is the foundation of our life. The love that God showed his people by, at the turning point of its history, leading it out of slavery in Egypt, is to have practical consequences as well. The Book of Leviticus gives it as the reason why Israel should not limit its love to its own tribe: "The alien who resides with you shall be to you as the citizen among you; you shall love the alien as yourself, for you were aliens in the land of Egypt" (Lev 19:34).

Love of God, Love of One's Neighbor, Self-Love

Love means that God loves us unconditionally, without our having to prove anything to him. We do not need to buy God's love. But it is our task to answer this love. And so Jesus answers the Pharisee's question about the most important commandment: "'You shall love the Lord your God with all your heart, and with all your soul, and with all your mind.' This is the greatest and first commandment. And a second is like it: 'You shall love your neighbor as yourself'" (Mt 22:37–39). Love of God and love of one's neighbor, then, are closely linked. And self-love is part of this, as well. Loving oneself has nothing to do with egotism. I love myself as a creature of God. I treat with care what God has given me, and I value it.

God's Love Permeates the World

The only question is how we can love a God whom we cannot see. We can answer this question only when we look at another aspect of God's love. The First Epistle of John states: "God is love, and those who abide in love abide in God, and God abides in them" (1 Jn 4:16). God is a Thou who loves me and whom I love, but God in himself is also love. love, in the view of the Greek philosopher Plato, is more than a feeling. It is a force that connects everything that had been separated. It is this force that Paul eulogizes in his song of love: Love "bears all things, believes all things, hopes all things, endures all things" (1 Cor 13:7). God as love permeates the entire world. Love is the foundation of the world. Current research on evolution, which sees love as the foundation for the development of animal life, confirms this: it is not the fittest who survive, but those who are successful in relationships. This love is within us, as well, as a source on which we can draw. But all too often, we are cut off from it. The words of Jesus want to bring us in touch with this love.

If we are in touch with this source of love, we love God, and this love will flow toward God as well. It connects us to God, the foundation of all being, to God who is himself love. In this love, deep at the bottom of our soul, we are already in God, are already one with God as the Epistle of John tells us. For the Christian faith, then, love is more than a moral imperative. It is a mystical experience. And it is only out of this deep experience that we can love God, love our neighbor, and love ourselves.

Jesus' Life and Death as Fulfillment of Love

When Jesus said: "This is my commandment, that you love one another as I have loved you. No one has greater love than this, to lay down one's life for one's friends" (Jn 15:12–13), he gave us love as the true commandment. Jesus modeled this love for us by how he lived and died. In the Gospel of John, Jesus' death on the cross is the consummation of love. And Jesus' love is a love for his friends. Friends are equals. In the Gospel of John, Jesus' death is not penance for our sins. Rather, Jesus consummates his love by dying for us. In his death, we are meant to recognize that we are his friends, that he made himself familiar to us by giving himself to us wholly and entirely. The cross itself is a gesture of loving embrace. In John, Jesus says: "And I, when I am lifted up from the earth [i.e., crucified], will draw all people to myself" (Jn 12:32). When we look at the cross on which Jesus is stretched, we can feel embraced by his love. And to John, this love is the force that connects all things. Even before Jesus' death on the cross, after all, the cross was a symbol of salvation. It symbolizes the unity of all opposites, the unity of heaven and earth, light and dark, men and women, old and young, rich and poor. And on the cross, we may feel embraced with all our injuries and wounds. This love with which Jesus died for us on the cross flows out as blood and water from a pierced side (see Jn 19:34) and flows into the whole world. God's love, this love that we can now see in the person of Jesus and his life and death, permeates the entire world, the entire cosmos. This love flows into us too. When we celebrate the Eucharist, we always remember the open heart of Jesus. From this heart, his love flows into our body and our soul to permeate everything, to heal our wounds, to unite all contradictions within us, and to enable us to love.

Jesus' Purifying Love on the Cross

But there is another effect of the love with which Jesus loved us so consummately on the cross: it purifies us. This is what Jesus shows us by washing the feet of his disciples before suffering. John sees the washing of feet as a symbol of Jesus' death on the cross. On the cross, Jesus bends down to our dusty, wounded feet in order to purify us there. To Peter, Jesus also offers the following interpretation of what his death on the cross means to him: "One who has bathed does not need to wash, except for the feet, but is entirely clean" (Jn 13:10). Jesus purified the disciples by his words, by his radiance, and by his deeds (see Jn 15:2). The cross completes this purification. It purifies us precisely where we keep getting dirty: at our feet. Another image that John links with Jesus' purifying love on the cross is that of cleansing the temple (Jn 2:13–22). Through his death on the cross, Jesus cleanses us of the noisy thoughts of the merchants, of the animal thoughts of the cattle, and of the superficial thoughts that flutter around inside us like doves. He cleanses us so that we can become temples of God. In the temple, God's glory shines out. And God's glory, God's beauty, is his love.

The Pinnacle of Love: Loving One's Enemies

Love, then, is the foundation of our faith. God is love. This divine love shines out to us in Jesus. Through Jesus' deeds and death, it entered into us to fill us, full, with love and to enable us to love. The pinnacle of this love that Jesus has enabled in us and to which he calls and challenges us is the love of our enemies. When we love our enemies, we are emulating God, who lets his sun shine on good and evil alike (Mt 5:45). Luke uses three behaviors to describe to us what such love might look like in practice: We love our enemies by doing them good although they treat us badly. We love our enemies by blessing them. By blessing them, they are no longer our enemies, but become blessed people we encounter in new ways. And we love our enemies by praying for them. In prayer, we become one with them, see them with the eyes of God, and recognize their longing for good that is behind the evil that they do. The Church Fathers considered love of one's enemies to be the true hallmark of Christians in the world of their time. Today too, love of one's enemies could be the way to overcome enmity between people, between tribes, between religions. It could be the way that the love preached by all religions flows to all people and connects them with one another.

2. Only the Lover Is Truly Spiritual

Ahmad Milad Karimi

The Unusual Nature of Love of God

Loving is a divine act. God, as the Qur'an testifies many times, is the insuperably loving (Arabic: *al-wadūd*). According to Ibn 'Arabī, Islamic mysticism (that is, Sufism) consists of adopting the names of God[56] so that God's self-revelation is wholly present in oneself. All names of God are to be realized in human beings. Love, for instance, is meant to change, transform a person, since love—as the Muslim mystic al-Junayd has put it—is meant to exchange the qualities of the lover and the qualities of the beloved for one another. But not infrequently, the Islamic spiritual tradition has given rise to voices doubting whether it is possible to love God at all, since he is beyond all human experience and above all human reach. What matters here is to distinguish between love of God and human love. As human beings, we know different forms of love: self-love, neighborly love, parental love, erotic love, or love of our friends. All these are expressions of love, but each is defined differently and they are indeed unmistakable.

We are speaking here of love as an encounter and meeting of differences, as mutual fulfillment and enrichment. This differentiation is significant because love of God (both divine love and love toward God) means an unmistakably different form of love. Al-Ghazālī further distinguishes several levels of love of God.[57] Divine love, for one, is fundamentally an unconditional, inexhaustible foundation of life. God loves humankind, to the extent that he sees, affirms, and completes

---

56. M. Ibn 'Arabī: *Al-Futūḥāt al-Makkīya* (The Meccan discourses), Book II, 267. Translated from the German.
57. See al-Ghazālī's writing on the "Way of Salvation" in his magnum opus, *The Revival of the Religious Sciences*, particularly books 31–36. Various English translations can be found online at: https://www.ghazali.org/rrs-ovr/.

his own deeds in them.[58] Love toward God, on the other hand, consists of recognizing my own createdness and praising God with devotion, since I have him to thank for my life and since I cannot find peace without him. Al-Ghazālī himself speaks of an inner sense of love toward God that enabled him to turn to God with his internal sense, the heart, and devote himself to God.[59]

According to Ibn 'Arabī, human beings have a beginning—since humankind is created—but no end, since the infinite love of God makes human beings unbounded. Love, then, is among Islam's central motifs, particularly in Islamic mysticism. What is known as the "mysticism of love" sees love as the completion of a life laid out as journey toward God.

Living as Longing

Living in love means understanding life as longing. It is in longing that human beings find their true attitude, one that does not let itself be nailed down to remaining with one person or another. Longing, Islam tells us, is not something we have but something we are. Being longing means tying one's heart to God. We live from this bond, so that the pulse of life is fulfilled as longing, as longing for God. But for which God? Not for a God who exits in parallel with other objects. The God on whom the Muslim faith rests knows no equal beside him. Longing for God means knowing oneself to be held in his eternal hand. Maulānā Rūmī writes: "I have no longing for worldly goods, nor greed. Of all the riches of the ground, palaces, only my longing is the bedrock."[60] This bedrock, this foundation on which we stand tall, which supports us and gives us stability, which comforts us and gives us serenity, is God alone.

The heart seeks fulfillment, but nothing can satisfy it except God. It is not longing for reward, for paradise, for the beyond: those who seek only these are trying to find peace in something besides God. In Islam, however, longing describes a journey

---

58. See al-Ghazālī, *The Revival of the Religious Sciences*, Book 36.
59. See al-Ghazālī, *The Alchemy of Happiness*, 101.
60. Rūmī, *Divan*, poem 441. Translated from the German.

in a person's heart. Living in the heart is what being a Muslim means. And this unquenchable heart seeks to find peace, peace in God, peace with God. Rūmī writes: "God created me from the wine of love / I am intoxication and my origin the wine of love / Tell me, what but intoxication could come from me?"[61]

Islam as a Religion of Lovers

To mystics in Islam, Islam is primarily a religion of lovers. To the extent that we love, we live in Islam, live in the pilgrimage of love. The Qur'an describes as love the relationship between humankind and God: "You who believe, if any of you go back on your faith, God will soon replace you with people He loves and who love Him " (Qur'an 5:54). It is a relation that immediately concerns every human being and uplifts them to the absolute. But there can be love only in freedom. That is why the relationship to God cannot be a compelled or forced act, since it is founded in love.

But what exactly this love is cannot be put into words, all the more as precise distinctions are made between different terms for love (*maḥabba, 'ishq,* etc.). In Islamic mysticism, spiritual love (which is not physical or romantic love) is understood as an entity that does not require thoroughgoing explanation because it is revealed in its fulfillment, the act of loving. A person who wants to know what love is has no choice but to love. We cannot remain indifferent or untouched in the face of love. The revelation of the Qur'an itself is an act of love. The Prophet Muhammad receives the qur'anic revelation not mechanically, but is gripped by the care and attention of God; the Qur'an happens to him. Muhammad is gripped by the act of revelation that lets his heart tremble and fills it entirely. This is the experience of love, which, in the moment of revelation, overwhelms him as the utmost experience being human. God's love gets under his skin. Muhammad stands motionless and is unable to take a single step. But his heart is touched by the first

---

61. Rūmī, *Divan*, poem 683. Translated from the German.

throes of revelation. The Qur'an breathes with the intensity of this profound experience by the Prophet. For the Qur'an can be understood as the living declaration of God's love. And our journey to God as a pilgrimage of love can be traced in Muhammad's journey. The Prophet Muhammad was intoxicated with God. As the German poet Rainer Maria Rilke put it in a letter dated December 4, 1912: "Like a river through some primal mountain range, he breaks through to the one God."[62] It is in this sense that he is seen as "an excellent example" (Qur'an 33:21) for Muslims, since he has wholly become love. Rūmī writes: "Only love, only love—we have no other deed. Only love, only mercy do we plant. Drunk are we, as if drunk off that one king. Come here, come here, let us outstretch our hands to God."[63] The way of God, accordingly, is the way of love, since—as the Muslim mystic al-Qushayrī says—"when someone loves the encounter with God, God loves the encounter with them."[64]

The Double Basis: Insight and Action

In Islamic mysticism, love is thus more than merely a fleeting feeling. Rather, love is founded on a double basis: in the first place, love represents a central form of insight, and secondly it is an action. As a form of insight, love does not refer to a rational-intellectual process of understanding. Rather, love articulates something for which there is no other language. Islamic mysticism takes a clear position on this matter: through

---

62. Rainer Maria Rilke, *R. M. Rilke und M. von Thurn und Taxis: Briefwechsel* [R. M. Rilke and M. von Thurn and Taxis: Correspondence.] Ed. by Ernst Zinn and introduced by Rudolf Kassner. Vol. 1. (Zürich: Insel, 1951), 246. Translated from the German.
63. Rūmī, *Divan*, poem 1475. Translated from the German.
64. 'A. al-Qushayrī, *Das Sendschreiben al-Qušayrīs über das Sufitum* [Al-Qushayrī's missive on Sufism]. Translated, commented, and introduced by Richard Gramlich. (Wiesbaden: Franz Steiner, 1989), 438.Translated from the German.

love, a person can achieve an experience of God, but to do so they must be in a state of love. That is to say: love is loving. Only lovers recognize themselves and their creator. Insight occurs in the act of love, so that in this act a person is enabled to transcend the boundaries of usual insight. "What is love? Flying toward the heavens. Tearing off the veil in each whisp of breath," writes Rūmī.[65]

Spirituality arises in this act of love, in the act of unveiling, when lovers let themselves be kindled with love. Love reconciles and unites and lets no disparity stand. But in the process, it also transfigures everything—the eye of the lover sees the beloved in everything. In Islamic mysticism, accordingly, love is considered a spiritual state. Though they are not the same, love of God and love of one's neighbor nevertheless belong together in Islam. Only lovers are spiritual, since only lovers seek peace with God, with themselves, and with creation. Meanwhile, Islam understands God to be the highest living creative activity, and he lets his beauty be experienced by himself loving and motivating love. Love, therefore, is considered the foundation, content, and practice of the world.

---

65. Rūmī, *Divan*, poem 1919. Translated from the German.

Tolerance and Truth Claims

I. The Meaning of Christianity's Claim to Absoluteness

Anselm Grün

Claim to Rule or Good News for All?

Christianity's claim to absoluteness and the commandment of tolerance towards other religions seem to be at odds. But this is true only if we misunderstand the nature of Christianity's claim to absoluteness. The Catholic theologian Cardinal Walter Kasper has pointed out that the "notion of the absoluteness of Christianity derives from the philosophy of German Idealism, not from theology itself."[66] Kasper understands the claim to Christian absoluteness not as an assertion that Christianity alone is factually true. Rather, the claim is that "with Christ's coming the fullness of time has come."[67] This claim therefore says nothing about other religions, nor does it denigrate them. Instead, "the absolute character of Christianity means an absolute acceptance and affirmation of man and the world . . . The absoluteness of Christianity is less a claim than the 'good news' that the world is not ultimately hollow and worthless, or absurd and insane, because God has accepted it, because he cherishes it with the absolute love of which only God is capable" (Jn 3:16).[68]

Accordingly, the claim to absoluteness does not mean that Christianity excludes all other religions' efforts to search for

---

66. Walter Kasper, "Christianity — Absoluteness of Christianity", in Karl Rahner, SJ (ed.), *Sacramentum Mundi Online* (Leiden: Brill, 2016). Accessed at: http://dx.doi.org/10.1163/2468-483X_smuo_COM_000712.
67. Kasper, "Absoluteness of Christianity."
68. Kasper, "Absoluteness of Christianity."

truth. On the contrary, the claim includes all these efforts. Such an understanding of absoluteness clarifies that "Christianity is less an exclusive than an inclusive religion; instead of repudiating other religions and other efforts to discover truth it embraces them, and therefore its very nature disposes it to dialogue with the religions of the world and with philosophy."[69] Moreover, the claim means that the Church and Christendom itself are subject to the judgment of God. They cannot merely declare themselves as universal truth, since the actual absolute truth is God, and we are all traveling towards this truth. The claim to absoluteness must therefore always be linked with freedom of religion and the freedom to follow one's conscience. Walter Kasper therefore does not see the mission of Christianity as ensuring that all people become Christians. Salvation, according to Kasper, is possible outside of the visible Church as well. Instead, the goal of Christian mission is "to represent and proclaim the love of God, to give testimony to hope, and so to be a sign among the nations.... What Christianity affirms, with its absolute claim, is not its dominion but its vicarious service of all mankind."[70]

Only God Is the Actual, Absolute Truth

Christian theology has always known that the actual truth is God. What we say about God is never absolute truth, but only ever aims at absolute truth. God, however, is beyond any terms or images used in Christian or Islamic contexts. Religious tolerance therefore demands that we humbly acknowledge the limited nature of our notions of and terms about God and that together we look for the truth of God beyond all terms and concepts.

However different our imagery and language may be, Christian and Islamic theologians generally agree that the nature of God is love. But, as Karl Rahner repeatedly emphasizes in the context of the suffering prevalent in the world, this love is

---

69. Kasper, "Absoluteness of Christianity."
70. Kasper, "Absoluteness of Christianity."

an incomprehensible love. No matter how little we comprehend the human condition and the suffering that is evidently part of every person's fate, we can still hold on to the fact that God is love—a love that transcends all our notions of love.

Whenever Christian theology maintains the Christian faith's claim to absoluteness, it is also indicating simultaneously that the explication of our faith is always also indebted to limited, temporal categories. Christ is God's absolute affirmation of humankind. But even our descriptions of Jesus Christ are shaped by history and culture, as well as subject to the limitations of the human mind. Christian theology recognizes that other religions are important paths towards God: journeys to the absolute mystery of God. Knowing that God is beyond all our terms and explanations, Christian theology is open to the statements of other religions, since they too are indications of God, whose true nature is beyond all human images, terms, and explanations.

Respect, Not Indifference

Therefore, it is important for Christians to have an attitude of tolerance toward other religions. Tolerance is not indifference. It involves neither unqualified approval, nor lack of interest, nor being resigned simply to suffering the other's presence. Rather, tolerance means respecting the convictions of the other's faith: I respect the faith of those who belong to another religion because I know that we all are on a path toward the incomprehensible mystery of God. And I am convinced that we should support one another on this path. For there are fundamental tenets we share: that we are people on the way to God; that God is the aim of our life; and that God is love, challenging us to love one another. What is more, all of us together know how relative what we say about God must be, since God is beyond all human imagining. Because we all are on the way to the absolute mystery of God, we should recognize this kinship not by fighting or lecturing each other, but by listening to one another and being open to the incomprehensible mystery of God, who is the aim of all our lives.

There are two traditional methodologies within Christian theology: affirming and negating statements about God. Apophatic theology—that is, theology that negates, also known as negative theology—views any affirmative statement about God as inappropriate, since God is always other than we think, always beyond the reach of our concepts. Such theology is related to mystical theology. Christian and Islamic mystic thought have long given another fruitful impulses. They have been open to one another in the knowledge of the biblical commandment not to make graven images of God. And they shared the conviction that all human beings—Christians and Muslims alike—are journeying towards the one God, who is always greater than all the ideas of him we might have and anything we might say about him.

But Christians and Muslims alike are also caught in the tension between statements and negations about God. We cannot merely be silent about God. We need words and terms and imagery to talk about God, despite knowing that God is beyond all of these. The Old Testament commandment against graven images applies not only to Jews, but also to Christians and Muslims. And yet we need imagery to be able to talk about God at all. And this imagery differs according to our traditions.

No Salvation Outside of the Church?

To us Christians, Jesus Christ is the "the image of the invisible God" (Col 1:15). In this image, the love and goodness of God shines out to us, and we are tasked with proclaiming this love to all people. And—as the First Epistle of Timothy instructs us, we are to pray for everyone, since God "desires everyone to be saved and come to the knowledge of the truth" (1 Tm 2:4). Some understand this sentence to mean that all people must come into the Church in order to be saved. This is also the usual interpretation of St. Cyprian of Carthage's statement *Extra ecclesiam nulla salus*—no salvation outside of the Church. But that is not the true meaning of the sentence. Rather, God wants all people to come to know the truth regardless of what religion they happen to belong to.

Today's theology views the Church as a sign of the power of salvation. And outside the power of salvation—which is active not only within the Church—no one can be saved. The Second Vatican Council gives the following interpretation: "Those also can attain to salvation who . . . sincerely seek God and moved by grace strive by their deeds to do His will as it is known to them through the dictates of conscience."[71]

A Life in Conscience as Path to God

We must not, then, interpret the saying of Cyprian of Carthage in an exclusionary way, but rather in a spirit of inclusiveness: those who seek God earnestly—and that is sure to be true of many Muslims, many Buddhists, and many Hindus—are already, again using the language of Cyprian, members of the "invisible Church." To some non-Christians, this statement may sound too possessive. If so, another way of putting it is: those who live according to their conscience are on the path to God. And in the Christian view, Jesus Christ is the savior along this path, even if he is not recognized as such, because Christ is the mediator between God and humankind. In the heart of every person, he acts as the messenger reminding that person of the God of their salvation, bringing that individual in touch with the incomprehensible God, who is a God of all humankind and all religions, beyond any dogmatic determinations.

---

71. Paul VI, *Lumen Gentium*, 16. Accessed at: https://www.vatican.va/archive/hist_councils/ii_vatican_council/documents/vat-ii_const_19641121_lumen-gentium_en.htmlhttps://www.vatican.va/archive/hist_councils/ii_vatican_council/documents/vat-ii_const_19641121_lumen-gentium_en.html.

2. A Muslim Perspective on Tolerance and Truth Claims

Ahmad Milad Karimi

Intolerance: Denigration of Difference, Rejection of Diversity

Ever since the emergence of Islam on the Arabian peninsula in the seventh century, the question of Islam's self-conception as a religion founded by God itself has been of utmost importance. For those secure in their faith, could there be any other paths to salvation, other points of view, or even other religions at all that would stand beside or after Islam as equally true and dignified? Or is Islam's claim to truth exclusive? Throughout Islamic history, there have always been stances—some of which are adopted by some (for example, extreme or militant) groups even today—claiming that Islam is the only true religion and all other positions are either utterly wrong or incomplete. That is, they are said to be either paths that mislead or paths that are less good than the Islamic path and therefore to be disapproved of.

However, such a disparaging view of others' differences reveals its instability already in the fact that what is held to be the true religion is not Islam, but only the adherent's particular interpretation. Intolerance is shown not only towards other religions, but also towards other forms, traditions, or interpretations within one's own religion. The real animosity, then, is against the idea of pluralism itself. Among other things, this intolerant attitude is linked with the fear that one's own religion becomes relative and watered down if others' views are recognized and valued. "There can be only the one truth," this view says, "and this truth is present only in my own religion (and only in the way I understand it)." This misinterpretation is virulent because its results are not confined to theological disparagement and mental denigration of the other. Instead, such a position has aggressive consequences in action, as well: "the others" are persecuted, threatened, imprisoned, and in the worst cases forced to convert or even killed. Such an exclusive and consequently intolerant claim to truth is an expression of hubris. Admittedly, it is not limited to Islam: a tendency toward overweening misinterpretation of one's own position can be found in all the world's cultures and religions, particularly religions based in revelation.

It is all the more important to engage matter-of-factly and reasonably with one's own religion's claim to truth. Such theologically reasonable engagement also raises the question of how one's own certainty in faith can be coupled with an attitude of tolerance toward others' convictions in their faith.

Truth Claims and Relationship to Other Religions

Contrary to the perversion of religion into religious fanaticism, the philosophical, theological, and mystical forms of Islam's spiritual tradition are actually extremely sophisticated and humble regarding questions of truth. In this context, the phrase "epistemic humility" is invoked to mean: "I recognize the preliminary and fragmentary nature of my own thinking and knowing, and I am aware that I can never make the claim that my understanding of truth is truth itself." Even the Qur'an testifies that Islam is not a populist, exclusive religion. Rather, Islam is a religion among religions, namely with reference to Judaism and Christianity. Accordingly, the Qur'an states: "We revealed the Torah with guidance and light. . . . We sent Jesus, son of Mary, in their footsteps, to confirm the Torah that had been sent before him: We gave him the Gospel with guidance, light, and confirmation of the Torah already revealed—a guide and lesson for those who take heed of God. So let the followers of the Gospel judge according to what God has sent down in it. . . . We sent to you [Muhammad] the Scripture with the truth, confirming the Scriptures that came before it, and with final authority over them" (Qur'an, 5:44–48). The Qur'an contains no general denigration of Christianity, nor of Judaism. The only thing that is criticized is these religions' horizons of understanding, to the extent that they violate either God's universal devotion or God's absolute oneness. However, the relationship between religions is expressly not meant to lie in war and violence. Nor should it be shaped by dogmatism and mutual disdain: "God is our Lord and your Lord—To us our deeds and to you yours, so let there be no argument between us and you— God will gather us together, and to Him we shall return" (Qur'an 42:15).

Plausibility: The Judgment of Reason and Revelation

Of course, Islam makes the claim that it does not represent untruth. But the truth it is striving for is a truth that is mediated historically. Reference to one's own historical position—that is, the knowledge of one's own historical contingency, or historicity—opens up a space for dignifying others, a space for tolerance, a space of humility.[72] Those who see themselves as situated in a gradual process of understanding are in principle conceding that someone else can reach a different understanding. Although Islam has no magisterium, that is, no highest religious authority (at least in Sunni Islam, to which most Muslims belong), the principle of plausibility has come to be accepted for the theological self-assurance of one's positions. The principle of plausibility means that all religious views must prove themselves before the judgments of reason and revelation. The general attitude that all religious knowledge is fundamentally plural knowledge guarantees that there can be neither complete arbitrariness of religious views nor a relativism that anyone can say what they like. But any talk of truth remains empty if it is not situated in life.

Truth Proved in Life and in Striving for Good

Truth in life is situated in integrity. Truth, however, reveals itself in action; it must prove applicable to practical life. Only to the extent that it does so can truth lay claim to authenticity: "If God had so willed, He would have made you one community, but He wanted to test you through that which He has given you, so race to do good" (Qur'an 5:48). Truth, Islam teaches us, is

---

72. See Qur'an 109.

revealed in authentic service for humankind, in preserving the environment, and in engagement for peace. It is not a matter of religious zeal but of tireless work for good, so that the lasting inner relation to other religions is understood as a relationship in striving for the good. This deeply religious stance always views encounter with others first of all as spiritually enriching. For true encounter is gratitude. Being able to see oneself through the eyes of another, becoming conscious of oneself in the face of another—these are spiritually fulfilling.

Tolerance: Enriching Encounters and Grappling for Truth

If tolerance meant merely toleration, a kind of indifferent forbearance in the face of error, it would be nothing other than contempt—and we would need to overcome tolerance, or at least the idea with which this conception associates the term. Because today more than ever, the challenge consists in living not side by side, but together. To achieve peaceful togetherness, we must recognize: those who believe do not have possession of the truth. Rather, the truth has possession of us. No devout Muslim would therefore claim to represent the sole truth, given that—as the Qur'an sternly admonishes—the essence of devoutness is humility rather than pious desire for status.[73] Fundamentally, the question of truth cannot be conclusively answered. The truth is God—and only God. But neither do we have possession of God nor can we lay any claim to him for ourselves.

In the face of this truth, life is lived in diversity. The diversity of life, the diversity of religious views is a constituent part of Islam's polyphonic nature. The result is by no means an indifferent relativism between religions, but their inner relationality: life is meant to occur in the striving for truth, so that Muslims approach other religious people and grapple and argue over this truth together with them. Such a culture of discussion does not indicate violent disagreement, but a rational and above all beautiful argument: "Argue only in the best way with the

---

73. See Qur'an 2:177.

People of the Book" (Qur'an 29:46). What is demanded of Islam, then, is tolerance in the sense of such a joint argument over truth that belongs to no one exclusively. The goal of this argument is to get to know one another, come to understand the other, and to learn together. Togetherness can succeed only if we accord one another respect and mutual dignity, so that abhorrent phenomena such as antisemitism rule themselves out absolutely. Being a Muslim is not a question of labels, but of constant, never-ending self-examination and doubt, a question of learning and gratitude, founded in striving for truth.

Mission or Testimony?

I. The Christian Call to Mission

Anselm Grün

Jesus' Mission: Testimony of Lived Faith

Jesus tells his disciples to go to all the nations of the earth and make them his disciples, "teaching them to obey everything that I have commanded you" (Mt 28:20). Often enough, this mission from Jesus has been misunderstood by the Church, as if the Church were meant to use violence in order to make people the disciples of Jesus. Often, the mission was also linked to the opinion that only those who have undergone Christian baptism would be saved. Today, the Church understands this command of Jesus to mean that his message applies to all people. The Church has a responsibility for all people. It stands in service to Jesus and, following his command, is supposed to spread his good news to all people and testify to it everywhere in the world. But its method is the word alone. We Christians are convinced that Jesus' message is one of loving kindness, one that helps people recognize God in his love and goodness and live a faith that is healing to humankind. People must have the opportunity to experience the word through testimony of lived faith, of lived love and mercy.

Baptizing "All Nations"?

In the nineteenth century, all Christian churches followed a narrow interpretation of Jesus' mission: only those people who are baptized have a chance of entering heaven. Consequently, Christian missionaries tried to baptize as many people as possible. In the process, they often attempted to extinguish the peoples' religious traditions, replacing them with Christian culture. Early Christianity followed a very different practice. It adopted the religious traditions of the Greeks, the Romans, and the Germanic and Celtic tribes, reinterpreting these traditions in a Christian light, giving them a kind of Christian baptism. In the religious practices of the "heathens," the early Church saw an earnest longing for God and viewed the Christian message as the fulfillment of these pagan longings. The early Church, then, understood "baptizing all nations" to mean opening the religious traditions of all people toward Christ and his message. And by "all nations," Jesus means not only pagans, but the entire world, which is to say Jews as well.

Mission Today

Today's understanding of mission no longer has the ambition of baptizing all people and converting them to Christianity. Rather, the mission today consists in going to all the nations and offering all people the Christian message as the path that Jesus has taught us. The path of Jesus leads us to God as the father of Jesus Christ, to the merciful and kind God who wants salvation for all people. And the path of Jesus leads us to be human well. It is a path of love and of forgiveness. The Church is convinced that this path of love and reconciliation is especially necessary for our world today, so that we may live in peace in the globalized world. The word must therefore always be linked with the spirit of reconciliation that proves itself in the fruitful togetherness of the various religions and cultures.

Mission today also includes dialogue with other religions. We listen to the answers that other religions give to the three fundamental questions of human existence: Where do I come from? Where am I going? What do I hope for? In such a dialogue, we do not intermix all religions. We respect other religions, but we nevertheless offer people of other religions the Christian message because we are convinced that Jesus spoke of God authentically, and that his love even unto the cross shows us a way to overcome the hate and animosity in the world. In that sense, for us Christians, Jesus is the way, the truth, and the life (see Jn 14:6).

A Global Ethic and the Path of Love

Jesus' mission includes the injunction to teach others "to obey everything that I have commanded you" (Mt 28:20). The crucial commandment of Jesus to his disciples is to love. This means that Jesus' mission is to teach all humankind in the "art of love." The commandment to love is also at the center of many other religions' teachings. Therefore, the Foundation for a Global Ethic, for example, does indeed correspond to Jesus' intent. Religions come close to one another in the kinds of acts they command. They all are concerned with justice, peace, reconciliation, and love. Though its justifications may be different, that love is the same. Therefore, religions today have the shared task of testifying to that love in the world.

What Religious Liberty Means

Today's understanding of mission is also shaped by the idea of freedom of religion. Religions offer people their message—but people should be free to decide which offer they accept. We Christians therefore have difficulty with Muslims' persecution of Muslims who have converted to Christianity. The religion I follow is a matter of my own conscience. Of course, we should be careful not to use force in mission. But part of a living faith is testifying to our faith. And as Christians, we firmly believe that Jesus' message is good news, is "Gospel" for all people. We trust that Jesus' message is a liberating message for the people of our own time too, as well as for people of all religions and cultures. We must therefore fulfill Jesus' mission to proclaim this Gospel among all nations of the world.

2. A Joint Mission

Ahmed Milad Karimi

An Invitation to Devotion to God

In the history of Islamic thought, the phenomenon of *da'wa* (invitation) might be viewed as the counterpart to the Christian idea of mission. But *da'wa* does not play the same central role in Islam as mission does in Christianity. On closer inspection, seeing the two as equivalents would actually be misleading, for invitation does not mean conversion to Islam. Rather, the invitation is to faith in the one and only God and to justice.

At the same time, the Qur'an does posit that all people are naturally oriented toward God (Qur'an 30:30). This *fiṭra*, a person's natural inclination towards living in devotion of God, is seen as a kind of universal anthropological constant. The invitation (*da'wa*) to faith in the one God is thus revealed as the "disclosing" of human devotion to God (*fiṭra*). The invitation can therefore be understood as a kind of reminder. For in the Islamic view, those who forget God will end up having forgotten themselves. Muslims can make this invitation their own to varying degrees according to their knowledge (see Qur'an 41:33 and 3:110), but it is primarily one of the fundamental tasks of the Prophet Muhammad (Qur'an 16:125).

Conversion of "Infidels" to the "True Faith"?

Admittedly, throughout the twentieth century and even in recent years, there have been an increasing number of groups misinterpreting—and thus undermining—the intention of *da'wa* as an explicit conversion of "infidels" to the "true faith" of Islam. Since 1911, a *da'wa* movement has arisen first under the reform theologian Rashīd Riḍā (d. 1935 CE) and later and more strongly through the Muslim Brotherhood under the leadership of Ḥasan al-Bannā (d. 1949 CE) in Egypt and instigated by his screed *Da'watu-nā* ("Our *da'wa*"). This movement seeks to advance the spread of Islam in an organized way.

That idea led to the founding of the Muslim World League in 1962, essentially a politico-ideological organization of the Saudi state seeking to promulgate the Wahhabi reading of Islam. There are two misunderstandings in these ideological movements: In the first place, they define the right guidance of human beings as a matter for human beings. And secondly they misunderstand Islam as the exclusive arbiter of truth. The delusional notion that Islam's ideal is the Islamization of all people fails to recognize the fruit of difference that is desired by God and protected by God. On this topic the Qur'an reads: "You [Prophet] cannot guide everyone you love to the truth; it is God who guides whoever He will: He knows best those who will follow guidance " (Qur'an 28:56).

In this respect, there is a clear distinction in Islamic history. For example, the promulgation (*tablīgh*) of Islam is given solely to the Prophet (see Qur'an 5:67, 5:99, 7:62). And even this promulgation is not actually what leads a person to faith, but should be understood only as the transmission of the message of God. That means that missionizing in Islam is neither a duty nor even recommended by the Qur'an.

Encounter as an Opportunity for Learning

To us Muslims—that is, in the collective memory of Muslims— the phenomenon of mission has a negative ring due to its Christian context. That may be because missionizing occurred not infrequently in a context of colonization. Or it might be due to the history of missionizing itself and to the behavior of missionaries, which has left many scars and a great deal of incomprehension in its wake. But it may also be due to our outside perspective, with the true meaning of mission not being adequately expressed. For mission is always also linked with questions about respect and tolerance for the people who are being missionized, for their culture and religious origins. Even if the missionaries' intentions are love and goodness and the act of missionizing occurs not with violence but only with the word, the question remains: in missionizing, can any encounter with the other person truly be on an equal footing?

The attitude behind mission seems dubious because in missionizing, I am setting myself patronizingly above the person I seek to missionize. Not to missionize, meanwhile, need not mean that I water down my own position or am not sufficiently rooted in my faith. The question, then, is whether missionizing does not in and of itself make true encounter impossible. Such encounters remain something we urgently need. In this question, Islam's stance is decisive: we are learners. In the defining words attributed to the famous Muslim theologian Abū Ḥanīfa (d. 767 CE): "From the cradle to the grave, I remain a learner."

Conversion and Apostasy

Given this context, we can say that a conversion to Islam is possible and meaningful only if it is freely and autonomously chosen. In the case of apostasy—the judgment of those who fall from Islam—the situation is more complex. Throughout the history of Islam, there have been traditions, which still persist in some countries such as Pakistan today, that punish apostasy harshly, sometimes even by death. But this tradition is not convincing because it understands faith as a mechanism of force. How can faith be a freely chosen matter of the heart (a position attested by all schools of Muslim thought) if it is also forced? There can be no worldly sanctions for apostasy because, and to the extent that, apostasy concerns a person's bond with God. And we can neither control nor judge this connection, or else faith would be subject to force and thereby deprived of its own substance. For the Qur'an states: "There is no compulsion in religion" (Qur'an 2:256).

Taking a Stand Together for the Good

But does lived faith not include testifying to one's faith? And should not every person have the opportunity to live their life with God? From an Islamic perspective, the answer to these questions is certainly Yes, since Islam sees itself as God's universal devotion to all people. But the Qur'an also reminds us that it is not we human beings who lead other human beings or even ourselves to faith. Rather, it is God himself who captures people's hearts. As such, Islam sees the act of faith as an act of freedom (see Qur'an 2:256). If we Muslims want to testify to our living faith and thus understand Islam as an offer to all people, then this offer must be inherent in the effect of our actions. Standing up for more justice and more peace, for love and mercy, for people in difficulty—these things should testify to Islam, nothing else. The Qur'an explains: "If God had so willed, He would have made you one community, but He wanted to test you through that which He has given you, so race to do good" (Qur'an 5:48). We testify to Islam by living our lives in service of the good. Faith does not oblige us to lead others to faith. It obliges us to work toward the good. At its core, encountering God's creation and his creatures with respect means recognizing others in their otherness, and moreover: seeking a path toward others in order to work toward the good together. One could therefore say that mission in an Islamic understanding means mission toward a shared mission.

What Ought We to Do? Law and Ethics

I. Religion, Ethics, and Law from a Muslim Perspective

Ahmad Milad Karimi

Deeds as Measure of Faith

From the very beginning of the qur'anic revelation, the question of what we ought to do is closely linked to faith. Human deeds are the measure of faith, and in this context the Qur'an is understood as the means of distinction (Arabic: *al-furqān*).[74] However, the Qur'an is concerned not merely with a theoretical distinction between true and false, but also with the practical distinction between good and bad. As revelation, it seeks to be not only insight and realization, enlightenment and knowledge, but also right guidance. A conscious and considered faith therefore must include ethics as a reflection on fundamental questions of human deeds, their implementation in social custom, and their moral foundations. As ethical beings we humans are duty-bound. Nothing we do or fail to do is meaningless. Quite the contrary: it is not just our actions, but also our intentions that define us human beings. This existence as an ethical being is seen not as a burden but as an honor. That is why the Qur'an states programmatically: "We have honoured the children of Adam and carried them by land and sea; We have provided good sustenance for them and favoured them specially above many of those We have created." (Qur'an 17:70). The responsibility inherent in being human is emphasized in the Qur'an by the fact that God entrusts his creation to humankind as stewards (Arabic: *khalīfa*) in his place. At this, as the Qur'an records, the angels doubtfully remark: "How can You put someone there

---

74. See Qur'an 25:1–3.

who will cause damage and bloodshed, when we celebrate Your praise and proclaim Your holiness?" But God can see in human beings the dignity he has given them, and therefore replies: "I know things you do not" (Qur'an 2:30).

Islamic Conceptions of Ethics and Law

Since the eighth century, Muslim philosophers (al-Fārābī, Ibn Miskawayh), theologians, (al-Māturīdī, al-Ghazālī), jurists (Abū Ḥanīfa, ash-Shāfi'ī), and mystics (Junayd, Anṣārī) have all been concerned with developing an ethics, in the sense of a well-reasoned, internally consistent doctrine of morality. This tradition has left behind numerous works attesting to the diversity of ethical positions in Islam. Just as in Christianity, these scholars were trying to found a theological ethics that is bound to qur'anic principles and the prophetic tradition while still holding up to the "judgment of reason." In that sense, there is nothing unusual in Islam's distinction between a philosophical ethics seeking universally valid norms for action on the one hand and a theological ethics grounding its principles in its own religion on the other. Seen in this context, Islamic jurisprudence has developed not into a legalistic construct concerned with punishment—as outside perspectives often assume—but into an ethical one in which the plausibility of thoughts is always first and foremost.

Jurisprudence describes human beings' responsibilities toward God as well as an individual human being's rights and duties with regard to the community. The term *sharia* plays a crucial role in this context. It can have several meanings, describing the various forms of divine commands that apply differently in different societies, or the juridical systems ordering individual and communal life, or the different interpretations of religious principles as formulated according to their historical contexts.

Misinterpretations and Misunderstandings of Sharia

Admittedly, the term *sharia* is among the most misunderstood and misinterpreted concepts in all of Islam. In the face of the Islamic State's reign of terror and the inhumane practices of countries like Saudi Arabia, all of which speak of *sharia*, it seems understandable that so many would imagine *sharia* to mean draconian and repressive punishments. But this implementation is based on a perverted notion of *sharia* and cannot be justified by tradition. The fact alone that Islam supported multiple different schools of legal thought that respected and honored one another indicates a completely different practice and interpretation of *sharia*. Based on its own methodology and epistemology, each of these schools developed an understanding of *sharia* that competes with the understandings of other schools, based in turn on their methods and epistemologies. To put it archly: it is a matter of argumentative competition between rival interpretations, all of which coexist and constantly strive to refine their arguments. This process of interpretation remains unfinished by its nature. However, the validity of the ideas, concepts, laws, prohibitions, recommendations, maxims for action, etc., always depends on the persuasiveness of the arguments. They are therefore not to be seen as divine or otherwise immutable laws, but only ever as instances of understanding *sharia* in a particular way. Even a legal ruling (Arabic: *fatwa*) that a religious jurist (Arabic: *mufti*) formulates in answer to a very specific question cannot be simply or universally applied: it is dependent on historical context, on the circumstances and reasons for the consultation of the *mufti*, etc.

Right Guidance in Life, Not Rival Legal System

Sharia is not a legal text—in fact, it does not exist anywhere as a codified book. Instead, there are various and differing results of human efforts to understand *sharia*. This human reading (Arabic: *fiqh*) of *sharia* can never have any single, completely clear meaning. It is always plural, i.e., essentially related to human beings' contingent understanding. Islamic ethics and Islamic law, even in the narrow sense, therefore do not see themselves as rivals to a religiously neutral secular state or legal system. The talk of "instituting *sharia* law" is also highly misleading because Islamic jurisprudence does not constitute a system of administrative or regional law. The core project of *sharia* is not the strict ordering of Islamic life through a system of laws, but first and foremost the development of an ethical blueprint. This blueprint is based not in laws, but in signs of divine wisdom, which Muslims see predominantly in the Qur'an and the tradition surrounding the Prophet Muhammad. This also fundamentally determines Muhammad's position within Islam as an ethical one. The Prophet himself is said to have avowed: "I have been sent to fulfill your morality." Nevertheless, the normative nature of the Prophet should not be seen as universal applicable, and there is actually a separate discussion within the Islamic tradition about to what extent or even whether the Prophet and records of his actions have any normative force. This discussion distinguishes, for example, between his religious and worldly nature, between Muhammad as prophetic authority and as fallible human being. Emulating the Prophet as a role model does not mean rigidly interpreting all his actions and instructions as the blueprint for a religion defined by law. Instead, this emulation means right guidance for life, or more precisely: Islam obliges Muslims to be just, to recognize the fundamental equality of all human beings, and to open themselves to the good. This, however, can occur only if we also open ourselves up to distinguishing and precisely perceiving what is not good.

Criticism of Strict Interpretations

At the same time, it cannot and must not be denied that *sharia* is frequently associated with a strictness in Islam. It is beyond any doubt that people do commit violence and use "*sharia* law" as their justification. But *sharia* itself is not an acting subject. It is always people who—through their interpretation of *sharia* and thus of the entire religion—reach one or another conclusion and praxis. Even in a traditionalist understanding of Islam, however, the attitude of setting one's own interpretation of *sharia* as *sharia* itself is untenable. Moreover, such an attitude shows a callous disregard for human dignity, since its narrow imposition of religious normativity denigrates interpretations of Islam that are practiced by the majority of Muslims. On closer inspection, it is easy to see that the groups propagating such a distorted reading of *sharia* not only brook no interpretation other than their own, but also turn their back on the traditional Islamic principle of consensual scholarship in general. This break with tradition—from a religious point of view—violates and betrays everything. And there is another important point: ideas of morality that predominate in societies largely populated by Muslims need not automatically therefore be religious ideas. One typical example is a particular notion of honor, which has an ethno-cultural basis rather than an Islamic religious one.

Religious Norms: Translating Law into Contemporary Ethics

Since the eleventh century, the Islamic tradition has debated whether it would not be appropriate to develop a basic outlook, virtues, and fundamental goals of *sharia* that might establish a framework for moral action and provide a firmer footing for law and ethics. What deserves fundamental protection? The question has yielded five elements that should be protected: religion (Arabic: *dīn*), the intellect (Arabic: *'aql*), human life (Arabic: *nafs*), progeny (Arabic: *nasl*), and property (Arabic: *māl*). This idea, too, will need to stand up to the challenges of the present and perhaps be reformed, expanded, or redefined. Scholars recognize these principles as universal and attempt to see them as applicable to all human beings. It is especially this flexibility in dealing with our understanding of *sharia* that translates law into a contemporary ethics. So far from watering down religious norms, this process fills them with life in the first place. Conscience, personal and interpersonal morality, the purity of the heart, one's inner attitude, and education all play a central role in this context. Especially in Islamic mysticism, these aspects are therefore deeply appreciated and discussed, showing clearly that mysticism in Islam is not a peripheral phenomenon but constitutes an essential part of a successful religious life. For it is precisely in mysticism that collective norms are translated into a subtle individual morality, reflected upon, and embedded in daily practice. Pure intention (Arabic: *nīya*), sincerity (Arabic: *ikhlāṣ*), and perseverance (Arabic: *ṣabr*) are only a few examples. For instance, a saying attributed to the Prophet Muhammad instructs: "Ask your heart for a legal ruling, even if the jurists have already given one!"

The Islamic scholarly tradition teaches us that the question of what we should do can never be given a final, definitive answer. Rather, a religious person is constantly faced with the task of acting on their responsibility as a being released into freedom in the face of the all-merciful and just God. This task should be undertaken in humility and with care by understanding the path of life as a path to the source (which is the literal translation of the Arabic word *sharī'a*). No religious person possesses this source; we have no control over it, but we live in longing for it.

2. Ethics and the Spiritual Path from a Christian Perspective

Anselm Grün

Precepts on the Path to a Successful Life

The first question to which the Bible gives us an answer is: "Who am I?" First and foremost, a spiritual path is about our being. We are the daughters and sons of God, invested with a divine dignity. But the second question is just as important: "What should I do?" These two questions—who we are and what we should do—are central to human nature and thus also to Christians. The Bible is full of instructions for what to do. Asked by a rich young man how to find eternal life, Jesus answers: "If you wish to enter into life, keep the commandments" (Mt 19:17). By this, he means the Ten Commandments of the Old Testament. The Israelites understood these not as strict laws, but as precepts from God. And the Israelites praised the wisdom of God for having given them such wise precepts. The commandments show us paths to inner freedom and to living with others successfully.

Congruity of Thinking and Doing

On the other hand, Jesus does criticize the Pharisees, who often interpreted the commandments of the Old Testament rigorously and pedantically. Some Pharisees thought that simply obeying the commandments to the letter would make someone a good person. Jesus called on people to attend to their disposition instead. Those focused on rituals of cleanliness, he tells: "There is nothing outside a person that by going in can defile, but the things that come out are what defile" (Mk 7:15). One is therefore supposed to cleanse the heart of all tarnish. Once that has been done, ritual duty can also be observed, and the cups can be cleaned. Jesus does not lighten the commandments of the Old Testament, but he does internalize and radicalize them. That said, he does so not as a moralist trying to instill fear, but in an attempt to challenge us not to be satisfied with outwardly correct behaviors. Everything we do outwardly we should do with a pure heart. Our doing and our thinking should be consistent with one another.

Of the four Gospels, those of Matthew and Luke could be called the "ethical Gospels." The Gospel of Matthew is always also concerned with what Christians do. To Matthew, the goal of Christian behavior is the reconciliation of humankind. The rift that is torn into human society is to be healed by the love of Christians. Luke, on the other hand, has a different ethical emphasis. He is concerned above all with the sharing of goods, with how to deal rightly with the things of this world, with money and possessions. The core of his ethical message is: people should show solidarity with one another and share their possessions.

The Foundations of Ethics

Christian ethics is concerned not only with the distinction between good and evil, between just and unjust, but also with how the experience of human freedom on the one hand and responsibility toward God on the other go together in good deeds. In the Christian tradition, ethics as a guiding answer to these questions has never been developed out of Scripture alone, but always in dialogue with philosophy. In the Middle Ages, Thomas Aquinas provided a Christian interpretation of the four virtues that—independently of religion— Plato developed on the basis of human nature. Thomas Aquinas also adopted a Christian reading of Aristotle's *Nicomachean Ethics*, a guidebook in which the great philosopher of antiquity shows how one can become a good person by doing right and thus live a life according to *eudaimonia* (happiness as the highest good). Of course, Aquinas's ethics also presuppose biblical foundations: first, humanity's creation in the image of God, and then the instructions of Jesus and the ethical demands formulated in the Epistles of the New Testament. In these Epistles we find catalogs of virtues and vices. These are taken largely from Stoic philosophy, revealing that even within the Bible, ethics are founded with the aid of philosophical principles.

No "Moral Improvement Clinics"

Throughout ecclesiastical history, the first task of the churches was to lead people to a religious and spiritual experience of God. In the time of the Enlightenment, there was no sympathy for purely religious matters, much less for mysticism. As a result, according to one Church historian, the churches were reduced to something like moral improvement clinics. Morals, rather than religious experience, became the central message of Christianity. This roused resistance in many people, and particularly today, many people fight this idea. They feel that Christian morality comes from an earlier time, and that the Church, in its moralizing, is constantly seeking to impart a feeling of guilt.

Today, therefore, our task must be on the one hand to emphasize the spiritual dimension of the Christian message, but on the other not to neglect the ethical side of faith. Ethics as the discipline of doing right can never be set in stone once and for all. That is also the reason why in the Catholic tradition there are no ethical dogmas: dogmas refer solely to the salvation of humankind, to God's acts toward humankind. Ethics, on the other hand, must always also consider the specific circumstances.

Conscience as a Norm

The Catholic Church is often accused of paying too much attention to external norms—like the Pharisees in the Gospel. And indeed, some bishops do preach as if the external norms were set in stone. But since Thomas Aquinas, theology has emphasized that the highest norm a person must obey is one's own conscience. Of course, a conscience must be shaped, and it should grapple earnestly with existing norms—but the highest norm always remains the decision of conscience. Often, this decision is one I can no longer account for in words. It is formed from the innermost being of a person, and from the intensely personal relationship with God. An examination of my conscience means that in prayer, I am asking what God wants from me in the end. After all, there are norms that contradict one another, such as the norm not to kill and the commandment to protect others from heinous crimes. This, for example, was the dilemma faced by the German Protestant theologian Dietrich Bonhoeffer during the Second World War. His conscience told him that he should join the resistance, even at the risk of participating in the murder of Hitler. The decision of his conscience was not condoned by all theologians within his Church. A decision of conscience always also leads into loneliness: I am alone before God, to whom I must justify my decisions.

Cooperation of the Faiths: Tackling Problems Together

And so one of the tasks of the Church today is to confront, from the perspective of theological ethics, the problems brought on by the development of science, for example in controversial areas within the fields of human and animal medicine, biotechnology, or information technology. It is the task of ethics to develop ethical foundations for scientific action. For science itself researches without any regard for the ethical questions. But when there are no ethical yardsticks, such research can be to the detriment of humanity.

All religions can cooperate in questions of ethics and with a view to finding specific solutions for existing problems. Even if there may be differing views and sometimes differing terminology, there is nevertheless significant overlap in the ethical demands and formulations of fundamental values: protection and respect for human dignity and enabling a peaceful coexistence in reconciliation. Plato's four fundamental values—prudence, justice, courage, and temperance—are ones all religions would likely adopt. In his *Project for a Global Ethic*, Hans Küng has described the task thus: advancing a joint ethics of humaneness that—supported by all religions—knows itself indebted to the thought of reciprocity (the "Golden Rule"; see Mt 7:12, Lk 6:31, Rom 13:9; Gal 5:14 in the New Testament and Lv 19:18 in the Old Testament) but is also characterized by the idea of nonviolence, by the striving for sincerity and justice as well as partnership of man and woman.[75] In the interest of peace among all humankind, it is surely a worthwhile task that especially on questions of ethical yardsticks and norms religions should communicate, exchange views on joint actions and deeds in the world, and find common solutions.

---

75. See Hans Küng, *A Global Ethic for Global Politics and Economics* (Oxford: Oxford University Press, 1998).

The Individual and the Community

I. The Individual and the Community from a Christian Perspective

Anselm Grün

Following Jesus Individually and Communally

Jesus called each of us to follow him. According to the Christian view, the important thing is for every individual human being to follow the inner call with which God speaks to each of us. We are meant to realize individually the unique image of each of us that God has made of every individual. But Jesus also appoints twelve disciples. These twelve disciples are reminiscent of the twelve tribes of Israel. Jesus is trying to found a new people of God. A rift has come between the twelve tribes of Israel, and Jesus wants to gather the twelve tribes back into one community. In the early Church, the experience of communion of the faithful was seen as a sign that God's kingdom had already come. Luke describes this community of early Christians in very idealistic terms: "All who believed were together and had all things in common" (Acts 2:44). And elsewhere he writes: "Now the whole group of those who believed were of one heart and soul" (Acts 4:32). Evidently, to the early Christians it was a fascinating experience that Jews and Greeks, men and women, the poor and the rich, and people from all tribes could form a community that praised God together and shared goods with one another. The Apostle Paul also described this new form of Christian experience in his Epistle to the Galatians: because all were baptized in Christ, all were one, all were brothers and sisters of Jesus. "There is no longer Jew or Greek, there is no longer slave or free, there is no longer male and female; for all of you are one in Christ Jesus" (Gal 3:28).

The Church as Community of Jesus

The Church Fathers of the early centuries used many metaphors to describes the mystery of Church as the community of Jesus: The Church is the body of Christ, held together by the spirit of Jesus, with all faithful as limbs of this body. The Church is the mother of the faithful, since all faithful are born anew in the Church through baptism. Yet another image is that of the wandering people of God, as evoked in the Epistle to the Hebrews. All are journeying towards God together. Jesus accompanies them on this path. Jesus is the "pioneer and perfecter of our faith" (Heb 12:2). The Greek word *archegos* ("pioneer") used here means that Jesus walks ahead. We are meant to look to him. That will enable us to better withstand the hardships and afflictions of life.

As the wandering people of God, we are connected with all seekers. We are on a road with all people who seek God. The Church sees itself as a "traveling companionship of hope," in the phrase attributed to the German Jesuit theologian Medard Kehl. Metaphorically, the Church wanders together with all people and, in the midst of the globalized world and its rapid mobility and multifarious modes of communication as well as newly burgeoning conflicts, wants to be a place of hope: a place of hope for reconciliation and peace with all people. The Church, therefore, cannot have the divisive task of distinguishing between the faithful and non-faithful, between Christians and non-Christians. It has the task of representing, standing in for all people, for united humanity.

The Church Fathers did not particularly conceive of a constituted Church, nor of a Church hierarchically structured by an order of offices. Instead, they conceived of a community of the faithful. And so they create ever new imagery for the Church. To them, the Church is God's fruitful vineyard. It is the city of God, in which all the world's people gather together. It is the ship that navigates us safely through the storms of life. For the Church Fathers, the experience of the Church was always also the experience of salvation: *extra ecclesiam nulla salus*, or "no salvation outside the Church," as Cyprian of Carthage and others have said. This sentence must therefore be understood not as a statement of exclusion but as a positive assent that we need precisely this community to experience the salvation that faith promises us. By having faith together and gathering together for prayer and the Eucharist, we find that God resolves all our differences and connects us deep within us.

Separation from Organized Churches

Today, many Christians have separated from the organized churches. Among other reasons, one lingering cause of this turning away is the split of the Church into different denominations, as well as the fact that these denominations once fought bitter battles. Today, the efforts at dialogue between Christian denominations have the goal of a visible union that does justice to the biblically attested prayer of Jesus Christ: "I ask not only on behalf of these, but also on behalf of those who will believe in me through their word, that they may all be one. As you, Father, are in me and I am in you, may they also be in us, so that the world may believe that you have sent me" (Jn 17:20–21).

Although in many respects Christian denominations today practice reconciliation and coexistence, the experience of past schisms is still with us as a thorn meant to spur us Christians on to keep striving for unity. The goal, however, is not to make everyone the same, but rather to find unity in difference. A further reason why Christians are turning away from the Church is their disappointment in office holders, in priests and bishops, and in Church administration, which is becoming ever more bureaucratic.

Community in the Age of Individualism

In the age of individualism it is not easy to form a community that can withstand the differences of its members and still hold services together in spite of all disagreements. But people today, who feel more and more lonely, are also experiencing a growing longing for a more deeply founded connection and communion in faith. Many people can sense that we need the communion of the faithful. It supports us even when our faith is in danger or when, for a moment, we cannot feel a connection with God. That is why today we need—among other things—the concrete experience of prayer groups, joint services, a lively congregation, and the inner connection between all Christians in order to adequately answer present-day humanity's fear of isolation and loneliness.

Traveling Companionship with All People

The community of the Church as Jesus pictures it is not a community that casts out its members when they have transgressed the community's norms. Instead, it is a merciful group that takes in people who are in despair over themselves (see Lk 16:1–8). And the Church, as wandering people of God, is open to all who seek God, for all people of other religions who see God as the purpose of their life. "Ecumenicalism," which in its literal meaning refers to the "entire inhabited world" and thus to a universal and general dialogue, today no longer aims merely at the community of Christians, but has its eye on a "large" or Abrahamitic ecumenicalism, with dialogue between Judaism, Christianity, and Islam. Together, we are on a path to God, who is beyond all images we might make of God. And together with the faithful of all religions, we should work to create a humane, peaceful world. By acting together, we can sense the traveling companionship we form with all the people of this world.

2. The Individual and the Community as Understood by Islam

Ahmad Milad Karimi

The Individual: Immediate Relationship to God

It is the Muslim conviction that each individual human being, with all his or her definitive characteristics, is created, loved, wanted, and supported by God. God leads each individual to his or her own truth, and on the day of resurrection we all come before him individually. Justice and mercy are given to each individually. There is no mediating entity between the individual and God—neither sacraments necessary for salvation, nor a priestly caste. Rather, the individual human being relates immediately to God. Islam sees itself as a revealed religion in the sense that relation to God is opened up to each individual human being through the revelation given to the Prophet Muhammad. But each person's opening to God's reality is individual. One's relationship to God is thus immediate, not hierarchically mediated, because in our very existence we are inalienably single and unique. The nature of each person's own singularity is based in his or her individual action towards God. All of human life—and that includes death and all its eschatological implication—is irreplaceably rooted in the individual.

The Concept and Central Significance of Community (Umma)

At the same time, community has a central significance in Islam. From his earliest days as prophet, Muhammad values highly the power of community. This emphasis on community is understood in a two-fold sense: on the one hand, it is the community of the faithful, termed *umma* in Arabic; on the other, the inter-religious community of the Abrahamitic traditions. And finally, the community of all people, indeed all living beings, is in view as well. Over the course of Islamic history, there have been many changes of meaning in the term *umma*. For example, the first document that the Prophet Muhammad drew up after his arrival in Medina, a kind of charter of the community, includes the Jewish congregations among the *umma*. Even if the *umma* is understood solely as the community of the faithful—which is assumed in the majority of cases—the term should first of all be understood as a counterpoint to those worldviews that place people in, or perhaps under, categories of tribe, ethnicity, gender, etc. The idea of an *umma* is therefore meant to counteract the Ancient Arabic tradition, which sorted people by caste. And so a deep part of Muslims' collective memory in this context is the story that after the conquest of Mecca, the Prophet specifically accorded Bilāl the honor of calling the prayers from the roof of the Kaaba for the first time. Bilāl was a slave and a Black servant, likely from eastern Africa. Although Bilāl had the most beautiful voice and excelled in character and faith, this preferential treatment was not well received by the others. The reaction in the Qur'an is as follows: "People, We created you all from a single man and a single woman, and made you into races and tribes so that you should recognize one another. In God's eyes, the most honoured of you are the ones most mindful of Him: God is all knowing, all aware" (Qur'an 49:13). In the community as *umma*, all Muslims are united by faith.

Organic Unity and Inner Diversity

This connection in faith takes the form of an organic unity that is internally diverse. The Prophet, for example, compares the *umma* to the organs of the human body: "Usually you find the faithful in their mercy, their affection, and their empathy together like the body: if one part of it suffers, the entire body reacts with sleeplessness and fever!"[76] The unity of Muslims should therefore not be understood as uniformity brooking no distinctions and differences. And the concept of Muslims' community does not undercut their plurality, the factually given diversity. Instead, it is precisely this multiplicity that it honors. From the very beginning, the Prophet Muhammad prophesied that the *umma* was not meant as a community that made all its members same and self-similar, but offered a framework within which intra-Islamic plurality could grow: "The diversity of my community [Arabic: *ummatī*] is a mercy," the Prophet is often quoted.

This community binds the faithful in various ways. In the first place, only in community can faith that is otherwise individually lived become shared. Second, it is a liturgical community when ritual prayers are performed in community. Third, it is a social community in which Muslims strive for equality and work towards justice, help one another, share their worries, and "are mirrors for one another," to quote another

---

76. Cited according to: Ḥadīth, al-Bukhārī, no. 71.6011.

saying attributed to the Prophet. To be part of the *umma*, one does not need to sign any worldly contract, pay any taxes, or work to achieve membership. The attitude of being one of the faithful is sufficient for being part of this community.

Intra-Islamic Differences and Violent Conflicts

The present situation of Muslims is all the more devastating. Not infrequently, diversity burgeons into conflict and bellicose confrontation. The distinction between Sunni and Shiite—at root a theological difference over the question of succession after the Prophet's death, a matter one can debate without losing mutual respect—has often been reinterpreted politically, and the resulting conflicts go far beyond mutual insult and mutual disdain. The growing foothold of a particular reading of Islam that categorically excludes any other reading is lethal to the idea of community. Defamation of those within one's own religion who think differently lets a lively community fall apart into a splintered heap. That runs counter to Islam's intentions. It is thus all the more important to recall the true meaning of community.

The plurality of lived worlds in which Muslims move (for example in the diaspora) is currently encouraging a reevaluation of the idea of community. Migration may strengthen Muslims' feeling of community, but this can also be deceptive if the *umma* comes once again to be felt as a closed society.

Why Community between Religions Is Necessary

However, developing an inter-religious community is one of Islam's goals. Among other things, this aim is based on the idea that no community can realize its ideals, values, virtues single-handed. Community lives from the insight that it is encounter, communication, and learning from one another that make us a "We" in the first place. The reason for the immense significance of an interreligious community in the present is precisely that beyond existing differences (which should by no means be erased), interreligious community tackles the question whether there are in fact shared ideas, values, and experiences that, firstly, are shared by all people and, secondly, can only be adequately realized by all people together. Religion's role in society, for example, is one such fundamental question that touches all religious groups equally. Accordingly, there should be a redefinition of the relationship between Islam and Christianity with respect to ecumenicalism between religions, so that we can tackle the challenges of our time together.

And finally, Muslims must not be concerned with Muslims alone. Expanding the concept of community to encompass all people has its roots in the Qur'an itself. The claim of the qur'anic revelation is a universal one: it is not concerned with preferential treatment for a particular nation, nor a particular people, nor either of the two sexes. In the spirit of God's universal devotion towards all people, the community of the faithful opens itself in interpersonal connection to all people as the community of God. That is why Islamic mysticism has as one of its fundamental lessons that behind all the masks we wear in life, we must open our eyes to the human being. Muhammad Iqbal writes in his *Message from the East*:

> From clay and water thou art not yet free,
> Thou sayest thou art Afghan, Turkoman:
> First I am man, and have no other hue,
> Thereafter Indian, Turanian.[77]

At its core, the fear of all religious groupings hesitant to speak of a large human community is that such opening puts them at risk of losing their own identity, the specialness of their particular message. But in truth, the question is whether that uniqueness might not consist in the conviction to be a community of humankind in the service of humanity.

---

77. Muhammad Iqbal, *A Message from The East*, trans. by Muhammad Hadi Hussain, Arthur John Arberry, and Mustansir Mir (Lahore: Iqbal Academy Pakistan, 2014), 80. Accessed at: http://www.allamaiqbal.com/works/poetry/persian/payam/translation/02message.pdf

Men and Women: The Relationship between the Sexes

I. The Relationship between the Sexes from a Christian Perspective

Anselm Grün

The Equal Dignity of Men and Women

In assessing the relationship between man and woman in the history of Christianity, it is important to first point out that over the centuries the relationship between the sexes has always been viewed with ambivalence. It has also always been characterized by power dynamics. In patriarchal societies, whose fundamental values, norms, and behaviors are defined by men, male dominance goes hand in hand with the oppression of women and is often linked with their denigration. This denigration often grows out of man's fear of woman. However, the battle of the sexes, which has existed throughout all time, is independent of any one religion. It pervades all cultures and religions.

Looking into the Bible, we find a point of view that—for example in the Song of Songs—judges sexuality positively, as a source of vitality and joy, but in other sections—such as the story of David—does not overlook the potentially destructive effects of sexual desire (2 Sm 11–12). However, we find in the Bible no rivalries between men and women, and neither general supremacy of men nor general denigration of women. The first account of the creation states:

> So God created humankind in his image
> in the image of God he created them;
> male and female he created them.
> God blessed them, and God said to them,
> "Be fruitful and multiply." (Gn 1:27–28)

Men and women thus share the same human dignity, and only together do they form the image of God. The duality of the sexes, then, is something positive. Neither man by himself nor woman by herself is fully in the image of God. Both stand in relation to one another and thus jointly make up the image of God.

The second account of the creation describes God forming Eve out of Adam's rib. This too does not mean woman is subordinate to man. Instead, it is a metaphor illustrating that man and woman are deeply in relation to one another. Man feels a deep connection to woman:

> This at last is bone of my bones
> and flesh of my flesh;
> ... Therefore a man leaves his father and his mother
> and clings to his wife,
> and they become one flesh. (Gn 2:23–24)

Man and woman belong together. They have within them a deep longing for one another. The philosopher Walter Schubart sees the sexual union of man and woman as "leaving loneliness to return into divine wholeness," opining that "when two people who love one another find each other, in one place in the cosmos, the wound of individualization heals."[78]

The Fall from Grace and the Temptation of Patriarchy

After showing how deeply man and woman are in relation to one another, the Bible tells us of the Fall from Grace. In Christianity, this story has often led woman to be seen as a sexual temptress of man—but the true meaning of the story is very different. It is not about sexuality at all, but about the human temptation to want to be like God. The serpent tempts the woman by leading her to believe that if the two eat from the tree of knowledge, their eyes will be opened and they will

---

78. Walter Schubart, *Religion und Eros* [Religion and eros] (Munich: C. H. Beck, 1941), 84. Translated from the German.

be like God (see Gn 3:5). At the center of the story is actually the cowardice of man, who likes to hide behind woman and blame her for his misdeeds. This mechanism of wanting women to take the blame for evil persists in people's mentality to the present day. It is the great temptation of the patriarchal.

The Dignity of Women in the Bible

Ancient Israel was, of course, a patriarchal society. Nevertheless, Israel too has known great women, such as the prophetess Deborah; Miriam, the sister of Moses; and Judith, who saves the people of Israel from great danger. In the New Testament, women are accorded a new dignity, as shown in the Gospels, where women are the first witnesses and messengers of Jesus' resurrection. In the Gospel of Luke, women's dignity is exemplified in Mary, who (unlike Zechariah, the father of John the Baptist) opens herself up to the message of the angel, thus becoming the mother of Jesus. Luke also describes women accompanying Jesus and how Mary, the sister of Martha, sits at his feet and listens to him. She is just as much a disciple as the male disciples are. In the early Christian Church, women were accorded a new significance. Some, such as Lydia, led Christian congregations. And they spoke prophetic words during services. But then, already in the pastoral Epistles of the later New Testament, a different tendency arose, relegating women to the background. Exegetes attribute this tendency to pass over women to Roman social conventions of the time, among other factors. The early Christian community did not want to be accused of being disorderly or proclaiming a religion of women.

Sexuality and Marriage

Accordingly, only men were allowed to lead congregations. And even though the Bible treats sexuality as a gift of God to humankind, Christian tradition has long evinced a deep distrust of sexuality. In the early Church, this was due to the influence of Augustine, who held a negative view of sexuality, and the influence of Stoic philosophy, which rejected ecstasy and sexual desire, instead seeing equanimity as the ideal in relationships between the sexes, as well.

Until the Second Vatican Council, moral teaching therefore confined sexuality to marriage alone, and marriage's primary purpose was seen in reproduction. Since the Second Vatican Council, a different, more biblically appropriate view has won out against that narrow and pessimistic idea of sexuality as merely a means to reproduction. Sexuality is now seen as an expression of love, and the partners' mutual love for one another as the actual essence and meaning of marriage. Sexuality as the expression of amorous pleasure between man and woman is more than just a drive. But in order for it to culminate in the love between man and woman, it requires a personalization of sexuality and a culture of love, so that sexuality does not fall prey to the danger of exploitation of one partner by the other, particularly the woman by the man. Sexuality means devotion to the other, letting go of one's own ego in order to become one with the other in a profound way. The Church cannot legislate sexual morality. It can only set up theological principles in a dialogue with today's gender research and psychology.

Especially in questions of moral theology, however, there are no fixed dogmas, but rather a development in dialogue with the respective time period. In Pope Francis's Synod on the Family, testimony from the faithful on subjects of marriage and sexuality showed how widely opinion and practice of today's Christians diverge from the sexual morality proclaimed by the Church over centuries. Accordingly, it is the task of theology to develop, in critical dialogue with the people, a more positive view of sexuality—a view that does not simply copy the spirit of the times, but nevertheless takes into account psychological insights.

The perception of marriage has also gone through various phases over the course of Christian history. In contrast to Jewish skepticism regarding marriage, Jesus optimistically proclaimed marriages as indissoluble and built for eternal union. Throughout Church history, however, Jesus' words were often distorted into juridical thinking. And Jesus' words on refraining from marriage for the sake of the Kingdom of Heaven led to marriage's being devalued. The Protestant Reformation led to a reevaluation of marriage not only in the newly Protestant but also in the Catholic Church. An independent spirituality of marriage was developed which today is being defended against the dissolutionary tendencies of secular society.

Challenges for the Church on the Question of the Sexes

So far, the Catholic Church ordains only men as its priests and bishops. Many women feel hurt by this, and it is certainly a topic that the Church needs to reexamine. Theologically, there are no valid arguments for excluding women from the priesthood. Theology is one thing—but obviously a historically developed tradition cannot be simply overcome. It is therefore not a question that can be solved from an armchair. It requires a historical and cultural process of transformation that is sure to take some time. At any rate, women play a central and decisive role in the history of Christianity, and there have always also been great women, particularly mystics such as Hildegard of Bingen, Gertrude the Great, Hadewijch, and Teresa of Avila. In the Middle Ages, there was also the model of the Beguines: women who banded together in forms of economic self-sufficiency and together walked a mystic path, worked, and advanced the education of women.

Within the Catholic Church, there is the rather paradoxical situation that while spirituality tends to be shaped by women and women make up the majority of church-goers, the hierarchy on the other hand is shaped by men. This is certainly a challenge for the future. Protestant churches have had women pastors for some time. But it is not merely a question of ordination to ecclesiastic office, nor is it merely a question of power. Rather, it is a more fundamental matter of mutual respect between men and women and engaging with one another in mature ways. A man who truly accepts himself as a man will also accept a woman as she is. In turn, a woman who is at one with herself will not find it necessary to constantly accuse men of oppression. She will have enough confidence in herself to let men be men. And she will know how to protect herself from the tendency of denigration that some men still exhibit today. The Swiss psychologist C. G. Jung believes that all people carry within them *anima* and *animus*, female and male parts of the human spirit. The person who integrates both in him- or herself will be able to engage maturely with the man and the woman beside him or her.

2. The Relationship between the Sexes in the Muslim Tradition

Ahmad Milad Karimi

Fighting Discrimination and its Causes

In assessing the view of men and women in Islam, too, it is important to state that in human history, women have been the disadvantaged sex in almost all cultures and civilizations. Their rights are limited, their role reduced to tasks defined for them by men. And to this day, the position of women in society and in the religious communities is problematic, albeit to differing degrees. The very fact that institutions which are not religiously affiliated employ or have to employ people whose job is to ensure diversity and equal treatment, particularly of women, shows the fundamental disparity. Throughout the history of Islam, too, worrying and ambivalent positions can be identified. Under the cover of Islam and in reference to religion, men have ruled over women and their rights and duties: not infrequently unjustly, not infrequently with violence, and mostly to the benefit of men. The impression of widespread discrimination against women in the Islamic world is not wrong.

But what is the cause of this plight? Is it merely the effect of a patriarchal culture that has nothing to do with the core of Islam? Those who make such a claim are letting themselves off too easily. Abhorrent patriarchal culture is undeniable and affects most areas of life. But the goal of Islam cannot be to stand by in the face of obvious injustice and discrimination—

much less to absolve the religion of these problems. Islam must concern itself with fighting these tendencies. To that extent, an adequate reassessment of the relationship between the sexes is also a theological challenge that has been begun but is far from exhaustively completed. And more importantly, the insights and results of this process must be adopted into individual and societal practice. On the other hand, it is far too simple to reduce the entire problem to Islam.

Positive Links with Tradition

It is predominantly, though not only, in mysticism that women in Islam play a significant role: Rābiʿa al-ʿAdawiyya (d. 801 CE) and Fatima of Nishapur (d. 849 CE) are only two examples. Their spirituality is said to have been profound, and they have shaped the spiritual path of Islam. In Arabic, the word "soul" (*nafs*) is a feminine word, and in their interpretations of this fact, Muslim mystics point out that this can be no coincidence. Happily, especially in the twentieth century more and more voices have arisen that take up this tradition and demand a reevaluation of the relationship between the sexes, even developing independent theological approaches for arguing the fundamental equality of women and men. Amina Wadud (b. 1952 CE), Hatoon al-Fassi (b. 1964 CE), Shirin Ebadi (b. 1947 CE), and Leila Ahmed (b. 1940 CE), to name only a few, are academically qualified feminists who show that, on close inspection, treating men and women differently actually has no reasonable basis in Islamic theology. Neither have the exegetes of the Islamic intellectual tradition all been men, nor was the Prophet surrounded by male voices alone or influenced only by a male perspective on matters. On the contrary, the women of the Prophet's household appear as highly skilled, strong-willed personalities whom the Prophet consults for advice, whose perspectives he takes seriously, and whom he accords rights. They are also honored and revered in the Islamic tradition, particularly since they themselves are considered sources relating the deeds and words of the Prophet.

Women prayed in mosques in which there was no separation from men. Women were encouraged to seek knowledge; already in early Islam they were active both as teachers and as students. When the Prophet first receives the revelation of the Qur'an he doubts his vision, but the person who gives him confidence, who trusts him and finally convinces him, is a woman: Khadija (d. 619 CE), his beloved wife. She is more than twenty years his senior, a wealthy and successful businesswoman and widow, who married him and bore him several children. In the Islamic tradition, she is considered the "Mother of the Faithful," an honorable and spiritual woman.

Women Making Choices as Autonomous Subjects

Living "honorably"—that is, placing a value on the lived practice of purity, gracefulness, and shame and thereby distinguishing between what is rightfully inward and outward—is commanded of both women and men. Living inner purity means to live righteously, to not fall into an attitude of carelessness and vulgarity, and to not present oneself in superficial ways (i.e., to not bare oneself), including bodily. The twenty-fourth surah does call on women to cover their charms, but this is not intended to subjugate women as objects of male desire; rather, it describes a distinction between honorable women and scantily clad women of the lower classes.[79] The same surah also addresses men, telling them to live honorably and with a sense of shame, to cast down their eyes and be pure. Within Islam, there is a culture of discourse engaging with these topics on the level of ethics, Islamic jurisprudence, and theology.

Many critics in modern societies have a general suspicion of women who wear any kind of headscarf. They suspect that these women are discriminated against in the sense that the women are forced to act in such a way. But this is true only in

---

79. On this topic, see also A. Schimmel, *Meine Seele ist ein Frau: Das Weibliche im Islam* [My soul is a woman: The feminine in Islam], (Munich: Kösel, 1996), 23–24.

exceptional cases. Muslim women who want to be neither the objects of others' gazes nor the object of others' interpretations, but instead subjects of their own narrative and recognized as such regularly come out in favor of headscarves because they see wearing a headscarf as respect of their religious dignity. In this understanding, wearing a headscarf is an internally felt religious act, or more precisely, a religious stance. As such, it is worthy of respect, particularly if one wants women to have the right to control their own lives—including their religious lives. However, if the woman is not given autonomy in this choice, it should indeed be seen as religiously questionable and dubious in its purpose.

A Positive View of Sexuality

In Islam, sexuality is not linked with sin or with God's punishment for Adam and Eve's sin in the Garden of Eden, as for example Augustine assumed with such far-reaching consequences for Christianity. On the contrary: Islam's positive and relaxed attitude towards sexuality has been documented since its earliest days. Debate over the problematic aspects of the relationship between the sexes cannot, therefore, be reduced to the subject of sexuality. With reference to Islam, it would also be a misunderstanding to suppose that only the man is seen as a sexually active being, with woman as an object of desire meant to do everything in order not to seduce the man in whatever way, through her voice or otherwise through her appearance, lest the man be unable to control himself. In this regard, a clear shift of emphasis is evident from the Bible to the Qur'an: Eve is not a seducer, nor was she taken from Adam's rib. Rather, the Qur'an reads: "People, be mindful of your Lord, who created you from a single soul, and from it created its mate, and from the pair of them spread countless men and women far and wide " (Qur'an 4:1). The assessment of woman as sinner or temptress is absent here; the same shift and higher valuation of women can be noted in the description of Potiphar's wife, from the story of Joseph in the Book of Genesis. This woman, too, is described in the Bible as a seducer, but in the Qur'an she is explicitly appreciated and her behavior excused.[80]

Equality between Men and Women in Principle

Women and men are equal in their status as religious and ethical beings. Both women and men are absolutely the same in faith, in prayer, in fasting, in their obligation to give alms, in their call to pilgrimage, and indeed in all religious matters. The Qur'an addresses them both equally. In his final sermon, the Prophet Muhammad is reported to have emphasized this equality of all people by saying: "All humankind is descended from Adam and Eve. Neither does an Arab take precedence over a non-Arab, nor a non-Arab over an Arab; White takes no precedence over Black, nor Black any precedence whatever over White." Before God, there is preferential treatment neither because of one's sex nor for any other reason. The thirty-third sunnah contains a verse that explains this in clear language and purposely mentions both sexes:

> For men and women who are devoted to God—believing men and women, obedient men and women, truthful men and women, steadfast men and women, humble men and women, charitable men and women, fasting men and women, chaste men and women, men and women who remember God often—God has prepared forgiveness and a rich reward. (Qur'an 33:35)

Differences that are mentioned in the Qur'an do occur in reference to those points that cannot be adequately read or understood without putting the revelation in its historical context. Such points include on the one hand matters of jurisprudence and on the other societally important questions on the relationship between the sexes (such as questions of inheritance).

---

80. See Qur'an 12:30–34

Indeed, it is a historical fact that even in these questions the Islamic message was a substantial step forward for women compared with the rules that applied in the pre-Islamic Arab world. These verses refer to the context of the seventh-century Arabian peninsula. If we examine them in the light of that time—which is essential—and if we assume that the Qur'an must be understood anew for each new era, it raises the question of whether we should judge the passages based on the letter of the text or based on the spirit of the Qur'an, the message behind the letter. The answer is obvious.

The Status of Marriage and the Question of Polygamy

These fundamental considerations apply equally to the question of polygamy. It is incorrect to generalize lazily that Muslims can or should live polygamously. But marriage does enjoy a particularly high status, since its highest commandment is above all that wives be treated justly by their husbands. While the Qur'an does suggest the possibility of marrying more than one woman under specific circumstances—mostly limited to four women, with reference to Qur'an 4:3—the conditions formulated for doing so have led Muslim scholars to conclude that it is almost impossible to posit polygamy as the general rule. Specifically, the Qur'an passage 4:129 is a counterargument: "You will never be able to treat your wives with equal fairness, however much you may desire to do so." And just treatment is considered the precondition for any possibility of marriage at all.

The decisive issue for evaluating the relationship between men and women in Islam, then, is the following: before God, men and women are of equal worth, equally loved, and equally respected. This ideal is hardly achieved in real life, but it is demanded in the spirit of Islam. Accordingly, dignifying women and realizing their rights is a challenge that women and men should accept together.

How to Live: The Art of Spiritual Living

I. Experiencing Reality through the Spirit as the Art of Spiritual Living in Islam

Ahmad Milad Karimi

Seeing the Visage of God in the Visage of the World

The common Arabic translation for the Latinate word "spirituality" is *rūḥāniyya*. It is formed from the root *rūḥ*, meaning "spirit." But what are spirit and spirituality? The Qur'an says: "They ask you about the Spirit [*rūḥ*]. Say, 'The Spirit [*rūḥ*] is part of my Lord's domain [*amr*]'" (Qur'an 17:85). Since the spirit is subject to God's judgment, "spirit" and "spirituality" have always been used with great caution in the Islamic tradition. In addition, particularly in Persian, the word *ma'nawīyat* has come to mean "spirituality." Its root word, *ma'na*, refers to "meaning." Islamic spirituality, then, is fundamentally concerned insight into the inner meaning of things. The intention of such spirituality is to see the visage of God in the visage of the world.

'Aṭṭār says: "Until you travel within yourself, you will not reach the inner meaning of yourself."[81] Opening oneself to God opens a person's inner space. "Wherever you turn," the Qur'an tells us, "there is His face" (Qur'an 2:115). Translating this inward-facing spirituality into one's life is an art: an art of living to which Islamic mysticism has dedicated itself.

---

81. Quoted in Hellmut Ritter, *Das Meer der Seele: Mensch, Welt und Gott in den Geschichten des Farīduddīn 'Aṭṭār* [The sea of the soul: Man, world, and God in the stories of Farīduddīn 'Aṭṭār] (Leiden: Brill, 1978), 619. Translated from the German.

Perceiving the Uncommon in What Is Common

Perceiving the uncommon in what is common—that would be a way of describing this attitude: it does not distinguish matter from spirit, nor does it turn away from this world in an impractical ascetic spirituality, but rather sees spirit and dignity in all those places where one would otherwise see mere objects. Aḥmad al-Ghazālī put it aptly when he wrote: "Open the eye of your inward face! For in being there is nothing but Him."[82] Accordingly, the Qur'an describes God not only as "the Inner" but also as "the Outer."[83] This spiritual relationship with the world and with oneself transforms one's perspective, deepens one's vision and opens up a searching, yearning, but also healing and mindful way of seeing and approaching the world. In Islam's mystical tradition, this relationship with the world, a relationship supported by spirituality, is traced back to precisely distinct different forms of insight, such as spiritual tasting (*dhawq*), spiritual unveiling (*kashf*), spiritual clear-sightedness (*firāsa*) and spiritual observing (*baṣīra*). Each of these forms of insights, taken on its own, describes a separate spiritual experience of reality.

Reality as Sign: Transforming Our Sight and Perception

The spiritual art of living is to see the world and everything in it as if being seen for the first time; experiencing and perceiving things in their uniqueness and their mystery. Such an attitude does not romanticize the common and everyday, but rather transforms our sight and perception. However, the everyday can touch us only if we create and offer a space in ourselves

---

82. Ahmad al-Ghazālī, *At-Targīd fī kalimat at-tauḥīd: Der reine Gottesglaube. Das Wort des Einheitsbekenntnisses.* [*At-Tarjīd fī kalimat at-tauḥīd*: Pure faith in God. The words of the confession of oneness]. Introduced, translated, and with commentary by Richard Gramlich (Wiesbaden: Steiner, 1983), 18. Translated from the German.
83. See Qur'an 57:3.

where it can. We must find and devote time. As small and insignificant as things may seem to us, they are full of miracles. This symbolic nature of the world allows its objects to attain their own radiance, so that they can be perceived in their aweworthy beauty. Suddenly, there is nothing anymore that is common and a matter of course, because things are disclosing to us their deeper meaning. The Qur'an contains a touching passage in which God says that he would not be ashamed to compare himself even to a gnat. And the ungrateful, inattentive people would answer derisively: "What does God mean by such a comparison?"[84] A gnat is more than simply an insect with string-like, many-layered feelers. A gnat is also a symbol, a mystery of God, a living parable.

This "more" is not simply given, but it can disclose itself to us—in the simple and the every day. The art of spiritual living is revealed in insight into reality's nature as a sign. The Qur'an says: "There are signs in the heavens and the earth for those who believe: in the creation of you, in the creatures God scattered on earth, there are signs for people of sure faith; in the alternation of night and day, in the rain God provides, sending it down from the sky and reviving the dead earth with it, and in His shifting of the winds there are signs for those who use their reason" (Qur'an 45:3–5). Everything in the world becomes a sign, becomes a revelation of the greater truth of God in which we participate and in which we are permitted to take joy and in which we may grow.

The Miracle in the Simple

When the Prophet Muhammad and his companion Abū Bakr have to flee from Muhammad's birth city of Mecca because his life is threatened and the pursuers are at their heels, the two seek refuge in a mountain cave. When their pursuers approach, the companion says: "If one of them were to look down, they would see us!" The Prophet answers: "Oh Abū Bakr! What

---

84. Qur'an 2:26.

should one think of two who have God as their third?" And in that moment, a spider appears and spins its web across the mouth of the cave, the branches of a tree incline downward and block the entrance, and two doves lay eggs directly in front of the cave. This makes the pursuers suppose that no one could be in the cave, and they turn around. Cobwebs, doves, branches: from that moment on, they are anything but simple matters of course, and much more than common things. No irrational miracle has occurred. The spider is doing nothing it would not usually do. But precisely that is what becomes the unusual, the miraculous: it protects life. Immediately afterward, the Prophet is filled with gratitude. He feels supported by the eternal hand that has inscribed itself into the temporal. A simple cobweb becomes something significant, because what is special was revealed in its very simplicity.

An Approach of Reverence—Everyday Rituals

We must approach everyday life not just with humility, but with reverence as well. The art of spiritual living is revealed also in interpersonal relationships that can become true encounters when we approach one another mindfully and with awe. Seeing one another anew again and again requires both mindful wakefulness and sensitive care. Every seeing is a new beginning, represents a new opportunity to let ourselves be touched deep within us by one another in an encounter. A mindful approach in life can also occur through daily practice and repetition. Repeated actions provide contours for our everyday life and let it lose its ordinariness.

Rituals thus open up a different way of accessing the world. Through rituals, we can enter into conscious contact with reality. Muslims take off their shoes when entering a mosque or standing up in ritual prayer. Suddenly, the floor of a mosque comes quite close. The floor, which we otherwise step on only with our shoes, gains its own profundity and significance through such mindfulness. The repetition of this action creates a consciousness that remains with us not only in the mosque, but transforms our attitude towards the simple floor in general. In truth, it is we ourselves who are changed.

2. The Art of Spiritual Living in the Christian Tradition

Anselm Grün

What Does Us Good: The Art of a Healthful Life

Ancient Greek physicians saw their most important duty not in healing the sick but in teaching the art of living healthfully. To them, this art included religion as well. Opening oneself up to God does one good. Legend has it that the evangelist Luke was a doctor. Certainly in his Gospel he described Jesus as the true physician. He sees Jesus as the *archegos tes zoes*, which could be translated "leader (or instructor) towards healthful life." This life is revealed in Jesus' instructions and in the way he himself lived, in his repeated withdrawal for solitary prayer, in his opening up to the rituals handed down in the Jewish religion.

The Greek Church Fathers followed both ancient Greek physicians and the evangelist Luke. Again and again, they understood Christian spirituality as the art of healthful living, as well. In the Gospel, Jesus is always also the teacher of wisdom. He teaches us how our life can be successful. Early Christian theologians interpreted Jesus' words of wisdom with a view to the Greek art of living healthfully. That is why all statements of Christian spirituality should be understood in such a way as to do people good, to heal people. Jesus himself made the fundamental pronouncement: "The sabbath was made for humankind, and not humankind for the sabbath" (Mk 2:27). This principle applies to all spiritual forms, to prayer, to the liturgy, to asceticism. All these are meant to orient human beings toward God. And when individuals are oriented toward God, they will live according to their nature, they will live healthfully.

Drawing from the Wellspring of Spirit

The essence of Christian spirituality consists in living from the wellspring of the Holy Spirit that flows forth at the base of our soul. This wellspring is inexhaustible because it is divine.

We can draw from this source if we become permeable to the spirit of Jesus Christ. We cannot misuse the Holy Spirit for our own ends in order to puff up our ego with his energy. The Holy Spirit wants to pervade us with the spirit of Jesus. And only if we open ourselves up to the spirit of Jesus will our life draw on this inner wellspring and bear fruit; only then will we become a blessing to other people and to the world. Those who draw on this wellspring of the Holy Spirit will never become exhausted in their work. They will be permeable to the spirit of Jesus. The spirit of Jesus will shape their actions. And Luke is convinced that if we let ourselves be pervaded and shaped by the spirit of Jesus, we will live according to what the ancient Greek physicians meant when they spoke of the art of living. Jesus is the inner healer who leads us to a life in health.

God Shining through Reality

What is more, the Bible message reveals another facet of the art of living in how it relates to the objects of the world. Especially in the synoptic Gospels, Jesus often speaks of entirely earthly things in the form of parables: of the sower sowing his seeds, of the birds of the sky and the lilies of the field, of the merchant who seeks a fine pearl, of weeds among the wheat, or of the way in which people deal with money entrusted to them. By speaking of the things of this world, he is simultaneously speaking of God. Everything becomes permeable to this relationship. Objects, everyday occurrences, what we do every day—in all these things, the nature of the heavenly Father appears to us. In the Gospel of John, earthly things become a metaphor for the mystery of Jesus Christ, for his significance to us and his effect on us. Jesus says of himself: "I am the true vine" (Jn 15:1). In the Greek, the words *he alethine* occur at the end of the sentence: "I am the vine, the true one." All too often, we see only what is external. But Jesus' eyes probe deeper: if we look at the vine and understand its nature, its truth, we will recognize the mystery and the truth of our own life. Truth means: the veil that lies across everything is drawn away. And the mystery of being appears to us, the mystery hidden behind everything and lying at the foundation of everything.

Martin Heidegger has translated the Greek word *aletheia*, most often rendered as "truth," as "un-concealedness" (*Unverborgenheit*): what is concealed shines out to us, reveals itself. Recognizing this truth means: all things and activities, in the end, are transparent to that foundation, to the power that pervades all things, to the Spirit who works in all things, to the energy flowing through everything, to the love woven into the world: God is within me and outside me. We encounter him not only when we attend to the foundation of our soul and withdraw from the world. We encounter him in the midst of the world. But doing so requires openness of the eyes and openness of the heart, and it requires mindfulness, wakefulness, and presence in order to perceive behind and within all things this fullness of being, in order to see in all things a path to him and everywhere a place where we may encounter his presence. This is the deepest hallmark of such an art of spiritual living.

Different Expressions

Throughout history and into the present day, Christian spirituality has expressed itself in many different ways. For example, Benedictine spirituality emphasizes liturgy as a site of encounter with God while linking prayer and work; Franciscan spirituality breathes something of the freedom of St. Francis of Assisi; Jesuit spirituality grapples with making a clear choice in favor of God. But mystical movements in Christianity have existed in all eras. This was the case among the Greek Church Fathers, with the medieval Hildegard of Bingen, among the women who banded together as Beguines, with Meister Eckhart and Johannes Tauler, and then later among Spanish mysticism as exemplified by Teresa of Avila and John of the Cross. For a long time, Christian mystics were not given sufficient attention, but in the last thirty years, renewed interest has arisen in these figures of Christian mysticism. We sense that mystical spirituality is a way to experience the depth of faith and grow closer to one another.

A Connection through Mystic Spirituality

Mystical spirituality connects Christians and Muslims. I have always enjoyed reading the texts of Sufi masters such as Rumi. As a Christian, I can wholly and completely understand and accept these texts. And I can learn from the mystical experiences of Sufi mystics. In its turn, Sufi mysticism was obviously also influenced by Christian ideas. There was, then, a healthy spiritual and theological exchange between Christianity and Islam. The mystics who have experienced God do not try to pin God down to rigid dogmas. Rather, they describe the experience of God in images that are open to all who have set out toward God.

All religions' mystical paths understand one another because they speak of similar experiences. They merely interpret these experiences on the basis of their own theological tradition. But not everyone can walk a path of mysticism. It is therefore legitimate to walk other spiritual paths, as well. One of these paths, for example, involves fixed rituals. "Ordinary" Christians begin their day with a prayer and end it with a prayer. During the day, they let themselves be reminded of God's presence again and again—by small prayers, by the churches they walk past, or by the ringing of church bells. These rituals are not chores we need to fulfill for God. God does not need our rituals. But they do us good because they open us to God. Every day, they remind us that we live before and in God. They are concrete practice in faith and simultaneously a good expression of our faith.

Celebrating the Liturgy

The Christian path of the art of spiritual living values the celebration of the liturgy. In the liturgy, we praise God here on earth and are thus joining in with the songs of praise sung by the angels as an eternal liturgy in heaven. The Eucharist makes this function of the liturgy particularly clear. We are celebrating the holy feast here while the departed are joining in the heavenly marriage feast above. The Eucharist thus connects heaven and earth, the living and the dead. We feel that our faith is supported by all those who have lived and believed before us and who are now with God. At the same time, the Eucharist is persistent practice of Jesus' disposition. We celebrate his devotion with which he loved us to the utmost. We celebrate so that we may learn to devote ourselves to God and our fellow human beings in the same way.

Transforming Our World: Prayer and Work

The connection between prayer and work is crucial to Christian spirituality. *Ora et labora*, pray and work, became the encapsulation of Benedictine life. Spirituality must always also express itself in a new approach. And it should have the power to shape this world. Accordingly, Christian spirituality is never unworldly, but always oriented toward healing and transforming this world. Benedict of Nursia believed that our spirituality should reveal itself particularly in the way we work and interact with one another in our daily business. Spiritually shaped work should glorify God.

That is the goal of all our spirituality: the glorification of God. A saying is attributed to the Church Father Irenaeus: *Gloria dei homo vivens*—"God's glory is living man." If humankind gains life through the spirit of God, then in that spirit God is glorified in this world, then living humankind becomes testimony to the presence of the living God.

Mysticism and Secular Society

I. Hearing God's Word and Finding New Action

Anselm Grün

Insight into God, Replete with Experience

Christian spirituality has always also been shaped by mysticism, which Thomas Aquinas defines as *cognitio dei experimentalis*—an experiential knowledge of God. Mysticism, then, is not about believing in particular teachings about God, but about experiencing God. Mystics have always been free-spirited because they trusted in their own experience. And Christian mystics have also been close to mystics in other religions. Those who have once experienced the mystery of God in the depth of their own soul will feel at one with all people who are also seeking this deeper experience of God, even if these experiences are described in a different language.

Evagrius Ponticus, a fourth-century monk, distinguishes between two forms of mysticism: a mysticism of nature, (*theoria physike*) which recognizes God's all-pervading presence and love in nature, and a mysticism of simplicity. Evagrius sees this latter form as the higher mysticism and refers to it as the mysticism of the Trinity (*theoria tes agias triados*). To him, this type of mysticism leads to insight into the nature of things (*gnosis ousiodes*). It is a way of seeing God without all form or metaphor. It is wholly simple. Many Sufi mystics will understand and use similar terms for what Evagrius writes about this type of mysticism. And presumably, the Sufi mystics—who we as Christians also enjoy reading—were likewise influenced by Christian ideas. This showed that a deeper experience of God unites people, rather than dividing them the way insistence on religious orthodoxy does.

An Open Heart: The Aim of Mysticism in Practice

In its mystical understanding, the Christian faith does not lose sight of the state of society. The idea that mysticism requires open eyes to the suffering of people is inscribed into the biblical worldview from its inception. Unlike the priest and the Levite in the parable, a Christian must not walk past the man who was robbed and beaten by the robbers. The parable of the Good Samaritan (Lk 10:27–35), who looked out for and cared for the wounded person, reveals what the goal of Christian mysticism looks like in practice. The Greek word for "caring" in the parable is *meletao*, which literally means "to have a heart for someone." But the Samaritan showed not only pity— that is, an open heart— he acted as well. He poured oil and wine onto the wounds of the injured man, set him on his donkey and brought him to an inn (Lk 10:33–35).

Struggle and Contemplation: Eyes Open to the World

Many Christian mystics, both male and female, were far from leading lives of mere contemplative interiority. On the contrary, they always perceived and spoke out against the problems in society. Hildegard of Bingen traveled through all of Germany, admonishing the priests to live lives of God. The thirteenth-century mystic Hadewijch of Brabant criticized not only the state of the Church but also that of society. Catherine of Siena remonstrated with the pope that he should live in the spirit of Jesus. This linking of mysticism and activism for the world has been described in various images over the course of the Christian tradition.

Benedict of Nursia uses the formula: *Ora et labora* —prayer and work. This means that prayer should also be expressed in work on the world and for a more just world. Mysticism always also means shaping the world. A mysticism concerned only with removing itself from the world does not correspond to the tradition and nature of Christian spirituality. Brother Roger Schütz (who during the Third Reich gave refuge to Jewish and other opposition members, and whose confreres later did good works in poor regions of Algeria, Latin America, Africa, and elsewhere) terms this tension inherent to Christian spirituality "struggle and contemplation": according to Brother Roger, living in God's present also meant engaging in the world of today. Pastoral theologian Paul Zulehner describes the connection of "politics and mysticism" as "diving into the mystery of God and resurfacing among the people."[85] Dorothee Sölle titled her writing on Christianity's power for social criticism "Mysticism and Resistance."[86] Her fundamental insight was that where God loves and is loved, justice and peace embrace; the reality of a liberated world is manifested in such practice. Johann Baptist Metz, finally, in his "political theology"[87] speaks of a "mysticism . . . with the eyes open"[88] and emphasizes the *memoria passionis*, that is, the Christian faith's sensitivity to the suffering and its hope for the humanization of the world in openness towards its eschatological completion.[89] As lived practice, we find this attitude in "mystics of action," such as the leprosy doctor and nun Ruth Pfau, who for over fifty years dedicated her life to the poorest of the poor in Muslim Pakistan and did so out of her understanding of her faith as a "lived prayer" before God.

---

85. Paul M. Zulehner, *Unterstützung für und Widerstand gegen Papst Franziskus' Kirchenpolitik* [Support for and resistance to Pope Francis' church politics] (Vienna: self-published, 2019), 78. Available online at: https://www.zulehner.org/dl/tqKsJKJ-mOJqx4kOJK/190825_Bericht.pdf. Translated from the German.
86. Dorothee Sölle, *The Silent Cry: Mysticism and Resistance*, translated by Barbara and Martin Rumscheidt (Minneapolis: Fortress Press, 2001).
87. Johann Baptist Metz, *Love's Strategy: The Political Theology of Johann Baptist Metz*, edited by John K. Downey (Harrisburg, PA: Trinity Press International, 1999), 26.
88. Metz, *Love's Strategy*, 175.
89. Metz, *Love's Strategy*, 140.

Experience of God is Expressed in Behavior

The connection between mysticism and politics is also one that Jesus makes in the Sermon on the Mount. If we understand the Sermon on the Mount only as a series of moral demands, it will be too much for us. But at the center of the Sermon is the Lord's Prayer. In this prayer of Jesus, we experience God as our father and our mother; we become open to God. And this experience of God in prayer is the precondition for a change in our behavior. Only from a deep experience of God can we fulfill the demands of the Sermon on the Mount. These are not strict commandments, but rather instructions for how to react creatively to the evil done to us from outside. But our experience of God must also express itself in new behavior, in action. If the Lord's Prayer is spoken without any outward effect, the prayer becomes narcissistic orbiting around one's own self. But prayer and action belong together. Being oriented toward God in prayer is the basis for the transformation of behavior. Prayer must express itself in new action in order to become true prayer.

At the end of the Sermon on the Mount, Jesus tells us: "Everyone then who hears these words of mine and acts on them will be like a wise man who built his house on rock" (Mt 7:24). In prayer, we hear the words of God. But only if we act according to them do we build our life's house on a rock.

Looking at Society Critically—and Taking Healing Action

Christian mysticism has always also looked to its neighbors and oriented itself towards society. In the first century, Christian mysticism consisted mostly of cult mysticism and scriptural mysticism—that is, it involved services together and meditation on Holy Scripture as a means of experiencing God. To Christian mystics, experiencing God was always linked to a new way of seeing one's fellow human beings. There is a monastic saying: "If you have seen your brother, you have seen God." A mysticism that looks past the sufferings of our neighbor has no connection to the spirit of Jesus. Jesus himself identified with poor people and foreigners, with the homeless and hungry, with the unfree and the sick. So a person who does a good deed for a stranger—no matter whether Christian or not—is encountering Christ in that person. In this way, Christian mysticism always relates to the person.

And Christian mysticism also looks at society critically. Old Testament prophets always decried injustices as well. In the same way, Christian mystics have always criticized those political or societal tendencies that ran counter to the dignity of human beings or to justice between people and between peoples. Mysticism also engages in politics. Without telling politicians what to do, it nevertheless stands up for the values of justice, freedom, respect, love. The relationship between mysticism and secular society, therefore, does not mean that religion should form the basis of all social order. Far from it, especially in modern secular society, which is shaped by a plurality of world views and by the independence of the different magisteria, and in a nation-state whose self-conception and normative claims are not freighted with religious meaning. All the same, especially in such situations, spirituality is not independent from social, economic, and politic reality, nor indifferent to misery, suffering, or injustice.

Mystics are convinced that they are contributing to cleansing society's atmosphere when they let themselves be cleansed, through God's spirit, of all the unclarities that darken our human spirit and make social togetherness that much more difficult. Those who open themselves up fully and completely to the spirit of God will also have a healing effect on their environment. And those infused with hope will be able to communicate this hope to their environment, as well.

2. Shaping the World as a Spiritual Task in Islam

Ahmad Milad Karimi

No Separation between Secular and Religious

Although mysticism and spirituality naturally emphasize the inner, spiritual dimension of religious life, followers of Islam's mystic tradition nevertheless largely subscribe to the position that—for all necessary cleansing and letting go of worldly desires—one should by no means renounce the world entirely. Rather, the creative shaping of the outer, societal, and political reality is approached from the inner, spiritual dimension. In the twentieth century, it was predominantly Muhammad Iqbal who pointed out this task of mysticism: according to Iqbal, it must never be "blind" to political realities, philosophical and scientific/rational insights, or social circumstances. On the contrary, it should be "seeing" and engage in the practical purpose of shaping its surroundings in the matter of suffering and the misery of the world as well as the fight against injustice and intellectual backwardness. To Iqbal, who stands in the tradition of Ibn 'Arabī, 'Attār, and Rūmī, outward deeds begin with an inner stance, with a fundamental view of the world. If we see the world from a dualistic point of view by categorizing it into sacred and profane on principle, it is all too easy to see the profane—the secular—as secondary.

Islam, says Iqbal, takes a fundamentally different stance: "The Ultimate Reality, according to the Qur'an, is spiritual, and its life consists in its temporal activity. The spirit finds its opportunities in the natural, the material, the secular. All that is secular is, therefore, sacred in the roots of its being."[90] This view does not deny the existence of the secular; it does not claim that all of reality is theocratically determined. Only a clear distinction between religion and politics enables the development of a political consciousness in the first place. Iqbal

---

90. Iqbal, *Reconstruction of Religious Thought*, 123.

is instead pointing out that the perception of reality through religious eyes will fundamentally have a conciliatory tendency for the mere reason that it assumes the unity of material and immaterial things. Religion, in Iqbal's view, reveals that "the merely material has no substance until we discover it rooted in the spiritual. There is no such thing as a profane world. All this immensity of matter constitutes a scope for the self-realization of spirit. All is holy ground."[91]

Religion's Task: Endowing Society with Meaning

Those who live their lives from a place of spiritual fullness and an experience of divine reality can, through their actions, endow the world with meaning. That is especially necessary in a society that measures all life by quantitative yardsticks and according to material values, subordinating everything to the guiding categories of production and performance. Islam's spiritual tradition teaches one to find meaning even in the apparently meaningless. In one's own weakness, in one's own failure, in aging, and even in misery and illness, sadness and death, Islam sees hidden wisdom, strength, and dignity. Concretely and with reference to political reality, this means that even in the faces of refugees, the sufferers of our time, the faithful see not only misery but also especially hope, courage, and the trust that there can be a future shaped not by war and destruction but by peace and humanity. From the point of view of religious experience, these people are not foreigners who should be turned away from the borders. Instead, all of them, as individual beings, carry the entire dignity of humanity in them. Each one deserves an own name, an own story, an own reverence, because each hopes for a time in which life can succeed. That is the time towards which religions are working.

What is more, the way religion endows meaning must never be anti-intellectual, or indifferent to science, or apart from rationality—much less in a time in which it is primar-

---

91. Iqbal, *Reconstruction of Religious Thought*, 123.

ily rationality and algorithms that govern the development of society. Islam's understanding of spirituality has always been guided by a stance permeated with philosophy and reason. Ibn Sīnā, Ibn 'Arabī, Mulla Ṣadra, and Iqbal were all shaped by both philosophy and mysticism. Mysticism's contribution has always been to point out that rationality alone—without spirituality's inner dimension and without an ethical grounding—reduces the development of society to optimization and maximization.

Coherent Politics: Harmony of Values and Deeds

Word and deed must be at one. This is what the Qur'an teaches. The precondition for sustainability is a politics that is coherent in this particular sense. Uncontrolled progress at any price is regressive, is in truth spiritual poverty. Real development in the best sense can succeed when it is pursued mindfully and in a spirit of solidarity, but also in responsible consideration of the whole. Especially nowadays, the holistic, global perspective borne by the idea of the plurality of societies demands connection and obligation: it refers to values that apply to all, so that no human being is considered illegal anywhere, and no refugee can be bargained over or otherwise treated as a commodity. In that sense, religion's spirituality is not in competition with the rationally shaped development of society, but rather anchors this development inward. Social cohesion is a problem not just of political action, but with an existential quality, as well. While a secular society's social cohesion is based on a constitution, that constitution can no longer guarantee cohesion if the value convictions it presupposes are no longer lived and if the certainties at its core are factually no longer there. These fundamental experiences to which even a secular constitution refers rely on crucial contributions not only by art and culture, but by religion as well. The actual cohesive matter is that which connects, which is mutual, which is shared, which has developed, which has been created out of joint experience, that which communicates itself from one period to the next and must be continually defined anew. Under this view, especially, religion is an institution that offers more than just individual orientation.

The Political Claims of Religion

Present-day Islam, even encompassing its foundation in mysticism, cannot be content to distance itself from political or societal challenges. Nor, however, can contemporary Islam politicize the religion itself. Those who turn Islam into a political tool give up the openness of this faith in favor of narrowing its theology. The standard must be to formulate political and social responsibility out of an internal understanding of the religion and thus encourage people to participate in politics and become active in society. Religions themselves are part of the reality of society. They can and should formulate their own calls to participation and take a stand for the shaping of a free society, especially in the era of globalization. Religions have a rich experience of virtues and values. This is exactly what our time, more than ever, needs to think back on in reference to peace, tolerance, a responsible approach to the environment, the preservation of creation, the thoughtful construction of coherent animal rights ethics, and the like. All these represent universal values with a clear goal, even though the explicit formulation of their contents and the specific coupling to principles can always change. According to Islamic mysticism, religious service is insight into the ways in which God works that can be seen everywhere—including in the realities of politics and society. One must simply sharpen one's gaze.

Suffering: God's Will?

I. Christian Answers to the Question of Suffering

Anselm Grün

*Cosmic Drama? Suffering as a
Fundamental Question for Religion*

Why we suffer is one of humanity's most ancient questions, and biblical authors too are profoundly concerned with the very fact of suffering: "We know that the whole creation has been groaning in labor pains until now" (Rom 8:22). Not only Christianity and Islam, but all religions attempt to answer this question. Nature-based religions perceive suffering as part of a cosmic drama—between life and death, darkness and light—but also memorialize a primordial state in which the world was still whole. The major religions engage with the mystery of suffering, but always also view it as a challenge to create meaning in life. Additionally, they are concerned with the freedom and dignity of those who suffer. This is true whether (like in the ancient religions) suffering is understood as a challenge to perceive the essence that lies behind the ephemeral world, or—*per aspera ad astra*—considered to be a path to higher values, or (like in Eastern religions) seen as the result of a mistaken attachment to the world and advocated as the renunciation of all painful desire as the core of wisdom and the path of liberation.

Where is God in Suffering? Biblical Answers

In the Jewish and biblical tradition, too, questions of suffering—about comfort and hope, about how to act well, about God's absence or nearness when we suffer—repeatedly play a role. They find particularly vivid expression in the story of the suffering of Job. But suffering is not merely a fundamental part of human experience. Sufferers are also those who are promised that God

> will wipe every tear from their eyes.
> Death will be no more;
> mourning and crying and pain will be no more,
> for . . . see, I am making all things new. (Rv 21:4–5)

In the face of this tension, Christian spirituality to this day asks about suffering. As soon as we suffer, we automatically ask: Why? Why does suffering affect me in particular? Some people immediately link suffering with the question of punishment: Is this suffering a punishment from God because I have not lived according to his will? Christian theology responds to this question as follows: God is not a punishing God. We can say this much with certainty. But despite all theological attempts, we cannot answer the question of why we suffer. If we could, we would be setting ourselves above God and know exactly what God was thinking. We can only try to understand the suffering we experience and to find an appropriate answer to it.

Between Submission and Resistance

In the history of Christian piety, one attempt at an explanation was to refer to a saying from the Book of Proverbs: "the LORD reproves the one he loves" (Prv 3:12). That often led to an unhealthy mystification of suffering, in which suffering was sought out to express love to God. Others have interpreted suffering as a disciplinary measure God sends so that we repent. Some have even understood Jesus' saying that in order to follow him every disciple must bear his or her own cross (see Lk 14:27) to mean that we should intentionally and purposely take on suffering as our cross. Today, however, we understand Jesus' words differently. To C. G. Jung, the cross we all must bear is accepting our own contradictory nature, a cross that he sees as a necessary path to individuation as a full human self. The cross can also be a metaphor for things that come into conflict with our plans. Then it becomes a metaphor for suffering. Suffering happens to us whether we want it to or not. We should not seek it. But when it comes, the words of Jesus can help us bear it. Before bearing it, however, we should first try to solve what is causing us to suffer. Some people prefer to suffer instead of solving the problems that make them suffer. We always need to do both: fight against suffering and overcome it as far as we are able, and then bear the suffering that we cannot prevent. Medieval Christianity developed a mysticism of suffering that can help us bear this suffering; in our time, Dietrich Bonhoeffer described this tension between fighting and accepting suffering with the words "resistance and submission."[92]

Christian hope refers not just to the next world, but to this one. Full of hope, we should work on making this world more just and preventing or reducing suffering. But despite all resistance to unjust structures, we will always also have to suffer situations that we have to accept. In those moments, we are strengthened by the Christian hope that suffering is not the last word, but that after suffering, eternal life awaits us.

Theodicy: A Reaction to Suffering

The German philosopher Gottfried W. Leibniz referred to the question of God and suffering as "theodicy." Leibniz asked himself how faith in an all-powerful and loving God might be reconciled with the experience of evil, darkness, and suffering. He undertook to place God before the judgment of human reason. But Leibniz did not accuse God. Rather, in the face of all the suffering in the world, he defended him. Leibniz felt that God had created the best of all possible worlds. This answer has never quite satisfied Christian theologians, and the Bible itself contains an injunction not to argue with God (Rom 9:20). There have been other attempts to interpret suffering as the price of freedom or as a pedagogical measure on the part of

---

92. Dietrich Bonhoeffer, *Letters and Papers from Prison*, translated by Reginald H. Fuller (New York: Macmillan, 1962), 138.

God. But Karl Rahner counters all these theological attempts with the claim: Suffering is incomprehensible. It cannot be grasped, and this is part of how God cannot be grasped. To Rahner, this is the only possible honest answer that we can give to our searching minds.

So we cannot explain suffering. But we can ask ourselves how we should respond to it.

Coping with Suffering: Answers from the Bible

And to that question, the Bible gives us many good answers. In the first place, Jesus himself is a role model. He passed through suffering, and by passing through it reached resurrection. By resurrecting Jesus from the dead, God gave us hope that our suffering too is not the last word, but that it will be lifted in resurrection. Jesus tells the disciples on the road to Emmaus: "Was it not necessary that the Messiah should suffer these things and then enter into his glory?" (Lk 24:26). The Greek word *dei*—translated as "Was it not necessary"—does not indicate an absolute necessity. It is simply how the Greeks describe fate. Suffering overcomes us like fate, but the thing that crosses our path is also the entry into glory—*doxa* in the Greek. This word means "shape," "image," "beauty." Thus, suffering could become the pathway to my true shape, to the original image of me God has made for himself.

Christian mystical readings of the Passion have seen Jesus' suffering as an expression of his love for us. Jesus himself says of his suffering and death: "No one has greater love than this, to lay down one's life for one's friends" (Jn 15:13). In the suffering that afflicted them, Christians have looked up to Jesus. Doing so, they experienced communion with Jesus. And they have experienced his love, which transformed their suffering, too. Looking to the suffering of Jesus has thus always helped people cope with their own suffering without losing their dignity. In their spirituals, enslaved African Americans sang about the suffering of Jesus. Memorializing Jesus' suffering gave them the strength to pass through their own suffering upright, and even within it to still experience their dignity.

The Search for Meaning

But after the question of how to cope with suffering, we are also faced with the question of the meaning of suffering. Viktor E. Frankl, a Jewish therapist who nevertheless espoused some Christian positions, maintained that suffering has no meaning in and of itself. But it is our task to wrest meaning out of suffering. Frankl believes: Fate can rob us of many things. It can rob us of our loved ones when they die. It can rob us of health or our occupation. But there is one thing it cannot take from us: the freedom to react to these losses. And this freedom consists in imbuing our suffering with meaning and thus transforming it. For example, a possible meaning could be to turn the suffering into devotion. That is how my mother, as a devout Christian, approached her illnesses. She accepted them and transformed them into devotion toward her children and grandchildren. This gave her the feeling that she was able to do something for her children and grandchildren through her suffering. And it did the people around her good as well—because equanimity and love emanated from her. It is this transformation of suffering into devotion that Christians celebrate with every Eucharist. Jesus did not choose his suffering: it happened to him. It crossed his path, foiled his plans. But he transformed into love all the things that crossed him. And so he says of himself: "I lay down my life for the sheep . . . No one takes it from me, but I lay it down of my own accord" (Jn 10:15–18).

Not Breaking Down but Breaking Open

Based on what Jesus told the disciples on the road to Emmaus, I would like to set out a principle for understanding the meaning of suffering: life breaks apart my idea of myself, of life, and of God. When I let suffering break apart my preconceived notions, I will not break down, but will instead be broken open to my true self, to new ideas about life, to all my brothers and sisters and the ungraspable love of God. I want to explain this abstract principle using the example of a healthy woman who was suddenly diagnosed with an autoimmune disorder. She immediately wanted to know what had caused the illness.

I answered her that seeking fault with herself for her illness held no meaning: The illness happened to her. We do not know why. The illness breaks apart her previous view of herself, her idea that she always has the capacity to do what she wants to do. When this self-image of the strong woman is broken apart, she can ask herself: Who am I really? What is my true self? The illness also shatters her notions of life, such as that she will always be able to do athletic sports. But now she can look for other ways to keep living a rich life: taking small walks, having a good conversation, enjoying nature. And her suffering breaks apart her conception of God. She had gone to church every Sunday. Why does God allow this illness? The idea of a merciful and all-powerful God breaks apart: If God is all-powerful, he is able to prevent this illness. And if he is merciful, he must prevent it. But he has not done so. That is incomprehensible.

But if I accept that God is incomprehensible, I am broken open to the true God, to God beyond all human conceptions and imagery. On the other hand, if I hold on to my preconceived notions, the illness will cause me to break down. For example, if I hold on to "a healthy lifestyle will guarantee me a long life of health," then the illness will lead me to blame either myself or others who might be at fault. But doing so makes me bitter, and I will break down sooner or later. The meaning of suffering, then, is that it breaks us open to our true self, to new opportunities in life, and to the ungraspable, incomprehensible God, who with all his incomprehensibility remains love—but a love that is incomprehensible.

What We Gain from Equanimity

The Psalms teach us that when we are suffering, we should not simply submit in God. Often, the one who prays the Psalms struggles with God, calling to God to deliver him from the pit of despair and from the hands of the wicked. And then amid these pleas, he confesses that God is his refuge, that God helps and liberates. We can lament with the psalmist and remonstrate with God. But all lament and remonstration should, at some point, be transformed into the trust that despite all suffering God has not deserted me, that he will transform the suffering of the helpless. We can lament to God, can entrust our anger to him. And we can plead with him to heal us. We should bring before him all our needs. But in the end, every prayer turns to the plea: "thy will be done." This is not resignation. We may try to move God with our pleading. But at the same time, we trust that God's will is good for us. God's will is not arbitrary. God does not enjoy making others suffer.

The Christian tradition distinguishes between two types of will. The first is superficial will, often associated with the word "want": I want to drive there, eat this, do that. The second is the will we discover at the bottom of our soul when we are completely still and listen into ourselves. This will at the base of our soul is identical with the will of God. And this will of God grants us an inner freedom. I know that God's will is always in my best interest. But this does not necessarily mean that God will lift my suffering or preserve me from illness. Nevertheless, I trust that in the end, God's will seeks my salvation. Whether my suffering continues or is lifted from me, I am always held in God's good hands. And these good hands will carry me regardless of what happens to me. That gives me an inner freedom and equanimity.

2. Suffering as a Spiritual Challenge in Islam

Ahmad Milad Karimi

The Stereotype of "Muslim Fatalism"

We would like to keep from experiencing suffering in our lives. This is mostly due to how we judge our experiences of suffering. The mere intention of living a life beyond any experience of it creates fear and anxiety of being afflicted by suffering, injustice, and pain in any way. But it is part of human life to experience it, as well. Muslims, too, ask: But why are there suffering and evil at all if there is a God who himself is unsurpassably good? Why would the good and kind God inflict suffering on his own creation? In contrast with the Christian tradition, however, Islam has not developed theodicy in the sense of a systematic theological attempt to answer the problem of suffering or justify God through reasoned explanation. The Islamic spiritual tradition by no means ignores suffering, but nor—unlike the Christian theology of the cross—does it theologically exaggerate it or interpret it as necessary for salvation. From the outside, this has sometimes created the impression that Muslims fatalistically subjugate themselves to God and his will, accepting suffering in a kind of blind submission to destiny. In this negative context, Leibniz has spoken of the *"fatum Mahomedanum."*[93] This, however, is a stereotype.

Suffering as Existential Experience:
Wisdom that Must Be Plumbed

When they look at the suffering in the world, Muslims see no contradiction of God's goodness. It is not suffering itself that is the object of their reflection, but rather suffering as an existential experience. Muslim spirituality is convinced: no suffering takes hold of us meaninglessly. What is important is not suffering in and of itself, but our spiritual approach to it. Accordingly, Muslims primarily see suffering as a kind of wisdom that must be plumbed. This, however, is the opposite of a mere fatalistic, passive acceptance. The spiritual challenge in the experience of suffering lies not in rejecting it, remonstrating with God, or justifying, but instead patiently withstanding the suffering. What, then, does this mean? The Qur'an dignifies the practice of patience as an important spiritual virtue. "Behold, God is with the patient," reads a

---

93. See Gottfried Wilhelm Leibniz. *Theodizee II. Philosophische Schriften* [Theodicy II: Philosophical writings], vol. 2.2, edited by Herbert Herring (Frankfurt: Suhrkamp 1996), §55 and §59.

central passage (Qur'an 8:46, translated from the German). But this does not refer to a stance that lets everything come as it may. Being patient shows inner maturity and greatness of soul. For in patience—which the Qur'an often emphasizes in the same breath as prayer[94]—faith in God is strengthened. A man once asked Muslim mystic al-Shibli (d. 946 CE) what type of patience the already patient might find most difficult. "He answered: 'Patience in God.' The man said: 'No!' Shibli: 'Patience for God.' The man: 'No!' Shibli: 'Patience with God.' At that, Shibli became angry and said: 'Hey you, then what is it?' The man answered: 'The patience (of bearing up) without God.' At that, Shibli let out such a cry that he almost gave up the ghost."[95]

God Loves the Patient

Patience shows us the extent to which we have given our hearts to God. Bearing up against a hardship, mastering it as though there were no God, means: I am aware of the full intensity of the suffering I am experiencing, I do not minimize it. And yet I do not despair. Such an attitude does not coopt God as a placeholder or scapegoat. On the contrary, we are alone with our hardship because we do not shirk our responsibility. But what patience reveals is how we deal with the hardships that afflict us. If our heart is filled with God, we are never truly alone. The actual intensity of patience consists in our being patient with patience, as well. We may articulate what precisely makes us suffer; we may name the injustice; we may lament; we may grapple with God; we may doubt him; but we may not despair. Because in the face of an experience of deep suffering, nothing is more difficult than patience itself. Perhaps, then, patience is the true test that is meant when the Qur'an

---

94. See Qur'an 2:45 and others.
95. Quoted from as-Sarrāj in Richard Gramlich, *Islamische Mystik. Sufische Texte aus zehn Jahrhunderten* [Islamic mysticism: Sufi texts from ten centuries] (Stuttgart/Berlin/Köln: Kohlhammer, 1992), 55. Translated from the German.

says: "God loves the patient" (Qur'an 3:146, translated from the German). Because precisely in the hour of our suffering he is with us, so that our experience of suffering can teach us. It can teach us when we see ourselves not as a plaything of divine will, but as learners on the path of our pilgrimage to God. Nothing could be harder suffering than to be distant from God. When we suffer, Muslims have no recourse to God as the perpetrator. Rather, in such a situation, we are thrown back on ourselves, because in this context suffering is the price of the gift of freedom we have received. That God created us as free beings also means that we ourselves bear the responsibility for our actions, even in situations in which we are afflicted with suffering.

Suffering as Place of Encounter with God

Understood in such a way, however, suffering can also be taken as an intimate place of encounter with God. Salvation occurs not after having made it through an experience of suffering, but with and within this experience, for example when we become aware of our fragility and ephemerality and question ways of living that pretend that we will live forever. The experience of suffering also reveals to us who wait for forgiveness and salvation whether we ourselves are ready to forgive. The experience of suffering is thus a profound spiritual experience that does not simply pass us by; rather, the experience of suffering changes people—for the better.

Islam, too, is familiar with prayers of lament. True faith proves itself in grappling with God (which does not mean accusing God). All too often, we are left uncomprehending in the face of the almost unbearable experiences of suffering that often afflict innocents. Doubting is part of faith itself. We should not suffer in silence. On the contrary, this view sees it as an integral part of religion to recognize suffering in the world and wonder what it means to be religious in such circumstances.

Divine Justice and Human Responsibility

What answers do we have in the face of the obviously unjust experiences of suffering that afflict good people and innocent children every day? May we hope for some kind of retributive justice from God? Islamic theology and mysticism emphasize this hope for God's retributive justice. It stresses the hope that in the end God will turn all things to good—but much more, it emphasizes the responsibility of human beings in the world. It is not always within our power to turn away unjust experiences of suffering, but often enough, it is. And when we do experience our own powerlessness—for example, being unable to prevent natural disasters or finding that circumstances give us no effective means to actively prevent suffering—we are called to go to those affected, offer them comfort, and share in their experience of suffering. The Prophet Muhammad makes this clear when, in words not unlike those of Jesus in chapter twenty-five of the Gospel of Matthew, he says: "In the beyond, God will ask a man: 'I was sick, and you did not visit me; I was hungry, and you gave me nothing to eat; and I was thirsty, and you gave me nothing to drink.' The man will ask, astonished: 'But you are God. How can you be sick, thirsty, or even hungry?' And God will answer: 'On such-and-such a day, an acquaintance of yours was sick, and you did not visit him. If you had visited him, you would have found me with him. One day, an acquaintance of yours was hungry, and you gave him nothing to eat, and one day, an acquaintance of yours was thirsty, and you gave him nothing to drink.'"[96]

---

96. Quoted after Ṣaḥīḥ Muslim, Ḥadīth no. 2569. Translated from the German.

Life, Dying, and Death

I. Christian Thought on the Connection between Living, Dying, and Death

Anselm Grün

The Thought of Death Strengthens Life

In the Christian tradition, living and dying belong together. There are different aspects to this connection. In the first place, the knowledge that our life is finite lets us live more fully. In every moment, we know that we might also die. This knowledge invites us to live consciously and mindfully, to perceive the mystery of life. The thought of death, then, strengthens life.

Another aspect is that we are constantly dying in order to permit new life within us. Life is a constant process of letting go in order to become new. Augustine tells us that we are already dying in each moment. The past dies so that we may fully engage with the present and become open to the future. We must let go of our childhood in order to grow up. To that extent, we should also let go of old conflicts in order to face up to current issues.

From the Ego to the Self: Dying as Spiritual Path

Dying, in the Christian tradition, always also refers to a spiritual path: dying to the world in order to be born to heaven. In psychological terms, our ego must die in order for our self to unfold. In the Christian tradition, this death of the ego in order to illuminate a person's true image is represented by John the Baptist. He says of himself and his relation to Jesus: "He must increase, but I must decrease" (Jn 3:30). The ego, which is always trying to garner recognition, must decrease in order for Christ to increase in us, that is, so that the spirit of Jesus can shine ever brighter within us, so that the unique image God has made of each of us for himself can radiate ever more clearly. To faithful Christians, the testimony of Christian funeral rituals holds true for the actual experience of true death, as well: faith in the resurrection and in Jesus' victory over death does not lift our grief. But it does help us deal with our grief through the perspective of hope. Grief consists not only in the pain of farewell or in the relationship with the departed beyond death. It always also consists in the question of my own identity and the meaning of my life.

Dying into New Being

Monks were fond of using the metaphor of death to express that the identity through which we tie ourselves to the world must pass away so that the new way of being gifted to us by Christ can blossom within us. We are in the world but not of the world. Therefore, our cleaving to the world must die in order for divine life to unfold within us. There is a story in which the Desert Father Macarius sends a young monk to a cemetery. He is to viciously insult the dead for one hour and then praise them for one hour. Naturally, the dead do not answer. When the monk returns to Macarius, the latter says: "Do as the dead do: care for neither praise nor insult. Then your life will succeed." This is not to say that the monk should give up his feelings. But he should let neither recognition nor rejection define him, but define himself solely from God. Those who have succeeded in this inner death can live in the midst of the world without being ruled by it.

Another patristic apothegm—a saying of the fourth-century desert monks—states that a brother asked Abba Moses: "I see before me a task and cannot fulfill it." The father answered him: "Unless you become a corpse like the buried dead, you will not manage it."[97] When we meditate on our own death, we come to

---

97. *Apophthegmata patrum*, saying 505. Translated from the German.

sense everything we carry around with us as excess weight that we should let go of. Possessions we cling to; opinions we hold onto; roles we play; masks we wear: all this would fall from us. And we could rise from the grave as new human beings. The idea of lying in the grave is not meant to sap our vitality. Rather, it can help true life unfold within us. Dying, the monks believe, seeks to enable us to live. It seeks to make us capable of fulfilling well those tasks that life gives us. The idea that we will die and lie in a grave can aid us in gaining true life, the life that shines out to us in Jesus' resurrection.

The Mystery of Jesus' Death and Resurrection

Nature models constant death and new life for us—and this cycle applies to our spiritual path, too. The old in us must keep dying in order for the new in us to grow. That is the mystery of Jesus' death and resurrection. Paul the Apostle explained it vividly in his description of baptism. Baptism, as he relates, is meant to show us that we die with Christ in order to be resurrected with him as new human beings: "We know that our old self was crucified with him so that the body of sin might be destroyed, and we might no longer be enslaved to sin. For whoever has died is freed from sin. But if we have died with Christ, we believe that we will also live with him" (Rom 6:6–8). In the rite of baptism, Christians experience this on our very bodies. We are immersed in water. Our old being dies. Then we resurface and are clothed in a white garment—as a sign that we have become new. For early Christians, this was an impressive experience. They felt themselves to have been born anew.

Practicing the Event of Baptism in Everyday Life

We are meant to practice this experience of baptism again and again in our daily lives. One ritual that reminds us of this death and resurrection is the cross we make with holy water. We dip our hand into the water and then touch our forehead, our breast, our left and right shoulders. As we touch our forehead, we are expressing that our thinking is renewed. Paul calls for us to "not be conformed to this world, but be transformed by the renewing of [our] minds" (Rom 12:2). We then touch our breast, so that our vitality and sexuality be permeated by the spirit of Jesus. Then we touch our left shoulder. This new life wants to penetrate deep into our unconscious, into the images of our dreams, and transform everything. And finally we touch our right shoulder. Our conscious deeds and words are to be shaped by the new spirit of Jesus, not by the old measures of this world.

Taking Part in Eternal Life

Paul experienced the mystery of living and dying, of death and resurrection, in his own body: Wherever we go, we are "always carrying in the body the death of Jesus, so that the life of Jesus may also be made visible in our bodies. For while we live, we are always being given up to death for Jesus' sake, so that the life of Jesus may be made visible in our mortal flesh" (2 Cor 4:10–11). We must not read into these words any longing for death. Rather, this experience gave Paul the strength and courage to proclaim the message of Jesus fearlessly, although he had to suffer many persecutions and afflictions in doing so. He faced up to life, unafraid of the dangers, because for him suffering was an experience of Jesus' agony and death. In this suffering, he experienced communion with Jesus. And to him, Jesus was precisely the one who was crucified and resurrected, that is to say: who transgresses all our conventional measures and breaks us open to new life, to a life that cannot be destroyed even by death.

That is how the mystery of our spiritual life is expressed in images of living and dying, of death and resurrection, of letting go of the old and admitting new life. The new life we experience even here will shine out fully within us when we die bodily, as well. But the Christian tradition knows: Already here, we take part in eternal life. The paradise awaiting us in heaven after our death is shining out to us even here.

2. A Muslim Interpretation of Living, Dying, and Death

Ahmad Milad Karimi

Life is Devotion: Islam as Conscious Life Before God

The word *islam* means "devotion" and describes living in the awareness of God in the face of God. What occurs with this devotion cannot be located outside the individual and his or her life. This devotion is not a desire seeking material fulfillment, but it is a yearning, an inner disquiet. Those who devote themselves are permeated with a passion that moves them. It is this dynamic that defines the Muslim conception of the meaning of life: devotion stands at the beginning of a journey to God, a journey inward. This devotion is not blind submission, no enslavement of humankind. Devotion, rather, means opening oneself up to God. However, the path to God is not linear. The heart may desire God, but it does not cleave to him. The inward journey does not end. Every inner step opens up another one, paths upon paths that finally open the finite and limited heart towards the infinite. "The Opening" is also the name for the first surah of the Qur'an as the beginning of a journey that never stops transcending boundaries within us. In this spirit, the Prophet Muhammad is said to have recommended: "Die before you die!" In Islam, then, life and death belong together.

Death as Part of Earthly Life

Death is part of humankind. We are reminded of this awareness in the Psalm:

> As for mortals, their days are like grass;
>   they flourish like a flower of the field;
> for the wind passes over it, and it is gone,
>   and its place knows it no more. (Ps 103:15–16)

Living an authentic life, then, consists in accepting death as part of reality, not trying to avoid it or building one's life around the fear of death. Those who live carry death inside them.[98] It is inescapable: "Death will overtake you no matter where you may be, even inside high towers" (Qur'an 4:78). But in the face of this reality, Muslims believe in a living God who supports and completes the ephemeral lives of human beings. The Qur'an states: "Say, 'My prayers and sacrifice, my life and death, are all for God, Lord of all the Worlds" (Qur'an 6:162). Just as we have no control over the creation of our life, we have no control over our death. In death, our earthly life finds the temporal end that was determined for it.

Recognizing the Essential: On the Meaning of Death

Yet through faith, death gains a new meaning: "So say, 'The death you run away from will come to meet you and you will be returned to the One who knows the unseen as well as the seen: He will tell you everything you have done'" (Qur'an 62:8). In Islam, therefore, death does not constitute a fall or a catastrophe, but the return of life to its origins.[99] The knowledge of my own impending death is also linked with the idea that I am devoting myself to God, whose justice and mercy will judge my life.[100] "On that Day, people will come forward in separate groups to be shown their deeds: whoever has done an atom's-weight of good will see it, but whoever has done an atom's-weight of evil will see that" (Qur'an 99:6–8). Insight into our mortality lets us recognize the essential matters of life—a life that is not infinite on Earth. This insight allows us to recognize what we

---

98. "God takes the souls of the dead and the souls of the living while they sleep—He keeps hold of those whose death He has ordained and sends the others back until their appointed time" (Qur'an 39:42).
99. See Qur'an 5:35.
100. "He does not wrong anyone by as much as the weight of a speck of dust: He doubles any good deed and gives a tremendous reward of His own" (Qur'an 4:40).

are living for, what we strive for in life, what we should keep, possess, leave behind. "The people are sleeping. When they die, they awaken," the Prophet is reported to have said.

Life in Relation to Death: Three Stages

In the Islamic tradition, a distinction is made between three stages of life as related to death: life before death, life after death, and life during death. Before death, death is meant to be a constant companion in life. Thinking of death, the Prophet tells us repeatedly, puts life into the correct perspective and shows that each moment of life is infinitely precious and valuable because it can be neither repeated nor extended. Life during death, which is to say dying, is given particular recognition in Islamic spirituality. And life after death represents the ultimate stage of life, since it is based in the encounter with God, enriched by the experience of earthly life and one's own death.

Death as a Special Spiritual Experience

Life during death, in other words dying itself, marks the point in our own lives at which we make our farewell to those lives. This gives dying a particular spiritual significance in the lives of Muslims. On his deathbed, a Muslim is surrounded by Muslim companions reciting the thirty-sixth surah of the Qur'an in gentle voices. The twelfth verse of this moving surah tells us: "We shall certainly bring the dead back to life, and We record what they send ahead of them as well as what they leave behind: We keep an account of everything in a clear Record" (Qur'an 36:12). Death occurs by the angel of death carrying us into death. And immediately after death, the eyes of the deceased are closed and the face and feet are turned towards Mecca, as if the deceased had stood up to pray. The corpse is then cleaned and undergoes a ritual ablution. The Muslim shroud is a plain white cloth in which we are wrapped: before God, all are the same, whether rich or poor. If the deceased has completed the journey to Mecca, he is further wrapped into his clothes of pilgrimage (another white cloth of several parts). Muslims are not cremated after death but buried: "From the earth We created you, into it We shall return you, and from it We shall raise you a second time" (Qur'an 20:55). At the grave, the ritual prayer for the dead is spoken and the deceased is oriented toward Mecca in the devoted posture of prayer.

"Wedding to Eternity": Death Is No End

The Qur'an tells us that death is part of being human, but not the last word: it neither extinguishes nor definitively ends anything. While our mortality shows that nothing has permanence, the Qur'an also teaches that our passing itself will pass: "How can you ignore God when you were lifeless and He gave you life, when He will cause you to die, then resurrect you to be returned to Him?" (Qur'an 2:28). The Muslim mystic Maulānā Rūmī writes:

> Behold the body, born of dust, how perfect it has become.
> Why should you fear its end?
> When were you ever made less by dying?[101]

Even when death does come upon us, our soul does not suffer it passively, but rather "Every soul will taste death" (Qur'an 3:185). This means that death represents both a natural process in life and simultaneously a culmination of life in expectation of the return to God. In another phrase attributed to Rūmī: "Our death is our wedding to eternity."

---

101. Quoted in: Andrew Harvey, *The Way of Passion: A Celebration of Rumi* (Berkeley, CA: Frog Books, 1994), 190. An alternative reading of the final line, as given in H. C. Meiser's German rendering of Jonathan Star and Shahram Shiva's English translation, is "It is only by death that you were created." See Rumi, *Das Lied der Liebe* [The song of love], translated by H. C. Meiser (Munich: Droemer Knaur, 2005), 191.

Life as a Valuable Gift that Must Not Be Killed

Especially in the face of death, life represents an incalculable good, a gift of God that must be preserved and honored: "If anyone kills a person—unless in retribution for murder or spreading corruption in the land—it is as if he kills all mankind, while if any saves a life it is as if he saves the lives of all mankind" (Qur'an 5:32). Accordingly, the Qur'an is considered the book of life, and the Prophet Muhammad the messenger of good news for life. Life is to be preserved as an untouchable good because it is understood to be on loan from God. I do not know of a single serious position that would take a theologically positive view of, say, assisted suicide, given that it usurps control of one's own end under the pretext of human autonomy. But today, when people refer to Islam in an attempt to religiously justify the killing of human beings, or when they use their own lives as so-called martyrs in order to destroy the lives of many other people, that simply means that they are committing murder against themselves and against others. By glorifying their death and the expectation of an afterlife in order to justify their murders, such people are misconstruing the Islamic insight and conviction that death is the culmination of life. According to the core of the Islamic tradition, therefore, their acts are utterly reprehensible, in fact a clear perversion of the divine message, a sin against life, against the work of God.

What Do We Hope for? Where Are We Going?

I. Muslim Expectations of the Beyond

Ahmad Milad Karimi

Belief in the Day of Judgment

The Qur'an records a prayer of Abraham's: "Lord, we have put our trust in You; we turn to You; You are our final destination" (Qur'an 60:4). In the Islamic view, the path of life is boundless: it not only originates with its creator, but leads back to him, as well. Already in the very first revelations of the Qur'an, belief in the Day of Judgment is affirmed alongside the oneness and uniqueness of God. The Qur'an contains a number of terms for that day: Day of Resurrection (Arabic: *yaum al-qiyāma*), the Final Day (Arabic: *yaum al-ākhar*), the Day of Reckoning (Arabic: *yaum al-ḥisāb*), the Day of Separation (Arabic: *yaum al-faṣl*), the Day of Awakening (Arabic: *yaum al-ba'th*), the Encompassing Day (Arabic: *yaum al-muḥīṭ*), the Day of Judgment (Arabic: *yaum ad-dīn*), or simply the Hour (Arabic: *as-sā'a*). The Prophet Muhammad describes this day in rich imagery: "Then will God say: 'O Angel Isrāfīl, arise and blow on your trumpet the signal for resurrection!' He shall blow and call out: 'O you spirits who have passed away! O you bones that have fallen apart and bodies that have rotted! O you sinews that have been parted and skins that have torn! O you hairs that have fallen out! Arise for the proclaiming of the judgment!'"[102]

---

102. Quoted in Iman 'Abd ar-Rahim ibn Ahmad al-Qadi, *Das Totenbuch des Islam: "Das Feuer und der Garten" – Die Lehren des Propheten Muhammad über das Leben nach dem Tode* [Islam's book of the dead: "The Fire and the Garden"—The teachings of the Prophet Muhammad on life after death],

And the Qur'an states: "Whoever has done an atom's-weight of good will see it, but whoever has done an atom's-weight of evil will see that" (Qur'an 99:6–8). This means that while the Day of Judgment is an event that touches the entire cosmos, we nevertheless come before God as individuals, with our good and bad deeds evident before him. Faith in the one God is linked with the hope for resurrection, for a life after death, for a beyond. On the Day of Resurrection, God alone will judge the deeds of human beings—in justice and mercy. The Prophet describes it as follows: "On the Day of Judgment the feet of the servant will not depart from the face of God before he has not been asked about his life and his possessions."[103] Human beings neither have any control over the judgment of God, nor do they know when the Hour (Arabic: *as-sā'a*) will occur (see Qur'an 79:42–44).

Visions of Paradise and Hell

Those who have dedicated their lives to the good will find the "best place to return" to God (Qur'an 3:14):

> Such people will have Hell for their home and will find no escape from it, but We shall admit those who believe and do good deeds into Gardens graced with flowing streams, there to remain for ever—a true promise from God. Who speaks more truly than God? It will not be according to your hopes or those of the People of the Book: anyone who does wrong will be requited for it and will find no one to protect or help him against God; anyone, male or female, who does good deeds and is a believer, will enter Paradise and will not be wronged by as much as the dip in a date stone. (Qur'an 4:122–124)

---

      translated by S. Makowski and S. Schuhmacher (Bern: Scherz, 1981), 105. Translated from the German.
103. al-Qadi, 135. Translated from the German.

In both the Qur'an and the prophetic record, we find an extraordinary richness of imagery to describe paradise. According to the Qur'an, as the Garden of Eden and site of bliss, it represents the appropriate place for humankind. As the Qur'an attests, humankind was fundamentally created for paradise: "But you and your wife, Adam, live in the Garden" (Qur'an 7:19). Accordingly, the revelations and the selection of the prophets are seen as God's merciful devotion, meant to uplift humankind to its best: "We have honored the children of Adam" (Qur'an 17:70). That is also why the revelations of God are considered right guidance, and the prophets as voices of warning and admonition, so that human beings do not let themselves be seduced into injustice and evil. In one of the first surahs, revealed at the very beginning of Muhammad's prophetic mission, we read: "You, wrapped in your cloak, arise and give warning! Proclaim the greatness of your Lord; cleanse yourself; keep away from all filth; do not be overwhelmed and weaken; be steadfast in your Lord's cause" (Qur'an 74:1–7).

Reward and Punishment: Admonitory Parables

On this basis, the metaphorical and richly ornamented descriptions of paradise and hell must always be seen as parables with pedagogic intent: God is trying to use them to admonish human beings. When we speak of a parable, that primarily means that we cannot imagine the beyond. Muhammad al-Ghazālī writes:

> This life . . . is of the material world while the hereafter is of the transcendent world. . . . We speak now while being in this life of the next. Because, we speak in this life, it being the sensible world, but our purpose is the explanation of the hereafter, which is the world beyond the senses, and it is inconceivable to describe the transcendent world within the sensible world except by adducing parables. That is why it is said AND THOSE PARABLES, WE COIN THEM FOR THE PEOPLE, BUT NONE UNDERSTANDS THEM SAVE THOSE WHO

KNOW. . . . This is because compared to the transcendental world . . . the temporal world is like slumber. That is why the Prophet said: "men are asleep, and when they die they awaken." . . . That which will occur in the waking state becomes clear to you during sleep only [through] parables which are in need of interpretation. Likewise, that which will take place in the waking state of the hereafter cannot be explained in the sleep of this life except through a multitude of parables.[104]

Regardless of whether these parables speak of heavenly maidens with large eyes and blinding beauty (Arabic: *al-ḥūr*) or of flowing rivers, or whether they describe hell as the place where "people will be like scattered moths and the mountains like tufts of wool" (Qur'an 101:4–5), the unimaginable is always communicated metaphorically to people through imagery, motifs, comparisons, and parables in order to give an impression of what is intended in the beyond. This is equally true for God's reward (paradise) and punishment (hell). But it would be a misreading of the punishment of God, which is mentioned in the Qur'an as well, to assume that it was a matter of a vengeful, strict God interested in causing humans pain. In the first place, what God's punishment precisely means is barely conceivable. At one point, the Qur'an says of those who make mischief: "God will neither speak to them nor look at them on the Day of Resurrection" (Qur'an 3:77). In parallel, those who do good deeds are said to be rewarded by seeing God: "On that Day there will be radiant faces, looking towards their Lord" (Qur'an 75:22–23).

---

104. [Muhammad al-Ghazālī], *Al-Ghazzali on Repentance*, translated by M. S. Stern (New Delhi: Sterling Publishers, 1990), 65–66. Brackets are as given in the original volume; capitalization indicates a quotation from the Qur'an (29:34) and is likewise given in the original. Ellipses, however, mark elisions by Prof. Karimi.

Return to God: Hope in His Retributive Justice

These parables memorialize the fact that everything we do or leave undone has an eschatological significance. That means: our actions receive a definitive, final judgment—shaped by the awareness that God's mercy exceeds his punishment. "Anyone who does good of his own accord will be rewarded, for God rewards good deeds, and knows everything" (Qur'an 2:158). The Prophet Muhammad once remarked on this matter: if a person's evil deeds outnumber the good deeds, but even a single eyelash of that person trembles with reverence before God, then "God will forbid hell from touching it! . . . So God will forgive him."[105] For God takes no pleasure in punishing human beings, since "whoever purifies himself does so for his own benefit" (Qur'an 35:18). Rather, he wants to lead human beings to bliss through love and mercy; this is also why the qur'anic imagery on hell is so drastic and terrifying. As free agents, human beings are advised to let themselves be admonished so that their souls may find peace: "The one who purifies his soul succeeds and the one who corrupts it fails" (Qur'an 91:9–10). However, Islam does not espouse the idea of automatic salvation. To that extent, the hope for a hereafter is also the hope for God's retributive justice. "The beyond is as a sea and the world is like its foam," says Rūmī.[106]

Being human means action. And it is from action that heaven or hell arise. That is why human deeds in this world gain such an immeasurable significance: "Good and evil cannot be equal" (Qur'an, 41:34). But how ought one to counter a bad deed? The Qur'an enjoins us: "Repel evil with what is better and your enemy will become as close as an old and valued friend" (Qur'an 41:34). The return to God as completion of

---

105. al-Qadi, 171–172. Translated from the German.
106. Annemarie Schimmel, *Weisheit des Islam: Ausgewählt, übersetzt, und herausgegeben von Annemarie Schimmel* [Wisdom of Islam: Selected, translated, and edited by Annemarie Schimmel] (Stuttgart: Reclam, 2003), 53. Translated from the German.

universal divine devotion is a matter that concerns not only Muslims, but all human beings, who will be judged based on their deeds: "You will all return to God, and He will make you realize what you have done" (Qur'an 5:105). As the Prophet Muhammad pithily put it: "All creatures are God's family."[107] The cosmic dimension of Islamic eschatology is revealed by the fact that numerous sayings of the Prophet refer to the "animals of paradise."

The hope for encounter with God and the return to our own origins put into correct perspective an inappropriate fixation with paradise and hell. In a phrase attributed to Maulānā Rūmī: "Neither do we worry about hell, nor do we aspire to paradise. Unveil Your face. For You are our entire longing."

2. Christians' Hope for the Beyond

Anselm Grün

Biblical Imagery and Theological Interpretation

We Christians too hope that in death we will be admitted to paradise. The Bible uses a great many images to describe what awaits us after death. For one, there is the image of the celebratory feast to which we are invited; for another, the image of paradise as a beautiful garden; then the image of God's maternal and paternal arms into which we die and by which we are embraced in death. But the Bible also speaks of the Day of Revelation and of the judgment in which God will judge all human beings. Theology has attempted to understand and interpret these biblical images through reason.

And so theology tells us: in death we will encounter the one and the true God. This is the one God whom all religions venerate, but whom they imagine in different metaphors. But all human beings, no matter of which religion, will encounter

---

107. Schimmel, *Weisheit des Islam*, 62. Translated from the German.

the one God in death. And this God is love. By encountering God's love in death, however, we are also encountering ourselves. And in God's love we recognize that we are far from the image that God has made himself of us. We have darkened and stained this image through our faults and our sins. Theology speaks of purgatory, the cleansing fire that purifies us of these dark blotches. But we must not imagine purgatory as a place or time. The love of God that we will see in death purifies us of our faults and sins, which we will see in utter clarity once we encounter God. The more darkly the image of God in us is obscured, the more painful our cleansing will be.

Theology also speaks of hell. But God does not cast people into hell. Those who close themselves off to God's love are closing themselves off from paradise. They are isolating themselves, and it is this isolation that is hell. We must expect the possibility of hell. Human beings can fail if they close themselves off from God. But we may hope that hell is empty, that in the face of God's love, people will let themselves fall into that love.

The Day of Judgment: Threat or Symbol of Hope?

The Bible also speaks of judgment. In the past, many saw that as threatening—but actually, judgment is a symbol of hope. The philosopher Max Horkheimer was convinced that there is a fundamental principle of human justice dictating that murderers must not triumph over their victims. If murderers are admitted to heaven just as their victims are, then this goes against our sense of justice. But there is hope for the perpetrators. If they subject themselves to the judgment of God and let themselves be oriented towards God, then they too can enter heaven. But the victims, too, must be oriented towards God by judgment. Sometimes people say to me: I would love to go to heaven, but I would hate to meet my neighbor or my work colleagues there. Such sentences show that we all must let judgment orient us toward God and toward absolute love. Only then can we love the people in heaven that we have difficulty with here on earth. Only then can we share heaven with all people. The Bible describes the end of the world and the Day of Revelation, on which God's glory will be revealed and Christ will appear as judge over the living and the dead. Theology has interpreted these metaphorical ideas of the Bible as saying that when an individual dies, that person's world ends. For every dying person, that is the Day of Revelation. That is when judgment occurs. What the Bible describes as the end of the cosmos is the revelation of the ended worlds of the many individuals.

Paradise, Heaven, Resurrection

The Bible describes paradise as a beautiful garden, as a feast with rich foods and old wines, as a joint praise of God together with the angels. In dialogue with Hellenic philosophy, theology interpreted these metaphors as follows: In death, we become one with God. Heaven is the *visio beatifica*, the blessed vision of God. In death, we see God as he is, and in seeing him we become one with God and in God become one with humankind. That is why theology also says that after death we will be reunited again in God's glory. But this is not like a class reunion, where we swap old memories. It will be becoming one in God, which we cannot fully imagine.

Theology takes the biblical message of the resurrection seriously. Faith in resurrection is not identical with the ancient Greek belief in the immortality of the soul as Plato taught it. We will be resurrected body and soul. This body, of course, will decay. But resurrection with the body also means transformation of the body. And it means that each individual is saved into God. In the First Epistle to the Corinthians, Paul attempts to imagine the heavenly body: "What is sown is perishable, what is raised is imperishable. It is sown in dishonor, it is raised in glory. It is sown in weakness, it is raised in power. It is sown a physical body, it is raised a spiritual body" (1 Cor 15:42–44). But in the end, we cannot imagine what the resurrection of the dead will be like. Just like God, the resurrection of the dead is beyond all images. We need images of God and of eternal life. But at the same time, we should know that reality is beyond all imagery.

Final Union: All Die into God's Love

In death, we human beings—Christians and Muslims, Jews, Buddhists, Hindus alike—will die into the love of God. It is the one God who awaits us all. When we see God, our images and imaginings, our theological doctrines cease. And together we gaze on the God beyond all images, on the God of absolute mystery. But in this God, we will all be one, if before God we let ourselves be judged, justified, oriented toward him and the absolute love in which we become one with one another and with God. In that sense, looking to what awaits us is also a way to be oriented toward God even now, not to fight among each other, but to prepare for the fact that there will be no more differences in death. We will all be one in God.

Conclusion

Stories as Means of Approach

Ahmad Milad Karimi

Where We Seek God

Seek God, but do not seek where he lives.
—Sisoës the Great (d. 429 CE)

The Desert Father Sisoës the Great, who gained renown in early Christendom through his deep spiritual wisdom, encourages human beings to seek God. We are not meant to seek him occasionally, from time to time, nor only when we think we need him most. What this Desert Father—venerated as a saint in the Orthodox and Catholic traditions—means is: "Seek God" in such a way that your entire life becomes search and longing. Those who set out to seek God are not seeking some object in the world or some unknown place. What are we looking for when we seek God? In the first place, the search for God demands contemplation, pausing, but also orienting ourselves. Those who seek the place where God lives, as Sisoës advises against doing, are fixing God in a particular place and thus to delimitation. But God does not reside anywhere. And yet there is no place where he is absent, as the Qur'an says: "The East and the West belong to God: wherever you turn, there is His Face" (Qur'an 2:115). The search never ends, because God is endless. At root, the search for God in the Christian as in the Muslim tradition describes the path of life. We are to seek God everywhere, and we can find him everywhere. Accordingly, the following story is attributed to the Muslim mystic 'Aṭṭār: "A man in the raptures of ecstasy spoke to God: 'O God, finally open the gate to me!' A mystic named Rabia was sitting close by, and she said: 'You fool, when was the gate ever closed?'"

How Does God Enter Our Hearts?

> Who will grant me to find peace in you? Who will grant me this grace, that you would come into my heart and inebriate it, enabling me to forget the evils that beset me and embrace you, my only good?[1]
>
> —Augustine of Hippo (d. 430 CE)

The great Christian thinker Augustine calls for God, but the call is not abstract in the sense that it is made outward from him, into emptiness. Rather, he is calling for how God enters into the hearts of people, touches them and takes away all disquiet, all trembling. He is calling for God with God, and is seeking to be intoxicated with God. He is speaking in the voice of longing, the voice that yearns for fulfillment. God is appealed to as the entity of peace with ourselves. After a turbulent life, Augustine was one of the most renowned theologians of his time but reflecting on God—as important as it is—had not sated his thirst for a personal God, who is what we all learn for in the depth of our existence. To Augustine, like to many Muslim mystics, God represents not a philosophical and theological concept, the first cause, foundation of being, etc. God is primarily a beloved without whom we can find no peace and no completeness. In the meantime, Augustine asks for a mediator, for an entity of revelation that will lead the glory of God inside me and keep it awake. These revelations of God, which we Muslims recognize in the Qur'an and Christians recognize in God's self-revelation in the person of Jesus, promise one and the same thing: a path on which God enters into our life. In our different revelations, we experience a beating memorialization of God in our hearts. And through this memorialization, we come into contact with a truth that transcends our human reality and simultaneously lifts us to the eternal: it is our "only good."

---

1. Augustine of Hippo, *The Confessions* (Second Edition), translated by Maria Boulding, O.S.B. edited by John E. Rotelle, O.S.A. (Hyde Park, NY: New City Press, 1987/2012), 41–42.

The Meaning of Our Life

If man is not made for God, why is he happy only in God? If man is made for God, why is he so unlike God?[2]

—Blaise Pascal (d. 1662 CE)

In note no. 438 of his posthumously collected *Pensées* ("thoughts"), the scientist and Christian philosopher Pascal wonders about the meaning of human life in relation to God: What are we made for? And why do we long for God and see and feel our ultimate happiness and peace in him alone? He also realizes: at the same time, we not infrequently live in direct contradiction of him. This we do on the one hand by rejecting this ultimate authority that endows life with meaning, because we cannot recognize any meaning in God. On the other hand, we live in contradiction of God to the extent that we do not accept our own destiny of being created for God; we let ourselves be seduced by what removes us from our own truth. According to Pascal—and the Islamic spiritual tradition shares this conviction—our being created does not represent a mere and empty given. Rather, our existence is a meaningful deed of God which immediately concerns us and gives us enthusiasm for life. By our very living we are confronted with the question of why we live and what we yearn for. Being in contradiction to God, then, means living in forgetfulness of God; for our life is not completed merely once we see our ultimate happiness in God. On the contrary: being created for God represents the beginning of the life of a person seeking meaning, admonishing God, grappling with him in order to be close to him, to learn to taste him who yet turns every contradiction of him to the good.

---

2. Blaise Pascal, *Selections from the Thoughts*, translated by Arthur H. Beattie (Wheeling, IL: Harlan Davidson, 1965), 85.

How God Uplifts Us

Do not pray for a lighter load, but for a stronger back.

—Teresa of Avila (d. 1582 CE)

At the end of the second surah of the Qur'an, there is a prayer that runs: "Lord, do not burden us as You burdened those before us. Lord, do not burden us with more than we have strength to bear" (Qur'an 2:286). Human life is self-evidently shaped by the experience of not infrequently being confronted with tasks and impositions that it is hard even to just accept. Why do such things happen to us, and how should we behave in relation to them? Often enough, our first impulse is to flee from our responsibility by, for example, not wanting to view it as our responsibility at all. This applies not only to us, our tasks, and our own experiences of suffering, but also to everyone else who is experiencing hardship. Are others a burden to which we shut our eyes? Or are they signs of God that, while they may challenge us and push our boundaries, nevertheless encourage us to transcend every boundary if it is a matter of the good, the just, the merciful? Especially whenever we are at home in our faith—whether Christian or Muslim—the question of the right attitude and the right action is significant because there is nothing we do or leave undone, bear or do not want to bear, in which we are alone. We live in the visage of God, but also with him, by unceasingly understanding our life from our relationship to God. Here, Teresa of Avila is asking us what we should pray for when we offer ourselves up to God in prayer. The path of faith, as Muslims are convinced as well, is not the most comfortable path, not the path of cowardice, laziness, or ignorance. Those who pray for a stronger back, then, are also praying for greater courage for justice, greater fortitude for standing up for the good, and more strength to take up responsibility. The stronger back that lifts us up is simultaneously uplifting us to God.

Anselm Grün

The Energy of Blessing

> One day, several people poured out invective on Jesus as he was walking through their quarter. But he answered by saying prayers in their names. Someone said to him: "You prayed for these people. Did you not feel anger against them?" He answered: "I could spend only what my purse contained."
>
> —Farīduddīn 'Aṭṭār (1136–1221 CE)

The Islamic tradition honors Jesus as a great prophet. The story attributed to Jesus by 'Aṭṭār is, ultimately, an interpretation of the saying of Jesus related in the Gospel of Luke: "Bless those who curse you, pray for those who abuse you" (Lk 6:28). Jesus does not give those who curse or abuse him power by letting them provoke him into anger or a negative mood. He stays with himself—in inner peace. And he gives only what his purse contains, that is, what is in his heart. He prays for the people who inveigh against him. He does not take the role of the victim but prays from his heart for those who insult him. Prayer and blessing are an active energy that Jesus sets against the negative energy of his abusers. This positive energy makes him the stronger one in the end. Prayer gives him hope that the people who are abusing him will confront themselves with their own truth. If he does not react to them as they would expect, they are thrown back upon themselves. For them, that is then the chance to face up to their own truth. And Jesus trusts that his prayer will transform the people he is praying for, so that they come into contact with the good core inside themselves. Then they will no longer need to shower him with invective.

Where We Find God

I tried to find him on the cross of the Christians, but he was not there. I went to the temples of the Hindus and to the ancient pagodas, but I could find no trace of him anywhere. I sought him in the mountains and the valleys, but neither in the heights nor the depths did I see myself capable of finding him. I went to Mecca to the Kaaba, but he was not there either. I questioned the learned and philosophers, but he was beyond their understanding. I examined my heart, and there he reposed, when I saw him. He can be found nowhere else.

—Rūmī (1207–1273 CE)

Rūmī, the Muslim poet and mystic, seeks God in all places where God is venerated: on the cross, in the temples, but also in nature. Those are all places we can experience God. But Rūmī experiences God not in an outward place, not even the place that is sacred to Muslims: the Kaaba in Mecca. And neither does he experience him in conversation with theologians and philosophers. Only when he examined his heart did he find God in his heart. Christian mystics might describe this experience in similar ways. To Evagrius Ponticus, the fourth-century monk, the heart is the site of God within human beings. Augustine had a similar experience. All the time that he sought God in the external, he did not find him. Then he recognized: God is more inward to me than I am myself. Some mystics speak of God dwelling within us at the base of our soul. Others describe the heart as the place where God dwells within us. The heart is simultaneously the place of love. It is in the heart that we feel love. Evidently we can feel God, who is love, best in the heart that is filled with love. The first Johannine epistle expresses it as follows: "God is love, and those who abide in love abide in God, and God abides in them" (1 Jn 4:16). If we place our hand on our heart and perceive the love that warms our heart, then in our heart we can experience God himself as that love. But we cannot hold on to God, just as we cannot hold on to love. Love flows, and God wants to flow in us. Mechthild of Magdeburg (1210–1294 CE) is said to have addressed God as follows: "O you flowing God in your love song." When love flows within our heart, we experience the flowing God who is love.

Rising up in God

> There was a man who one night called out to God for so long that his lips became quite sweet from the name. At that, the devil came to him and said: "What now, you endless prattler: where is the answer 'Here I am' to all your clamor for 'God'? There has not been the slightest answer from his throne. So how long will you keep calling pointlessly for him?" Broken, the man laid himself down to sleep. But in his dream, he heard God's voice: "Your call 'God!' is my call 'Here I am.' Your ardent plea is my message, and all your striving to reach me is nothing other than my hands, releasing the bonds around your feet and pulling you up to me. Your love and fear are the nostrils through which you breathe my mercy. And to each of your cries 'O my God!' I answer a hundredfold: 'Here I am.'"
>
> —Rūmī (1207–1273 CE)

What Rūmī is describing might just as well come from a Christian mystic such as Meister Eckhart or Johannes Tauler. The pious man calls out to God unceasingly, so much and so intensely that his lips become sweet with the name. This means: already in his longing call, he is experiencing God's healing and blissful nearness. God's fulfilling nearness can be experienced already in opening oneself toward him. This nearness has a pleasant taste. There is nothing in it of harshness or denial of life. Prayer alone transforms people and lets them taste the sweetness on their lips. But the devil makes the pious man uncertain. The devil wants to prove to him that his cries go out into emptiness. This diabolical suggestion lets the pious man doubt whether his prayers so far have not indeed been pointless and unanswered. But in his dream, God explains to him that his call for God already contains the divine answer "Here I am." And then, in two beautiful images, God explains his nearness: The pious man's attempts to reach God are themselves God, are God's hands loosening the pious man's shackles. And in his love and fear, the pious man is as if breathing in God's grace. These are beautiful metaphors for the intimate nearness between God and human beings.

I as a Christian can let these metaphors enter into me just as easily as I could with images by Christian mystics. In the experience of another religion, they show me that God himself is present already in my longing for him and that God's answer is already resonating in my calls to him

Bibliography

al-Azmeh, Aziz. *Islams and Modernities,* 3rd ed. London: Verso, 2009.

al-Ghazālī, Abu Hamid. *The Alchemy of Happiness.* Translated by Claud Field. London: John Murray, 1910. Available online at: https://archive.org/details/alchemyofhappine00algh/mode/2up.

al-Ghazālī, Abu Hamid. *Confessions, or Deliverance from Error.* Translated by Claud Field. Ed. by Jerome S. Arkenberg. Available online at: https://sourcebooks.fordham.edu/basis/1100ghazali-truth.asp.

al-Ghazālī, Ahmad. *At-Tarġīd fī kalimat at-tauḥīd: Der reine Gottesglaube. Das Wort des Einheitsbekenntnisses.* [*At-Tarjīd fī kalimat at-tauḥīd*: Pure faith in God. The words of the confession of oneness]. Introduced, translated, and with commentary by Richard Gramlich. Wiesbaden: Steiner, 1983.

[al-Ghazālī, Muhammad]. *Al-Ghazzali on Repentance.* Translated by M. S. Stern. New Delhi: Sterling Publishers, 1990.

al-Kindī, Ya'qub ibn Ishaq. *Al-Kindi's Metaphysics: A Translation of Ya'qub ibn Ishaq al-Kindi's Treatise "On First Philosophy."* Trans. Alfred L. Ivry. Albany: State University of New York Press, 1974.

al-Qadi, Iman 'Abd ar-Rahim ibn Ahmad: *Das Totenbuch des Islam: "Das Feuer und der Garten" – Die Lehren des Propheten Muhammad über das Leben nach dem Tode* [Islam's book of the dead: "The Fire and the Garden"—The teachings of the Prophet Muhammad on life after death]. Translated by S. Makowski and S. Schuhmacher. Bern: Scherz, 1981.

al-Qushayrī, 'Abd. *Das Sendschreiben al-Qušayrīs über das Sufitum* [Al-Qushayrī's missive on Sufism]. Translated, commented, and introduced by Richard Gramlich. Wiesbaden: Franz Steiner, 1989.

Augustine of Hippo. *Confessions*, Second Edition. Translated by Maria Boulding, OSB. Edited by John E. Rotelle, OSA. Hyde Park, NY: New City Press, 1987/2012.

Augustine of Hippo. "Exposition of Psalm 121." In Boniface Ramsey OSB. and John E. Rotelle OSA., eds. *Expositions of the Psalms: Volume 6, Ps. 121–150*. Translated by Maria Boulding. Hyde Park, NY: New City Press, 2004, 13–28.

Augustine of Hippo. "Sermon 109." Translated by Edmund Hill O.P. In John E. Rotelle O.S.A., editor.*Sermons, III/ 4 (94A – 147A) on the New Testament*. Hyde Park, New York: New City Press, 1992, 133–34.

Bauer, Thomas. "Islamisierung des Islams" [Islamization of Islam]. *Aus Politik & Kultur* no. 11: 178–180. Available online at: https://www.kulturrat.de/wp-content/uploads/2016/04/pdf_Islam_AusPolitikUndKultur_Nr11.pdf

Benedict of Nursia. *Saint Benedict's Rule*. Translated and introduced by Patrick Barry, OSB. Mahwah, NJ: HiddenSpring, 2004.

Bonhoeffer, Dietrich. *Letters and Papers from Prison*. Translated by Reginald H. Fuller. New York: Macmillan, 1962.

Buber, Martin. *I and Thou*. Translated by Walter Kaufmann. New York: Charles Scribner's Sons, 1970.

Clark, Mary T. "Die Dreieinigkeit in der lateinischen Christenheit [The trinity in Latin Christendom]." In Bernard McGinn and John Meyendorff, eds.

Geschichte der christlichen Spiritualität [History of Christian spirituality], vol. 1. Würzburg: Echter, 1993.

Gandhi, Mohandas K. *The Mind of Mahatma Gandhi.* R. K. Prabhu and U. R. Rao, eds. Available online at: https://www.mkgandhi.org/momgandhi/main.htm.

Gramlich, Richard. *Islamische Mystik. Sufische Texte aus zehn Jahrhunderten* [Islamic mysticism: Sufi texts from ten centuries]. Stuttgart/Berlin/Cologne: Kohlhammer, 1992.

Guillaume, Alfred. *The Life of the Prophet: A Translation of Isḥāq's Sīrat Rasūl Allāh.* Karachi: Oxford University Press, 1967.

Harvey, Andrew: *The Way of Passion: A Celebration of Rumi.* Berkeley, CA: Frog Books, 1994.

Iqbal, Muhammad. *Javid Nama* [Book of eternity]. Translated by Arthur J. Arberry (no place or date). Available online at: http://www.allamaiqbal.com/works/poetry/persian/javidnama/translation/index.htm.

Iqbal, Muhammad. *A Message from the East.* Translated by Muhammad Hadi Hussain, Arthur John Arberry, and Mustansir Mir. Lahore: Iqbal Academy Pakistan, 2014. Available online at: http://www.allamaiqbal.com/works/poetry/persian/payam/translation/02message.pdf.

Iqbal, Muhammad. *The Reconstruction of Religious Thought in Islam*, Stanford, CA: Stanford University Press, 2013.

Karimi, Ahmad Milad. "Zur Frage der Erlösung des Menschen im religiösen Denken des Islam" [On the question of salvation of human beings in Islamic religious thought]. In Klaus von Stosch and Aaron Langenfeld, eds. *Streitfall Erlösung* [The dispute over salvation]. Paderborn: Brill, 2015: 17–38.

Kasper, Walter. "Christianity — Absoluteness of Christianity." In Karl Rahner, SJ, ed. *Sacramentum Mundi Online.* Brill Online Publishing, 2016.

Available online at: http://dx.doi.org/10.1163/2468-483X_smuo_COM_000712.

Küng, Hans. *A Global Ethic for Global Politics and Economics*. Oxford: Oxford University Press, 1998.

Leibniz, Gottfried Wilhelm. *Die Theodizee II. Philosophische Schriften* [Theodicy II: Philosophical writings], vol. 2.2. Edited by Herbert Herring. Frankfurt: Suhrkamp, 1996.

Metz, Johann Baptist. *Love's Strategy: The Political Theology of Johann Baptist Metz*. Edited by John K. Downey. Harrisburg, PA: Trinity Press International, 1999.

Pascal, Blaise. *Selections from the Thoughts*. Translated by Arthur H. Beattie. Wheeling, IL: Harlan Davidson, 1965.

Paul VI, Pope. *Lumen Gentium*. Available online at: https://www.vatican.va/archive/hist_councils/ii_vatican_council/documents/vat-ii_const_19641121_lumen-gentium_en.html.

Plato. *The Republic*. Trans. by James Adam. Cambridge: Cambridge University Press, 1902. Available online at: http://www.perseus.tufts.edu/hopper/text?doc=Perseus%3atext%3a1999.04.0094.

Rilke, Rainer Maria. *R. M. Rilke und M. von Thurn und Taxis: Briefwechsel* [R. M. Rilke and M. von Thurn and Taxis: Correspondence.] Edited by Ernst Zinn and introduced by Rudolf Kassner. Vol. 1. Zürich: Insel, 1951.

Ritter, Hellmut. *Das Meer der Seele: Mensch, Welt und Gott in den Geschichten des Farīduddīn 'Aṭṭār* [The sea of the soul: Human, world, and God in the stories of Farīduddīn 'Aṭṭār]. Leiden: Brill, 1978.

Rūmī, Jalāl ad-Dīn. *Von Allem und vom Einen* [Of all and of the One]. Translated and prefaced by Annemarie Schimmel. Munich: Diederichs, 2020.

Schimmel, Annemarie. *Das islamische Jahr: Zeiten und Feste* [The Islamic year: Seasons and celebrations]. Munich: C. H. Beck, 2002.

Schimmel, Annemarie, ed. *Die Botschaft des Ostens: Ausgewählte Werke* [The message of the East: Selected works]. Tübingen: Edition Erdmann, 1977.

Schimmel, Annemarie. *Jesus und Maria in der islamischen Mystik* [Jesus and Mary in Islamic mysticism]. Munich: Kösel, 1996.

Schimmel, Annemarie. *Meine Seele ist eine Frau: Das Weibliche im Islam* [My soul is a woman: The feminine in Islam]. Munich: Kösel, 1996.

Schimmel, Annemarie. *Muhammad Iqbal: Prophetischer Poet und Philosoph* [Muhammad Iqbal: Prophetic poet and philosopher]. Munich: Diederichs, 1989.

Schimmel, Annemarie. *Weisheit des Islam: Ausgewählt, übersetzt, und herausgegeben von Annemarie Schimmel* [Wisdom of Islam: Selected, translated, and edited by Annemarie Schimmel]. Stuttgart: Reclam, 2003.

Schubart, Walter. *Religion und Eros* [Religion and eros]. Munich: C. H. Beck, 1941.

Sölle, Dorothee. *The Silent Cry: Mysticism and Resistance.* Translated by Barbara and Martin Rumscheidt. Minneapolis: Fortress Press, 2001.

Thunberg, Lars. "Der Mensch als Abbild Gottes: Die östliche Christenheit" [The human being as likeness of God: Eastern Christianity]. In Bernard McGinn and John Meyendorff, eds. *Geschichte der christlichen Spiritualität* [History of Christian spirituality], vol. 1. Würzburg: Echter, 1993.

Tillich, Paul. *Systematic Theology: Volume One: Reason and Revelation, Being and God.* Chicago: University of Chicago Press, 1951.

Zulehner, Paul M. *Unterstützung für und Widerstand gegen Papst Franziskus' Kirchenpolitik* [Support for and resistance to Pope Francis' church politics]. Vienna: self-published, 2019. Available online at: https://www.zulehner.org/dl/tqKsJKJmOJqx4kOJK/190825_Bericht.pdf.

FOCOLARE MEDIA
Enkindling the Spirit of Unity

The New City Press book you are holding in your hands is one of the many resources produced by Focolare Media, which is a ministry of the Focolare Movement in North America. The Focolare is a worldwide community of people who feel called to bring about the realization of Jesus' prayer: "That all may be one" (see John 17:21).

Focolare Media wants to be your primary resource for connecting with people, ideas, and practices that build unity. Our mission is to provide content that empowers people to grow spiritually, improve relationships, engage in dialogue, and foster collaboration within the Church and throughout society.

 Visit www.focolaremedia.com to learn more about all of New City Press's books, our award-winning magazine *Living City*, videos, podcasts, events, and free resources.

Printed by Libri Plureos GmbH in Hamburg, Germany